Gangs and Delinquency in Developmental Perspectiv

Gang membership has long been understood to have a disruptive influence on adolescent development and to contribute disproportionately to the rate of delinquency and crime. The exact nature of the impact and the long-term effects on individuals, however, have not been well understood. This book uses longitudinal data to examine for the first time the developmental consequences of gang membership, not just the short-term effects during membership itself, but its longer-term influence on the life course.

This longitudinal approach is made possible by data from a unique and important study of antisocial behavior, the Rochester Youth Development Study, which followed 1,000 adolescents through their early adult years. The subjects include adolescents who were gang members and others who were not, allowing the authors to compare motives, patterns of behavior, and recurring problems with caregivers and the law, education, peer relations, and career paths. The findings indicate that multiple, serious developmental deficits lead to gang membership and that membership, in turn, leads to an increase in serious and violent delinquency and lingering problems thereafter.

The authors, experts in criminal behavior and adolescent development, explain the social and psychological factors that lead some youths to join a gang. They show that gang members are responsible for the lion's share of serious and violent delinquency – including drug use and selling, and gun ownership and carrying – and that it is gang membership itself that facilitates these behaviors. Girl gang members, for example, exhibited higher levels of delinquent behavior than delinquent boys who were not gang members. Finally the authors demonstrate the ways in which gang membership generates "disorder" across the life course. Youths who join gangs are more likely to be arrested, to drop out of school, to become teen parents, and to exhibit other developmental problems. Gang membership has continuing effects into adulthood on educational achievements, job prospects, and economic status.

This book offers the most empirically informed explanation of the ripple effect of gangs on individuals and on society and the most compelling argument for early intervention for at-risk youths who join gangs.

Cambridge Studies in Criminology

Editors

Alfred Blumstein, *H. John Heinz School of Public Policy and Management, Carnegie Mellon University*
David Farrington, *Institute of Criminology, University of Cambridge*

Gangs and Delinquency in Developmental Perspective

Terence P. Thornberry
Marvin D. Krohn
Alan J. Lizotte
Carolyn A. Smith

University at Albany, State University of New York

Kimberly Tobin

Westfield State College

CAMBRIDGE
UNIVERSITY PRESS

PUBLISHED BY THE PRESS SYNDICATE OF THE UNIVERSITY OF CAMBRIDGE
The Pitt Building, Trumpington Street, Cambridge, United Kingdom

CAMBRIDGE UNIVERSITY PRESS
The Edinburgh Building, Cambridge CB2 2RU, UK
40 West 20th Street, New York, NY 10011-4211, USA
477 Williamstown Road, Port Melbourne, VIC 3207, Australia
Ruiz de Alarcón 13, 28014 Madrid, Spain
Dock House, The Waterfront, Cape Town 8001, South Africa

http://www.cambridge.org

First published 2003

Printed in the United States of America

Typeface   ITC New Baskerville 10/12 pt.   *System*   LATEX 2_ε [TB]

A catalog record for this book is available from the British Library.

Library of Congress Cataloging in Publication data

Gangs and delinquency in developmental perspective /
Terence P. Thornberry . . . [et al.].
      p.   cm. – (Cambridge studies in criminology)
   Includes bibliographical references and index.
   ISBN 0-521-81439-1 – ISBN 0-521-89129-9 (pbk.)
   1. Gangs – New York (State) – Rochester – Longitudinal studies.   2. Gang
members – New York (State) – Rochester – Psychology – Longitudinal
studies.   3. Juvenile delinquency – New York (State) – Rochester –
Longitudinal studies.   4. Adolescent psychology – New York (State) –
Rochester – Longitudinal studies.   I. Thornberry, Terence P.
II. Cambridge studies in criminology (Cambridge University Press)
HV6439.U52 N74   2003
364.1′06′60974789 – dc21   2002066520

ISBN 0 521 81439 1 hardback
ISBN 0 521 89129 9 paperback

To Malcolm W. Klein,
gang leader extraordinaire

Contents

Tables and Figures

Tables

Figures

About the Authors

Terence P. Thornberry is Distinguished Professor of Criminal Justice and Director of the Hindelang Criminal Justice Research Center at the University at Albany, State University of New York. He is the author of numerous books, articles, and book chapters and a Fellow of the American Society of Criminology. Since 1986 he has directed the Rochester Youth Development Study (RYDS).

Marvin D. Krohn is Professor of Sociology at the University at Albany with a joint appointment in the School of Criminal Justice. The author of numerous articles on adolescent delinquency, drug use, gangs, and gun use, he is a coprincipal investigator of the RYDS.

Alan J. Lizotte is Professor of Criminal Justice at the University at Albany and a coprincipal investigator of the RYDS. He is a nationally known expert on patterns of gun ownership and the impact of guns on criminal behavior.

Carolyn A. Smith is Associate Professor of Social Welfare at the University at Albany, as well as a coprincipal investigator of the RYDS. Her research focuses on the impact of the family, including parental abuse and maltreatment, on adolescent development.

Kimberly Tobin is Assistant Professor and Graduate Coordinator in the Department of Criminal Justice at Westfield State College and Director of Research for the Institute for Criminal Justice Studies and Research.

Preface

When you're a Jet
You're a Jet all the way,
From your first cigarette
To your last dyin' day.
      – *West Side Story*

American popular culture has built up a strong mythology about street gangs and their members. Some of it is fueled by movie and song – from the lyrics of Bernstein and Sondheim's classic Broadway hit to the grittier depiction of gang life in contemporary gangsta rap and Spike Lee movies. Some of it is fueled by the coverage of gangs in the mass media; some of it by autobiographies like Claude Brown's *Manchild in the Promised Land* (1976) and Sanyika Shakur's *Monster* (1998). Whatever the source, these images are entertaining and have taken firm root in popular views of gangs and gang members; their accuracy is another matter entirely.

Indeed, at one and the same time, they glorify and demonize gang members, presenting a warped picture that misses the mark in fundamental ways. For example, the idea that gang life is permanent, reflected in the lyrics that opened this book, is dead wrong. Gang membership, for the vast majority of gang members in America, turns out to be a rather fleeting, transient adolescent dalliance. It is the job of science to correct the record, to describe the phenomenon as accurately as possible, to attempt to explain why it happens, and to propose an appropriate response. This book is one contribution to this long-term effort.

It differs somewhat from previous approaches to this topic. For, unlike much of the scientific literature on gang behavior, we embed the study of gang members in a long-term investigation of a community sample of individual adolescents. Doing so allows us to examine the influence of the gang from a life-course perspective, to address old questions in a new way, and to address new questions about the origins and consequences of gang membership. We hope that the results of this analysis add to an accurate understanding of street gangs and help in the development of programs to reduce, and ultimately eliminate, street gangs from the American scene.

Acknowledgments

This study is part of a larger project, the Rochester Youth Development Study, a longitudinal investigation of antisocial behavior that began in 1986. Any study of that duration accumulates many debts along the way and owes its successes to many people. We would like to acknowledge some of them here.

The Rochester project would not have been possible without the continuing support of its funding agencies. The project was initiated by the Office of Juvenile Justice and Delinquency Prevention (OJJDP) in the U.S. Department of Justice, as part of its Program of Research on the Causes and Correlates of Delinquency. OJJDP was the primary supporting agency through 1992 and has supported us, without interruption, since 1986. It is rare for a research project to receive such enduring support from a sponsoring agency, and we are deeply appreciative of the confidence in our work that it reflects.

Over these 16 years we have benefited from working with many of OJJDP's professional staff. Pamela Swain and Barbara Tatem Kelley initiated this project and were our earliest supporters. They were followed by Donni LeBoeuf, Buddy Howell, Betty Chemers, Charlotte Kerr, Elen Grigg, and Kathy Browning. We have also had the support and encouragement of several OJJDP Administrators, especially Terrence Donahue, John Wilson, Shay Bilchik, and John Wilson (again).

Buddy Howell, now retired as OJJDP's director of research, deserves special recognition. He shepherded the project through difficult days, pushed us to expand the scope and quality of our work, and skillfully used our results in the development of comprehensive strategies to prevent juvenile delinquency. He was also the first to see the value of studying gangs in the context of a longitudinal design and was responsible for the particular grant to study gangs (grant no. 95-JD-FX-0015) that led to this book. After his retirement he read (all too often) these chapters, improving upon them every time. He is a remarkable friend and colleague.

The National Institute on Drug Abuse supported much of the data collection and research that led to this book. Our project officer, Mario De La Rosa, was always helpful. The Rochester project also received support from the National Science Foundation and currently the National Institute of Mental Health. Although their support is less directly focused on the issues addressed in this book, the overall project could not have been accomplished without their help and it is gratefully recognized.

We also want to recognize the contributions of Mac Klein, to whom this book is dedicated. Mac was a member of the National Advisory Board for the three projects of the Program of Research on the Causes and Correlates of Delinquency. In that capacity he was a strong advocate for the projects and helped steer us through difficult waters. Mac has dedicated his scholarly career to the study of gangs, and it seems to us that he never understood that the Rochester project was not really a "gang study"; he just assumed that, like all criminological research, we should study gangs! He was right, of course, and his focus led us to the importance of this topic and to this book. Along the way he served as a mentor, critic, colleague, adviser, and friend. Like Buddy, he was also forced to read too many versions of these chapters, but always to our benefit.

We also acknowledge the contributions of other veteran gang researchers who reviewed the manuscript, especially Scott Decker. Scott's careful reading of the manuscript and detailed comments have improved this book substantially. The authors, of course, are responsible for the final product but we recognize the positive contributions of many others, especially Mac, Buddy, and Scott.

Over the past 16 years we have benefited greatly from collaborative work with our companion projects in the Program of Research on the Causes and Correlates of Delinquency: the Denver Youth Survey and the Pittsburgh Youth Study. We have learned a great deal from our colleagues in Denver, particularly David Huizinga and Finn Esbensen, and in Pittsburgh, particularly Rolf Loeber, Magda Stouthamer-Loeber, and David Farrington. All of the projects are much stronger together than they ever could have been as separate research undertakings. We received excellent advice from our National Advisory Board – Alfred Blumstein, Dante Cicchetti, Malcolm Klein, Lloyd Ohlin, and Lee Robins – as well as the Rochester project's Advisory Board – Rand Conger, Rex Forehand, and Charles Wellford. Dante Cicchetti, a member of the University of Rochester faculty, pulled double duty, not only serving on the Advisory Board but also helping introduce us to the Rochester community.

We owe a debt of thanks to many, many people in the Rochester community. First and foremost are the 2,000 members of the Rochester study.

The 1,000 adolescents and the 1,000 parents in our sample gave unstintingly of their time. Their willingness to be interviewed and reinterviewed – for most of them 12 times – and to share their private thoughts, feelings, and behaviors with our staff was absolutely essential to our research. We can never adequately repay them, but we hope the impact that our research findings have on developing better programs and policies for youth offers them some compensation.

Special thanks is owed to the officials at the Rochester City School District. Without their help at the outset of the study we would not have been able to identify and select the sample to initiate this long-term effort. We are particularly grateful to Peter McWalters, the superintendent of schools, and to David Hunt, the supervising director of Student Data, Testing, and Records at the time. We were also helped by Ann Brown, Judy Klein-Henwood, and Warren Crichlow at various stages of our research. During the early waves of the study we conducted almost all of the adolescent interviews in the schools, a process greatly facilitated by the principals, vice-principals, and counselors. Despite our efforts to be nonintrusive, we did intrude and we appreciate their tolerance and help.

As we began this research project, two New York State cabinet officers introduced us to officials in Monroe County and in the City of Rochester. Lawrence Kurlander, a former Monroe County district attorney, was the director of the Office of Criminal Justice and Joseph Cocozza was the executive director of the Council on Children and Families. We benefited greatly from their advice, good judgment, and political savvy.

We have also collected information from many Monroe County and Rochester city agencies. At the Monroe County Department of Social Services we are particularly grateful to Diane Larter and Dan Ross, not only for providing access to crucial data files but for thoughtful readings of several of our papers. Over the years the Office of the Monroe County Executive has been very helpful. We particularly appreciate the assistance we received from Craig Osborne in the 1990s and from James Mulley more recently. The Mayor's Office of the City of Rochester has been equally helpful. In particular we thank Mayor William A. Johnson, and William Faucette and Earl Isaac of his staff.

The members of the juvenile and criminal justice communities in Rochester simply could not have been more helpful to our efforts. At the Rochester Police Department we appreciate the help we received from Chiefs Gordon Urlacher and, especially, Robert Duffy, and many of their division heads, including Deputy Chief Ann Marie Van Son, Captain Lynde Johnston, Captain Wayne Cannon, and Sergeant Stephen DiGennaro. The Monroe County Family Court and the State Supreme Court have helped us throughout. We are particularly grateful to Judge Francis Affronti who helped at both levels and to Judge Leonard Maas of the Family Court.

Howard Relin, the Monroe County district attorney, was also a firm supporter over the years.

We have received assistance from a number of New York State agencies. Leonard Morgenbesser, Dave Clark, and Karl Gohlke of the Department of Correctional Services were particularly helpful in arranging for us to interview subjects who were incarcerated. Charles Devane and William Baccaglini were equally helpful at the Division for Youth. Our collection of statewide arrest histories at the Division of Criminal Justice Services was aided by Richard Rosen, Bruce Frederick, and Steve Greenstein.

Finally, and closer to home, we want to recognize the tremendous contributions made by the staff of the Rochester Youth Development Study. One of the great strengths of this study is the very high rate of subject retention over the course of the study. That is entirely due to the herculean efforts of the Rochester staff and our field director, William Miles. Bill has held that position since the inception of the project and has masterminded the data collection effort with care, professionalism, and the utmost loyalty to the project and to the study families. Since the late 1980s he has been aided by Jacquetta Daniels, field coordinator; Carol Wright, our senior interviewer; and Raymond Specht, who was also a field coordinator through the mid 1990s. We have benefited greatly from their level-headed advice and sheer hard work. We also want to recognize the other staff members and the many interviewers – too many to mention by name – who worked for the project over the years. Theirs is a difficult job, locating and interviewing a large sample, often in poor neighborhoods and in all kinds of weather. We believe the level of retention and the quality of our data are testimony to their accomplishments and the leadership provided by Bill and Jacquetta.

We have also been graced with outstanding colleagues and staff at the University at Albany. Margaret Farnworth, then on the faculty of the School of Criminal Justice, was a coprincipal investigator and Susan Stern, then a faculty member at the School of Social Welfare, was a research associate at the outset of the study. We benefited greatly from their contributions in the early years, especially their knowledge of measurement issues for structural position and family processes, respectively. We also benefit greatly from the statistical and methodological advice of our colleague, David McDowall, of the School of Criminal Justice.

Over the years we have had the pleasure of working with a number of graduate research assistants and we are happy the project has been able to contribute to their doctoral education and professional development. We would like to thank Oscar Best, Beth Bjerregaard, Trudy Bonsell, Elizabeth Cass, Deborah Chard-Wierschem, Rebekah Chu, Lori Collins-Hall, Martin Gottschalk, Nicole Hendrix, Gregory Howard, Nancy Jakubowyc, Sung Joon Jang, Carolyn Levy, Jessica Mass, Cynthia Perez McCluskey, Craig Rivera, James Tesoriero, and Kimberly Young for their assistance. We would especially like to recognize Rebekah Chu and Craig Rivera for contributions to this book. After Kim Tobin finished her Ph.D. and joined the faculty of Westfield State College, Becky and Craig finished much of the data analysis reported here. Becky, in particular, checked and reestimated many of the models to ensure that our results are as precise as possible. We thank her for her care and diligence in this effort.

The Albany professional staff has been absolutely essential to the success of this project. First Sharon Wright and now Arleen DeGonzague have served as the administrative assistant for the Hindelang Criminal Justice Research Center, and Deb Coppola as secretary. Their efficiency in preparing and in monitoring the project's various budgets and administrative matters is remarkable and made our lives much easier. We also want to thank Jeanette Megas and Michele Carlton who served as the project secretaries and who, in their usual efficient ways, typed this manuscript.

Marilyn Hubbard, as director of data entry, is responsible for translating the massive amount of data collected in Rochester into precise, clean data files. She performs this task with care and diligence, thereby ensuring the quality of our analytic efforts. Marilyn helps in innumerable other ways to make the project run smoothly.

Patty Glynn was and Adrienne Freeman-Gallant is the project data manager/analyst. Their care for the accuracy of the data and our analytic approach has served the project exceptionally well over the years.

Finally, we want to express our deep appreciation to the project's research coordinator, Pamela Porter. As the coordinator she contributes to virtually all aspects of the project: administration, data analysis, measurement, proposal preparation, editing, liaison with the field staff, and more. She does so with an efficiency and commitment that is startling. Thank you.

And, finally, to all of the project staff, in Rochester and in Albany, we want you to know how much we know how much our success is due to your efforts. We realize that life on this project can be a bit chaotic at times, but it is well worth the effort, as is evident from results and policy recommendations found in this book.

A Life-Course Orientation to the Study of Gang Membership

SINCE THE EARLIEST DAYS of gang research, such as the classic study of 1,313 gangs in Chicago conducted by Thrasher (1927), scholars have noted the disproportionate contribution that gang members make to the level of crime in society. Indeed, the observation that gang members, as compared with other youths, are more extensively involved in delinquency – especially serious and violent delinquency – is perhaps the most robust and consistent observation in criminological research.

This observation has been made across time, geographical and national boundaries, and methods of data collection. Observational studies indicate that gang members are heavily involved in various forms of delinquent activities. This finding has been reported in the early research of Spergel (1964), Miller (1966), and Klein (1971), as well as in more recent observational studies, such as those by Moore (1978), Horowitz (1983), Vigil (1988), Taylor (1990), Decker and Van Winkle (1996), and Hagedorn (1998). Studies that rely on official data to compare gang members and nonmembers have also found a strong association between gang membership and delinquent activity (see Cohen, 1969; Huff, 1996; Klein, Gordon, and Maxson, 1986; Klein and Maxson, 1989). Finally, survey research studies report higher rates of involvement in delinquency for gang members as compared with nonmembers. These surveys include Short and Strodtbeck's (1965) study of Chicago gangs, as well as the work by Tracy (1979), Fagan, Piper, and Moore (1986), Fagan (1989, 1990), Huff (1996), and Esbensen and Winfree (1998). Moreover, there is general agreement that the relationship between gang membership and delinquency is particularly pronounced for more serious offenses and for violent offenses.

In recent years there has been an almost incredible proliferation of gangs to more and more American cities and a concomitant increase in the number of gangs and gang members in American society. Klein reports that between 1961 and 1970 there was a 74% increase in the number of gang-involved cities, an 83% increase from 1970 to 1980, and a phenomenal 345% increase from 1980 to 1992 (Klein, 1995: 90–91). As Klein notes: "gangs are no longer a big-city problem" but have spread to cities of all sizes (1995: 96).

Curry, Ball, and Decker (1996a, 1996b) report similar results in surveys of law enforcement agencies conducted in 1991 and 1993. Curry et al. (1996a) found that 57% of all American cities had a gang problem in 1993; 87% of the cities with a population of between 150,000 and 200,000 and 89% of the cities with a population of more than 200,000 reported a gang problem.

The National Youth Gang Center (1997) conducted a series of surveys of law enforcement offices throughout the country, beginning in the mid-1990s. In 1995, near the peak of gang activity, they surveyed more than 4,000 law enforcement agencies[1] and found that over half (58%) of the responding agencies, covering all 50 states, reported youth gang problems (National Youth Gang Center, 1997). The most recent law enforcement survey found "that a total of 3,911 jurisdictions in the United States experienced gang activity in 1999, a 19 percent decline from the high of 4,824 in 1996" (Egley, 2000: 1). Gangs were reported in 66% of large cities, as well in suburbs (47%), small cities (27%), and even rural areas (18%). Despite the fact that the estimates of gang activity declined somewhat in all these categories, the 1999 survey still reveals a very substantial level of gang activity throughout the country and much higher levels than those observed 20 or 30 years ago.

All of these studies rely on surveys of law enforcement agencies and, unfortunately therefore, may share common sources of bias. For example, part of the increase in the number of cities with gangs may be due to a heightened awareness of gang problems in American society, an increased willingness of law enforcement agencies to admit to gang problems, or a tendency to identify more generic delinquency problems as "gang-related." Nevertheless, the consistency of the results across these three independent surveys and the magnitude of the estimated increase suggest there has, indeed, been a substantial expansion of gang behavior in the recent past.

This increase is alarming for several reasons. The first is the sheer number of gangs and gang members in American society. The second is the percentage of cities that are currently experiencing gang problems; virtually all large cities, and well over half of all cities, report active gangs. The third is the rapidity of the spread of gangs throughout America; in the space of about 15 years, gangs have spread from being isolated in a relatively small number of large cities to being a regular feature of the urban landscape.

The spread of gangs throughout American society, coupled with the strong association between gang membership and serious, violent

---

[1] This was not a nationally representative sample of law enforcement agencies. Overall, 83% of the agencies surveyed responded.

delinquency, makes it imperative that we understand as fully as possible the role of the street gang in generating involvement in delinquency, violence, drug use, and drug selling. Doing so will add to our theoretical understanding of the causes of antisocial behavior and will provide important information for prevention and intervention policies. Although the importance of this research issue is obvious, Howell has recognized that the data, especially the longitudinal data, necessary to answer a number of fundamental questions concerning the nature, extent, and causes of gang behavior are "woefully lacking" (1994: 510).

Gangs in Developmental Perspective

The purpose of this book is to respond to at least one part of this gap in our knowledge by placing the study of gang membership in a developmental or life-course perspective. We are interested in identifying the characteristics of gang members and in examining the social and psychological forces that lead some adolescents to succumb to the lure of the gang while others manage to avoid it. We are also interested in understanding the consequences of gang membership for the developmental adjustment of gang members. Although we know that gang members are heavily involved in delinquency, especially serious and violent delinquency, we know much less about the extent to which gang membership plays a causal role in eliciting this behavior. Our analysis addresses this by trying to separate selection effects (the extent to which delinquents seek out the gang) from facilitation effects (the extent to which the gang enables the delinquent behavior of its members). We do this for a variety of criminal behaviors related to gang activity – delinquency, violence, drug use, drug selling, and gun carrying and use. As we will show in our analysis, gang membership appears to have a pronounced impact on facilitating all of these behaviors.

We are also interested in exploring the longer-term consequences of joining a street gang, a very understudied topic. Does involvement in this weakly organized but strongly deviant form of adolescent social network exact a toll on the later life course of the individual? Or, is gang membership merely a transitory adolescent phenomenon with few, if any, long-term consequences? We examine whether gang membership interferes with meeting the normal challenges of adolescent adjustment, such as completing high school, and whether it contributes to generating disorderly transitions to adult roles, such as teenage parenthood. As we document, gang membership appears to have a pernicious impact on many aspects of life-course development.

We examine these and related issues for both male and female gang members. While the pattern of the onset and duration of gang membership varies somewhat by gender, it has robust negative impacts on the life course of adolescent girls, as it does for the life course of adolescent boys. Under-standing how these patterns develop is an important issue for the expanding study of female gang members (see, e.g., Miller, 2001).

In addressing these and related questions, we adopt a somewhat differ-ent conceptual perspective and methodological approach than that found in most prior studies of gangs. We do not sample gangs and then ob-serve their members as so many classic, observational studies do. Instead, we embed the study of gang members in an individual-based longitudinal study of antisocial behavior, the Rochester Youth Development Study. Some of the Rochester study subjects became gang members while others did not, and the gang members remained in the gang for varying lengths of time and at varying ages. By following these subjects over time – before, during, and after the period when they were gang members – we are able to place the study of gangs in a developmental perspective and address several issues that have largely been ignored in prior studies. This perspective should complement prior work on the phenomenon of street gangs and add to a fuller understanding of the ways in which gangs influence the lives of their members. In the remainder of this chapter we introduce our conceptual and methodological approaches, approaches that are more fully developed in the subsequent chapters.

Conceptual Framework

Our understanding of gangs and gang members has, in large part, been shaped by observational studies in which a researcher gains access to one or more gangs and spends a substantial period of time on the street corners with them, observing their behaviors and social relationships. These studies have been tremendously influential in informing theories of gang behavior (e.g., Cloward and Ohlin, 1960; Miller, 1958), as well as gang prevention programs (e.g., Klein, 1971; Spergel, 1966). In spite of the extensive contri-butions made by these observational studies, they have a curiously myopic quality. Although they open broad windows into the lives of the gang mem-bers they observe, they do so for very narrow periods of time, that is to say, only during the person's period of active gang membership. These studies typically contain little, if any, information on the lives of gang members before or after their time in the gang.[2] As a consequence, the general litera-ture on street gangs often fails to highlight life-course development, thereby limiting our understanding of both the antecedents and the consequences of gang membership. This book, however, adopts a life-course perspective to provide a somewhat different angle on gangs and gang members that

---

[2] There are some exceptions, for example, studies by Moore (1978, 1991), Vigil (1988), Hagedorn (1998), and Tracy (1979).

should add to the understanding of the origins and consequences of gang membership.

Life-Course Perspective

The life-course perspective emphasizes the importance of treating behavior as constantly evolving as various demands, opportunities, interests, and events impinge upon actors as they age (Baltes, 1987; Baltes and Brim, 1982). Human development is not completed in childhood or even in adolescence; indeed, behavior that is initiated in adolescence can have important consequences for transitions to adulthood, and these transitions, in turn, can shape the course of adult development. Thus, within the life-course perspective, emphasis shifts from a focus on early socialization to one on the entire life-span (Elder, 1994). Given this general orientation, Elder defines the life course as "the interweave of age-graded *trajectories* such as work careers and family pathways, that are subject to changing conditions and future options and to short-term *transitions* ranging from leaving school to retirement" (1994: 5; emphasis added).

Human development is viewed as explicitly multidimensional because people simultaneously move along different trajectories (e.g., family and school) as they age. Not everyone enters all developmental trajectories, however, and people can be characterized in terms of the pattern of trajectories they do and do not enter. Trajectories also become interlinked over time (Elder, 1994), and entrance into some trajectories can impact movement along other trajectories. For example, educational attainment can alter family and career development. Similarly, trajectories of antisocial behavior can influence a variety of conventional or prosocial trajectories like school, work, and family formation.

A central theme of the life-course perspective is that the timing of transitions into or along trajectories has real behavioral consequences. Off-age transitions, especially precocious or early transitions, can create disorder in the developmental sequence and lead to later problems of adjustment because the person is less likely to be socially and psychologically prepared for the transition. To illustrate, becoming a teenage parent can reduce the chances of completing high school and of establishing a stable employment history.

Elder (1985) also emphasized that both the timing of transitions and the interlocking nature of trajectories can create *turning points*, a redirection or change in the life course itself. A precocious transition in one trajectory that has a ripple effect into others can alter the long-term prospects of successful adjustment into adulthood. Thus, the life course is never fully determined. It is always possible for new conditions and events to coincide so as to deflect even well-established pathways.

The characteristics, behaviors, and experiences of individuals will also influence the contexts they enter and their perceptions of those contexts. In turn, the changing contexts are expected to have an impact on the individuals' characteristics and behaviors. Thus, there is an explicit recognition of bidirectional relationships between the individuals' behaviors and significant contexts in their lives (Elder and Caspi, 1988; Hetherington and Baltes, 1988; Magnusson, 1988).

In this regard, there is also increasing recognition of the importance that antisocial behavior has in generating transitions and, via those transitions, the likelihood of success in the adult years (Jessor, Donovan, and Costa, 1991; Krohn et al., 1995; Newcomb and Bentler, 1988; Sampson and Laub, 1993; Yamaguchi and Kandel, 1985a, 1985b). Adolescent antisocial behavior leads to later disorder in the life course for several reasons. Participating in illegal behaviors may distract one from conventional pursuits; for example, drug use lowers performance in school (Jessor and Jessor, 1977). Involvement in antisocial behavior may also cause the individual to be officially labeled, making participation in conventional arenas such as school and work more difficult (Farrington, 1977). In addition, participation in antisocial behavior discourages friendships with conventional others and encourages involvement in deviant social networks. Because prosocial friends, teachers, and family can play an important role in assisting the individual in getting through school, obtaining a job, and selecting a mate, the loss of these sources of social capital can have deleterious effects on later life chances.

Gangs in Life-Course Perspective

The life-course perspective has a number of implications for the study of gangs and gang members, both theoretically and methodologically. Perhaps the most basic is that gang membership itself can be thought of as a trajectory. Some people enter that trajectory while others do not. Of those who do, the transition into the gang occurs at different ages. Some experience an unusually early entry and, based on the general life-course premise that off-time transitions generate problems of adjustment, gang membership may be particularly consequential for them. It may be the case that people who join gangs at unusually late ages may experience serious problems of adjustment as well.

People who do enter the gang trajectory stay for varying periods of time and become more or less involved in the life of the gang. The gang literature demonstrates clearly that not all gang members are created equal. Many are fringe members, circling the periphery of the gang; relatively few are core members, ensnared in the center of the gang world (Klein, 1971). One would expect that deeper penetration along this trajectory – either in terms of duration of membership or position within the gang – would yield stronger behavioral and developmental consequences.

If gang membership is conceived as a trajectory with real behavioral consequences, then it is also important to identify why some people enter it and others do not. In addressing this issue, the life-course perspective points to the importance of several sources of explanation. First, it is unlikely that the social and psychological forces that lead to gang membership are only those that are established early in the life course. The life-course perspective highlights the importance of unfolding relationships and developmental influences that are more proximal to the outcome. Second, the multidimensional nature of the model emphasizes that several domains are likely to be involved. Thus, for example, it is unlikely that the origins of gang membership are to be found only in social structural position or only in family relationships. Rather, the broader social ecology – structural position, neighborhood context, and family, school, peer, and individual characteristics – is likely to play a role. The empirical problem is to see which combination of these factors is most important for this particular outcome.

The life-course orientation also suggests that for many people gang membership may act as a turning point that has the potential to alter or redirect basic life-course pathways. In brief, these processes stem from the somewhat more formal structure and the highly deviant nature of the street gang (see Chapter 9). Gangs are social networks that embed their members in deviant routines and isolate them from prosocial arenas. To the extent to which that occurs, gang membership may serve as a turning point, redirecting the person's life. This redirection can unfold in several other behavioral domains. One is the person's delinquent or criminal career; entry into a gang ought to deflect delinquent trajectories upward. This upswing in deviant behavior need not be permanent, however; indeed, because the life-course perspective assumes that human development is always malleable, influenced by proximal events, it should not be. Thus, exit from the gang ought to deflect the delinquent or criminal career downward. The life-course perspective suggests a synchronous movement between gang membership and delinquent behavior.

The view of gang membership as a turning point also suggests consequences for other, more prosocial trajectories. Given the intensely deviant orientation of the gang, joining a gang should disrupt the normal course of adolescent development, for example, with respect to family relationships and school performance. As a result, gang members ought to be more likely to experience precocious transitions to adult roles and be less well equipped to make a successful adjustment to adulthood.

Finally, the life-course perspective suggests that the duration of gang membership ought to intensify these consequences. While emphasizing the malleable nature of human development, the life-course perspective does not view development as endlessly malleable. The longer anyone remains on any trajectory, the harder it is to avoid its consequences, and deviant trajectories are no exception (Thornberry, 1987). Indeed, the highly deviant nature of the street gang may have particularly negative consequences, generating what Moffitt (1997) refers to as a "knifing off" from prosocial trajectories.

In sum, adopting a life-course perspective raises a number of interrelated issues for investigation. They concern the antecedents of gang membership, its short-term, contemporaneous consequences, and its longer-term developmental consequences. The research literature on gangs has addressed all of these aspects of gang membership but tends to focus on the middle portion, the period of active membership. By systematically addressing the broader array of issues identified here and by examining life-course development before, during, *and* after the period of membership, we hope to expand our understanding of this phenomenon.

Methodological Approach

The life-course orientation that we adopt also has implications for research design. Previous studies of gangs and gang members typically relied on one of two research strategies. There are many observational studies in which researchers (e.g., Hagedorn, 1998) or detached workers (e.g., Short and Strodtbeck, 1965) gather detailed qualitative information about the activities of gangs and their members. Other studies are comparative quantitative analyses in which researchers sample gang members and compare their behavior and attitudes to those of nonmembers (e.g., Esbensen and Winfree, 1998; Klein et al., 1986). Some studies, of course, blend the use of quantitative and qualitative analyses.

Although these studies form the bedrock for our understanding of gang behavior, they are somewhat limited in their ability to address life-course issues. As noted, the typical gang study focuses on gang members when they are actively involved in the gang. Relatively little is known about their pre-gang characteristics, behaviors, and activities, except via retrospective data or official records. Thus, our understanding of developmental precursors is hampered by designs that sample either gangs or gang members. In turn, that limits our ability to identify risk factors for gang membership, to distinguish between the precursors and the consequences of gang membership and, therefore, to examine the more difficult issue of identifying the social forces that actually cause adolescents to join street gangs.

Previous studies of this sort are somewhat less hampered in their ability to study the postgang behavior and adjustment of gang members since, having identified gang members, they can be followed in time (e.g., Hagedorn, 1998). Nevertheless, many studies of gang members do not do so, and the gang literature has an overwhelming focus on life while in the gang. Thus, while we have a varied and rich understanding of the contemporaneous influences of gang membership on the lives of gang members, we have much less information on its long-term consequences in altering human development and life-course trajectories. As early as 1971 Klein noted that "though the need is great there has been no careful study of gang members as they move into adult status" (1971: 136), a situation that has not changed appreciably over the past 30 years.

To address these life-course issues, it is necessary to identify a community sample of adolescents – some of whom will become gang members and some of whom will not – and trace their growth and development beginning prior to their age of joining the gangs. Doing so allows us to identify antecedent risk factors and the causal processes associated with gang membership. Following the sample during their gang-involved years allows us to gauge the contemporaneous impact of gang membership on behavior, attitudes, and social relations. Finally, by continuing to follow the sample – both gang members and nonmembers – after the peak years of gang membership, the longer-term consequences of gang membership on life-course development and adjustment can be assessed. In other words, the way in which the trajectory of gang membership relates to other trajectories – both prosocial (e.g., schooling) and antisocial (e.g., drug selling) – can be more properly studied.

This book is based on a long-term project, the Rochester Youth Development Study, that has these design features. It selected a community sample at age 13 and followed the youths until age 22, spanning the peak ages of gang involvement, at least in this study site.[3] Longitudinal panel studies such as this one have both advantages and disadvantages for the study of gangs and gang members. In panel studies the *individual gang member* is the unit of analysis; in contrast, in many previous gang studies the *gang* is the unit of analysis. Among the disadvantages of panel studies is the limited ability to study group processes and the ways in which group processes influence the behaviors of gang members. This type of design also tends to decontextualize the deviant behavior of gang members and makes it difficult, if not impossible, to distinguish between delinquent acts committed by gang members as individuals and delinquent acts committed by gang members for the gang, or at least in the context of gang activities. Thus, some important analytic issues cannot be easily addressed using individual panel studies.

There is also an important limitation concerning the generalizability of the findings derived from the available panel studies of gang members. Virtually all longitudinal data sets that have measured gang membership have been conducted in newer or "emergent" gang cities. In particular,

---

[3] The design is described in detail in the next chapter.

they have been conducted in Rochester, New York (Thornberry, Krohn, et al., 1993), Denver, Colorado (Esbensen and Huizinga, 1993), Seattle, Washington (Battin et al., 1998), and Montreal, Canada (Lacourse et al., forthcoming). Because of this, it is not clear whether the findings of these studies are unique to emergent gang cities or whether they would be replicated if panel studies had been conducted in traditional gang cities such as Los Angeles and Chicago.

While having some distinct limitations, studies of gang members embedded within these longitudinal panel studies also have distinct advantages. They address substantive issues that cannot easily be examined when the gang is the unit of analysis. As mentioned earlier, longitudinal designs are well suited to the identification of antecedent characteristics and the estimation of time-ordered causal models. Panel studies also allow for the study of models of within-individual change, not just between-individual comparisons. These models, in which each individual serves as his or her own control, are powerful ways of examining the impact of social influences – such as gang membership – on behavior.

Overall, a developmental approach complements the very detailed understanding that prior observational and comparative research has presented about periods of active gang membership, and both types of studies are needed to understand fully the phenomenon of street gangs. By identifying areas of convergence and divergence in results – in combination with a firm understanding of the strengths and weaknesses of the different designs – perhaps we can move both our knowledge of gang behavior and our efforts to prevent it forward. We return to this issue in the final chapter when we discuss the theoretical and policy implications of our findings.

Research Procedures: The Sample and the Data

TO EXAMINE the origins and aftermath of membership in juvenile street gangs, we rely on data from the Rochester Youth Development Study, an ongoing, longitudinal investigation of antisocial behavior. This study, which began in 1986 with funding from the Office of Juvenile Justice and Delinquency Prevention, focused on the causes and correlates of serious, violent, and chronic delinquency. The study of gangs is just one aspect of this broader research initiative, but one that is very central to the core aims of the study. In this chapter we introduce the reader to the design of the Rochester study and describe the study's sample and measures, especially as they focus on issues related to gangs and gang membership.

The Rochester Youth Development Study

The Rochester Youth Development Study follows a panel of juveniles from their early teenage years through their early adult years. Figure 2.1 depicts the overall research design of the study. To date, we have collected 12 waves of data spanning the ages of 13 through 22.

Each subject and a primary caretaker (in the vast majority of cases this is the biological mother)[1] were interviewed at six-month intervals from the spring of 1988 until the spring of 1992. After a two-year gap in data collection, annual interviews began in 1994. By the end of Wave 12 in the spring of 1997, we had reinterviewed 846 of the initial 1,000 subjects in the study, a retention rate of 85%.

---

[1] At the first interview, for example, 85% of the parent respondents were biological mothers, another 10% were stepmothers, and the remainder (5%) were fathers, grandparents, and other relatives.

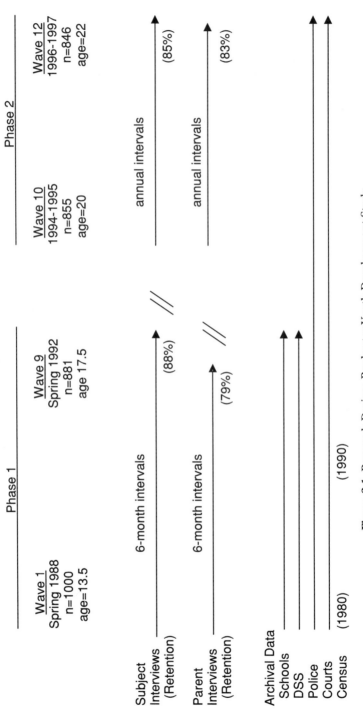

Figure 2.1. Research Design: Rochester Youth Development Study

The interviews lasted about an hour and covered a wide range of topics including social class position, family structure and processes, educational performance, peer relationships, neighborhood characteristics, psychological functioning, social networks, social support systems, and involvement in prosocial and antisocial behaviors. In addition to the interview data, we collected data from the files of official agencies that provide services to youth and families, including the Rochester public schools, police department, probation department, family court, and social services.

Sample

Research Site

The sample is drawn from Rochester, New York, a city of a quarter of a million people located on the shore of Lake Ontario in western New York State. According to the 1990 census, the population of the city was 230,356 and the population of the metropolitan area was 1,064,724. Rochester, the 69th largest city in the United States, contains a diverse ethnic population: 61.1% are white, 31.5% are African American, and 7.4% are of other races. In addition, 8.7% of the population is of Hispanic (mostly Puerto Rican) background.

Rochester is known as "The World Image Center" because of its historical role in the photography, xerography, and optics industries. Eastman Kodak, Bausch and Lomb, and Xerox corporations all were born in Rochester. The overall health of industry in Rochester is evidenced by a relatively low unemployment rate of 3.7% in 1990 and a per capita income that ranks 60th in the United States, above other New York cities of comparable size, such as Albany and Buffalo. Like other northern cities in the United States, however, Rochester has a declining manufacturing base. During the decade of the 1980s Rochester lost 27,500 manufacturing jobs. Although Rochester has a generally healthy economy and great wealth, these exist side by side with substantial levels of social disadvantage. For example, 21.1% of the families in Rochester lived below the 1989 poverty level and 38% of the residents under the age of 18 lived in poverty. Among 200 cities with more than 100,000 population, only 12 cities had more children living in poverty than Rochester.

Rochester also has a relatively high crime rate (Flanagan and Maguire, 1992). In 1990 its index crime rate was 11,039 offenses per 100,000 people, the violent crime rate was 1,237 per 100,000, and the property crime rate was 9,802 per 100,000. These rates far exceed the average rates in the United States. For the country as a whole the rates per 100,000 in 1990 were 5,820 for index crimes, 732 for violent crimes, and 5,088 for property crimes. If the comparison is limited to cities with populations between 100,000 and 250,000 the comparable rates are 8,230, 991, and 7,239 per 100,000 for index, violent, and property rates, respectively, still lower than those in Rochester. In fact, the rate of index offenses was higher in Rochester (11,039 per 100,000) than it was in New York City (9,699 per 100,000), although the latter had a substantially higher rate of violent crime (2,384 per 100,000 compared with 1,237 per 100,000). According to police and local community leaders, gangs became an emerging problem in the mid to late 1980s (Howell, Egley, and Gleason, 2002).

Rochester was chosen as the research site for several reasons, even though the research team is at the University at Albany, 250 miles to the east. The primary reason stemmed from the Office of Juvenile Justice and Delinquency Prevention's mandate to study a sample with a large number of serious, chronic offenders. Albany, and its neighboring cities of Troy and Schenectady, were not suitable because they are too small to yield sufficient samples for this purpose. For a variety of reasons associated with access to official records, it was desirable to remain in New York State and Rochester was the closest city that had a population large enough to support the aims of the study with the exception of New York City. The size, complexity, and bureaucratic scope of New York City's public schools, however, made it, in our judgment, a less than ideal research setting. Finally, the Rochester community, especially the Rochester City School District, simply could not have been more helpful or accommodating to our objectives. Thus, Rochester it was.

Sampling Procedures

To meet our study objectives we oversampled youth at high risk for serious delinquency and drug use because the base rates for these behaviors are relatively low. The following strategy was used. First, the target population was limited to seventh and eighth grade students in the Rochester public school system. Second, a stratified sample was selected from the target population so that high-risk youths are overrepresented, and the findings can be appropriately weighted to represent the target population.

To oversample high-risk youth, the sample was stratified on two dimensions. First, males were oversampled (75% versus 25%) because they are more likely than females to be chronic offenders and to engage in serious and violent delinquency (Blumstein et al., 1986; Huizinga, Morse, and Elliott, 1992). Second, students from high-crime areas of the city were oversampled based on the assumption that adolescents who live in high-crime-rate areas are at greater risk for offending than are those living in low-crime-rate areas. To identify high-crime areas, each census tract in Rochester was assigned a resident arrest rate reflecting the proportion of the tract's total population arrested by the Rochester police in 1986.[2]

There was a total of 4,013 students in the seventh and eighth grades at the start of the spring semester in 1988; of these, 3,372 (84%) were eligible for the sample.[3] All eligible cases were assigned to their census tract of residence at the beginning of sample selection. To generate a final panel of 1,000 students, 1,334 were selected, a number based on an estimated nonparticipation rate of approximately 25%. The 1,334 cases were selected in the following way. First, in the census tracts with the highest resident arrest rates (approximately the top one-third), all eligible students were asked to participate in the study. Second, students in the remaining census tracts were selected at a rate proportionate to the tract's contribution to the city's resident arrest rate. Tracts with lower resident arrest rates provided a proportionately smaller part of the sample. After the number of students to be selected from a tract was determined, the student population in the tract was stratified by sex and grade, and students were selected from those strata at random. A final panel of 1,000 students and their primary caretakers was selected for study. Because the probability of selection into the study is known for all the students, we can weight the data to represent the target population – the total cohort of seventh and eighth graders in the Rochester public schools in 1988. Unless noted, the data are weighted in the analyses presented here.

Field Procedures

Once the sample was drawn, we sent the parent (or legal guardian) of each selected student a letter signed by both the superintendent of the Rochester City School District and the principal investigator of the Rochester study. The letter described the study in general terms, asked for parental cooperation, and indicated that a project interviewer would shortly visit the family.

An interviewer then visited the prospective study member's home and described in detail the purpose and design of the study. The parent was asked to provide informed consent both for his or her participation and the participation of his or her child. If the parent agreed to participate, the Wave 1 parent interview was conducted. For Spanish-speaking parents,

---

[2] Each tract's resident arrest rate – not its crime rate – was used because there is a substantial gap between where crimes occur and where offenders live. Indeed, the correlation between 1986 arrest rates and crime rates across all of Rochester's census tracts was only .26. We assume that risk for being an offender is more highly related to coming from a neighborhood with a high rate of active offenders than coming from an area with a large number of crimes.

[3] Students were ineligible if they moved out of the Rochester school district before Wave 1 data collection began, if neither English nor Spanish was spoken in the home, if a sibling was already in the sample pool, or if they were older than the expected age for eighth graders given the Rochester schools' admission policy.

the interview was translated into Spanish and administered by bilingual interviewers from the local community. The children of all parents who consented were then contacted and asked if they would provide their assent to participate. Wave 1 student interviews usually were conducted at school, always in a private setting such as an empty office or classroom. Students who could not be interviewed at school (e.g., chronic truants) were interviewed at home.

Not all families agreed to participate in the study, of course. The overall refusal rate was 20%, and virtually all refusals were by the parents; only four students refused to participate after their parents had agreed. If a parent or student refused to participate, that student was replaced by another student similar in terms of grade, gender, and census tract of residence. In this way, minimum distortion was introduced into the final panel; the available data indicate that refusals were not differentially distributed in terms of race/ethnicity, gender, grade in school, or the resident arrest rate of the census tract of residence. These procedures generated a sample that is 68% African American, 17% Hispanic, and 15% white. Virtually all of the Hispanic respondents in the sample are of Puerto Rican descent. Males represent 72.9% of the sample and females 27.1%.

Subject Retention

Considerable effort was devoted to maximizing subject retention over the course of the study, particularly given the low income, highly mobile nature of many of our subjects, and the expectation that delinquent youth and gang members would be among those more difficult to contact and track (Krohn and Thornberry, 1999; Thornberry, Bjerregaard, and Miles, 1993). A number of steps were taken to minimize attrition. First, there was no a priori limit to the number of attempted contacts that were made with the subject at each wave. As long as the respondent did not refuse to be interviewed, the case was kept open until the end of each data collection period. Second, all subjects who moved from Rochester were followed and, whenever possible, interviewed. The Rochester study used a variety of sources to locate respondents who had moved, including friends and relatives nominated by the subject, mailings, directory assistance, data bases from official agencies, newspaper articles, military sources, credit bureaus, and schools. Third, even though the sampling frame was generated by the school roster and we conducted adolescent interviews in the Rochester schools whenever possible, adolescents who left the Rochester schools remained in the panel. Those retained included adolescents who were chronic truants, transferred to other schools, dropped out of school, or were institutionalized. Finally, we utilized a variety of specific strategies to maintain cooperation, including incentive payments that increased each year, a project newsletter that was

Table 2.1. *Subject and Parent Retention Rates,*
Wave 1 to Wave 12

	Number of Completed Interviews	Percentage of Total Panel (n = 1000)
Subjects		
Wave 1	956	96
Wave 2	947	95
Wave 3	931	93
Wave 4	928	93
Wave 5	920	92
Wave 6	907	91
Wave 7	898	90
Wave 8	877	88
Wave 9	881	88
Wave 10	855	86
Wave 11	857	86
Wave 12	846	85
Parents		
Wave 1	974	97
Wave 2	908	91
Wave 3	899	90
Wave 4	865	87
Wave 5	855	86
Wave 6	810	81
Wave 7	786	79
Wave 8	793	79
Wave 9[a]	–	–
Wave 10	826	83
Wave 11	833	83
Wave 12	827	83

[a]No parent interviews were conducted at Wave 9.

sent to all families annually, and routine reminders to the subjects about the importance of the study and of their participation in it.

As a result of these procedures, the Rochester study has an excellent record of retaining these relatively high risk and mobile youth over the nine-year period involving 12 waves of data collection (Krohn and Thornberry, 1999). Table 2.1 provides the retention rates for our target subjects and their parents over 12 waves of data collection. During the course of the study, we lost about 1% of the focal subjects per year. Even with the two-year gap in data collection between Waves 9 and 10 – when the subjects moved from

Table 2.2. *Demographic Characteristics of the Total Panel, Those Retained at Wave 12, and Those Not Retained (%)*

	Total Panel (n = 1000)	Retained (n = 846)	Not Retained (n = 154)
Gender			
Male	72.9	71.5	80.5*
Female	27.1	28.5	19.5
Race/Ethnicity			
African American	68.0	68.1	67.5
Hispanic	17.0	16.6	19.5
White	15.0	15.4	13.0
Family Disadvantage at Wave 1			
Yes	65.9	64.1	76.5*
No	34.1	35.9	23.5
Family Structure at Wave 1			
Both Biological Parents	25.0	25.4	22.7
Other	75.0	74.6	77.3

Note: Significance tests are for the comparison between those retained and those not retained.
*p < .05.

their high school years to the much more mobile and independent stage of young adulthood – retention dropped only from 88% to 86%.

Parent attrition is slightly larger and is more uneven across the waves. A larger than average drop in parent retention occurred between Wave 5 and Wave 6, by which time an increasing number of adolescents no longer lived with their parents. Because the vast majority of adolescent respondents still lived with their parents, the interview schedule was organized accordingly and the questions were somewhat inappropriate for the parents who had little or no contact with the adolescent subject. Starting in Wave 10, when a large number of respondents no longer lived with their parents, the interview schedule was revised and the parent retention rate increased to 83%.

To examine selection bias, we compare the respondents who were retained in the study with those who were not retained in terms of basic demographic characteristics (gender, race/ethnicity, social class, and family structure) and initial levels of deviance (Wave 1 general delinquency, violence, and drug use).

Table 2.2 presents the demographic characteristics of those retained and those not retained. We begin by comparing columns 1 and 2, the demographic characteristics of the initial panel of 1,000 subjects and of the 846 subjects who remained in the study at Wave 12, respectively. Only small differences in the percentages by gender, race/ethnicity, family disadvantage, and family structure are evident. For example, 72.9% of the initial panel is male and 27.1% female; at Wave 12 the distribution is 71.5% male and 28.5% female. The same level of similarity is evident for race/ethnicity groupings, family disadvantage, and family structure. Indeed, the largest absolute difference – the difference for family disadvantage – is only 1.8 percentage points.

A more formal way to examine differential attrition is to see whether those retained at Wave 12 are significantly different from those who left the study prior to that time on these variables. When this is done, comparing columns 2 and 3 in Table 2.2, we see that the study was more likely to lose males and disadvantaged respondents.

In any panel study a key concern is whether the respondents who are lost through attrition are the ones who are most likely to be involved in the behaviors that are being studied – in our case, deviant behaviors. One way to assess this is to compare the Wave 1 rates of delinquency and drug use of the respondents who were retained in the study at Wave 12 with the Wave 1 rates of delinquency and drug use for those who were not retained. Deviant behavior is measured at Wave 1 in these comparisons because it is the only wave for which we have data on all individuals who left the study at some time after Wave 1. Also, because the early onset of deviant behaviors is related to later involvement in those behaviors (Krohn et al., 2001), the Wave 1 measure is a reasonable proxy for more general involvement in deviant careers.

Table 2.3 provides the prevalence rates of delinquency and drug use at Wave 1 for the initial panel, those who were retained at Wave 12, and those who were not retained at Wave 12. Data are presented for all subjects and for racial/ethnic groups. Overall, the rates are very similar. For example, 49.2% of those retained at Wave 12 self-reported general delinquency at Wave 1. Of those not retained at Wave 12, 51.9% self-reported general delinquency at Wave 1. Neither this difference in the prevalence rate of Wave 1 general delinquency, nor *any* of the other differences in prevalence rates reported in Table 2.3 are statistically significant. This is also true when the panel is divided into racial/ethnic groups. To the extent that Wave 1 delinquency and drug use rates predict the likelihood that youth will continue to engage in these activities, the findings indicate that respondents who left the study are not significantly more likely to engage in deviant behavior than are those who remained in the study at Wave 12.

Overall the level of attrition in the study is rather low and there is little evidence of differential subject loss. The sociodemographic characteristics of the initial panel and the retained panel are quite similar, as is their early involvement in delinquency and drug use.

Table 2.3. *Prevalence of Delinquency and Drug Use at Wave 1
for the Total Panel, Those Retained at Wave 12, and Those
Not Retained (%)*

	Total Panel (n = 1000)	Retained (n = 846)	Not Retained (n = 154)
General Delinquency			
All Subjects	49.6	49.2	51.9
African American	51.6	50.7	56.7
Hispanic	45.9	45.7	46.7
White	44.7	46.2	35.0
Violent Delinquency			
All Subjects	30.6	30.6	30.5
African American	35.1	34.7	37.5
Hispanic	22.4	22.9	20.0
White	19.3	20.8	10.0
Drug Use			
All Subjects	8.0	7.9	8.4
African American	8.4	8.2	9.6
Hispanic	9.4	10.0	6.7
White	4.7	4.6	5.0

Note: Significance tests were done comparing those retained
and those not retained. None are significant.

A Note on Sample Size

Throughout the remaining chapters the number of subjects included in
analyses varies from chapter to chapter, and even across analyses within the
same chapter. This variability is produced by several factors. Some involve
missing data because not all subjects completed all interviews and some
subjects did not respond to all questions in an interview. Thus, depending
upon which variables are used, the number of cases can vary. Other reasons
involve cross-sectional versus longitudinal analyses. In the former, subjects
do not have to be interviewed at multiple waves to be included, whereas for
the latter they do.

Another source of variability concerns the statistical weighting of the
stratified sample to return it to a random sample of the 1988 seventh and
eighth grade cohorts. This weighting is necessary if proper estimates and
conclusions are to be drawn. Different weights are needed when conducting
subanalyses that select on variables that define the strata in the sample. For
example, the Rochester sample was stratified on gender (of the 1,000 cases,
750 are boys and 250 are girls). When conducting analyses where boys and

girls are combined in one analysis, the weighting procedure will return the sample to 500 boys and 500 girls because that is how they are truly represented in the population. To preserve the correct statistical power, the total sample size for any analysis must be 1,000 cases if there is no attrition or missing data. When attrition and missing data factors are taken into consideration, the number of cases after weighting must equal the total number available for the particular analysis. When analyses are conducted on boys and girls separately, however, the weighting procedure must return 750 boys for separate analysis and 250 girls for separate analysis. This preserves the proper statistical power for each gender while resulting in the correct overall sample size (1,000). As a result, the sample sizes for boys and girls in the analyses in this book vary depending upon whether analyses are combined or separated by gender.

These different sample sizes for boys and girls do not impact statistics like means and regression coefficients. They remain the same in total sample analyses and subanalyses regardless of the resulting number of weighted boys and girls. However, variances and standard errors do change depending on the number of cases in the total or subanalyses. In other words, tests of statistical significance depend on the number of cases. This is the reason for differences in weighting for total or subanalyses by strata, for example, by gender. (See Kish, 1965: 77–80, and Sudman, 1976: 127–128, for more detail on the weighting of stratified samples.) In sum, the number of cases presented in the results to follow varies. That variation is by design and reflects our decision to include the maximum number of cases possible in any particular analysis to maximize statistical power.

Measurement

The Rochester project contains a wealth of measures on youth behaviors, as well as measures on a range of environmental, social, and psychological factors associated with these behaviors. Because of the longitudinal nature of the project, we have multiple measures of the same variable over time, enabling us to track developmental progressions and changes in behaviors. In this section we summarize the measurement strategies and core measures that are utilized in this book.

Gang Membership

Gang membership is central to all the analyses, and we provide an overview of its measurement here. In the following chapters the particular measure of gang membership varies, depending on the objective of the specific analysis. For example, in several analyses gang membership is cumulated over several waves, in others it is measured at specific waves, and in yet others the focal variable is whether the subject ever reports being in a gang.

All of the measures are based on a series of questions about participation in gangs that were asked of all respondents starting at the second interview.[4] The core question is whether, during the six-month time period since the previous interview, they were a member of a street gang or "posse." The latter term was included in the item stem because it was the term Rochester adolescents used to refer to gangs, apparently derived from Jamaican posses. If they responded affirmatively, they were asked a series of follow-up questions about the nature of the gang including its name, the number of members, the role the subject played in the gang, whether their three best friends were in the gang, and why they joined.

In previous analysis (Thornberry, Krohn, et al., 1993) we found that the single self-report item asking subjects if they were a gang member worked as well and resulted in an almost identical list of gang members as when other items were used as selection criteria to define the existence of the gang and the youth's participation in it. For example, when we restricted gang members to those who belong to a gang that had a name, the number of gang members identified differed by at most three in any of the waves we examined (Thornberry, Krohn, et al., 1993). Because of these findings, we use the respondent's self-report as the key indicator of gang membership in this book.

While there is a rather large literature on the validity and reliability of self-reported delinquency data (see, e.g., Hindelang, Hirschi, and Weis, 1981; Huizinga and Elliott, 1986; Thornberry and Krohn, 2000), there is little comparable information on self-report measures of gang membership. The literature assessing the psychometric properties of self-reported measures of delinquent and other deviant behaviors, however, indicates that they have adequate reliability and validity for statistical analysis. Self-reported delinquency data also avoid a number of well-known problems associated with official indicators, such as underreporting and bias due to decision-making discretion.

Based on our interview experiences with these respondents, we know of no reason to suspect that self-reports of gang membership are any less valid or reliable. Adolescents appear to know what gangs are and whether they are a member of a gang. No doubt some respondents who say they are a gang member are not, and some who are deny it; that is the nature of self-reported survey data that forms the heart of most social science analysis. But in the end we agree with Curry and Decker's assessment that "the most powerful measure of gang membership is self-nomination" (1998: 6), which, as Esbensen and Winfree point out, is actually "law enforcement

---

[4] Gang questions were not asked at Wave 1 because we were told by city officials that gangs were not a problem at that time. Between Waves 1 and 2 they emerged as a serious problem confronting the Rochester community, and we began to track gang involvement.

officers' primary criteria for identifying 'official' gang members" (1998: 515).

The most comprehensive assessment of the validity of self-reported gang membership has been conducted by Curry (2000). Through a survey of 429 African American and Latino middle school students in Chicago, he first identified self-reported gang members and self-reported gang-involved youth.[5] He then searched the records of the Chicago Police Department to determine if the subjects were also identified by the police as gang members and whether they had an official police record. If the self-reports collected in surveys are a valid way of measuring gang membership, we would expect some degree of convergence among these measures.

Self-reported gang membership is significantly related to police identification of gang membership. Of the self-reported members, 37% were also identified as gang members by the police, as compared with 27% of the self-reported gang-involved youth and 12% of the nonmembers (Curry, 2000: 1262). From the other perspective, of the police-identified gang members, 56% were also identified as gang-involved in the survey. This level of concordance between self-reported and police measures of gang membership, while far from perfect, is similar to that observed when self-report and official measures of delinquency are compared (Thornberry and Krohn, 2000). A significant correlation also exists between the self-reported gang measures and the prevalence and frequency of police offenses: "The relationship between self-reported gang involvement and the presence of subsequent officially recorded delinquency [was] statistically significant when race, self-reported delinquency in early adolescence, and prior officially recorded offending were controlled" (Curry, 2000: 1268). Overall, the simple self-report measures of gang membership are correlated with the official police data of both gang membership and offending.

The other way to assess the psychometric adequacy of our self-report measure of gang membership is through construct validity. Construct validity is the extent to which the variable of interest – in our case, gang membership – relates to other measures, consistent with theoretically derived hypotheses. In our previous research we have shown that, on the basis of the single item asking about gang membership, gang members have higher rates of delinquency than nonmembers, particularly high rates of behaviors (e.g., violent crimes) that would be expected of gang members, elevated rates of delinquency and violence during periods of active involvement in the gang, high rates of associating with delinquent peers, and high rates of gun carrying and of drug selling (see Battin-Pearson et al., 1998; Bjerregaard and Lizotte, 1995; Thornberry, Krohn, et al., 1993). These relationships

---

[5] These youth responded positively to behavioral items such as wearing gang colors and being in gang fights.

suggest the fundamental adequacy of our self-report measure of gang membership. Moreover, we believe that the pattern of cross-sectional and longitudinal results presented throughout the remainder of this book provides the strongest evidence for the validity of this measure. Because of that, we defer additional discussion of validity until the final chapter, after the results have been presented.

Other Measures

In addition to the measure of gang membership, the Rochester project has collected data on a host of other concepts relevant for the study of gang behavior. The core measures used in this analysis are listed in Table 2.4, along with the source of the data, the mean, standard deviation, and range of the variable, and, where appropriate, Cronbach's α as an indicator of reliability. More detailed measurement information, specific to the individual analyses, is included in the later chapters. Here we present a brief description of the most commonly used measures.

Delinquency

Our measures of delinquency are extensive and enable us to investigate in some detail the offenses committed by gang members and nonmembers. At each wave respondents were asked if they committed each of 36 delinquent acts and, if they had, how often they had done so. All self-report responses were screened to determine whether they fit the type of delinquency measured by the item and are "actionable" offenses. The latter criterion is intended to screen out trivial offenses (e.g., sibling squabbles in response to a question about serious assault), pranks, and accidents that law enforcement officials would probably ignore.[6] After this screening, the items were grouped into categories used extensively in prior research. The analyses will be particularly concerned with offenses that are typically associated with gang activity. The General Delinquency index includes 32 nonoverlapping items covering a range of delinquent behaviors from status offenses, vandalism, and minor property crimes to serious violent and property crimes. Violent Delinquency comprises six items including attacking someone with

---

[6] We used a very broad notion of an "actionable" offense. If in our judgment there was any likelihood that a law enforcement officer would intervene to stop the behavior (and possibly record it), we considered it actionable. To determine that the offenses reported are "actionable," respondents were asked to describe the most serious (or only) act committed in a category. Coders rated the act as being actionable or not. The interrater reliability ranges from 90% to 95% for a given wave of data. If the most serious delinquency described is not rated as being actionable, the item is coded as zero, whereas the total frequency is counted if it is rated as actionable.

Table 2.4. *Description of Core Measures*

	Source	Mean	Standard Deviation	Range	α
Cumulative Frequency of Delinquency and Drug Use (Waves 2–9)					
General Delinquency	Adolescent	74.59	146.38	0–1,003	
Violent Delinquency	Adolescent	6.19	13.94	0–168	
Drug Use	Adolescent	28.90	93.16	0–1,051	
Drug Sales	Adolescent	13.05	49.25	0–512	
Arrests/Police Contacts	Police	1.30	2.52	0–23	
Frequency of Early Delinquency and Drug Use (Wave 2)					
General Delinquency	Adolescent	9.46	28.66	0–384	
Violent Delinquency	Adolescent	1.29	4.28	0–55	
Drug Use	Adolescent	1.80	11.41	0–140	
Drug Sales	Adolescent	.52	4.66	0–90	
Arrests/Police Contacts	Police	.88	1.87	0–17	
Area Characteristics					
Percent African American	Census	47.41	29.88	.27–99.13	
Percentage in Poverty	Census	27.14	12.04	2.72–55.70	
Community Arrest Rate	Police	4.19	2.07	.12–7.87	
Neighborhood Disorganization	Parent	1.61	.62	1–3	.95
Neighborhood Violence	Parent	1.63	.68	1–3	
Neighborhood Drug Use	Adolescent	2.19	.96	1–4	
Neighborhood Integration	Parent	15.66	4.66	7–28	.85
Family Sociodemographic Characteristics					
African American	Adolescent	.68	.47	0, 1	
Hispanic	Adolescent	.17	.37	0, 1	
Parent Education	Parent	11.08	3.28	6–13	
Family Disadvantage	Parent	.66	.47	0, 1	
Poverty Level Income	Parent	.39	.49	0, 1	
Lives with Both Biological Parents	Adolescent	.25	.43	0, 1	
Family Transitions	Parent	.20	.40	0, 1	
Parent-Child Relations					
Attachment to Parent	Adolescent	3.40	.44	1.18–4	.87
Attachment to Child	Parent	3.30	.36	1.82–4	.81
Parental Involvement	Parent	3.29	.90	0–4	.74
Parental Supervision	Adolescent	3.63	.40	1.25–4	.56

Table 2.4. (*cont.*)

	Source	Mean	Standard Deviation	Range	α
Positive Parenting	Parent	3.33	.48	1.60–4	.79
Report of Child	Social				
Maltreatment	Services	.15	.35	0, 1	
Family Hostility	Parent	1.75	.61	1–4	
School Factors					
Commitment to School	Adolescent	2.80	.29	1.78–3.90	.81
Attachment to Teacher	Adolescent	2.89	.44	1.40–4	.63
College Aspirations	Adolescent	3.57	.70	1–4	
Subject's College					
Expectations	Adolescent	2.63	.68	1–3	
Parent's College					
Expectations for Subject	Parent	2.32	.79	1–3	
Math Score	Schools	48.80	24.26	1–99	
Peer Relationships					
Delinquent Peers	Adolescent	1.38	.46	1–3.75	.88
Early Dating	Adolescent	.47	.50	0, 1	
Precocious Sexual Activity	Adolescent	.32	.47	0, 1	
Unsupervised Time with					
Friends	Adolescent	1.99	.62	1–4.67	
Individual Characteristics					
Negative Life Events	Adolescent	.38	.49	0, 1	
Depression	Adolescent	2.13	.46	1–3.79	.79
Self-Esteem	Adolescent	2.77	.33	1.64–4	.78
Externalizing Behaviors	Parent	.46	.34	0–1.83	.91
Delinquent Beliefs	Adolescent	1.25	.34	1–3.82	.84
Life-Course Transitions					
School Dropout	Adolescent	.44	.50	0, 1	
Early Nest Leaving	Adolescent	.14	.34	0, 1	
Early Pregnancy	Adolescent	.31	.46	0, 1	
Teenage Parenthood	Adolescent	.29	.45	0, 1	
Unstable Employment	Adolescent	.49	.50	0, 1	

Note: Unweighted values are reported here.

a weapon and throwing objects such as rocks or bottles at people. The Drug Use index measures the respondent's use of 10 different substances ranging from marijuana to harder drugs such as crack and heroin. Finally, the Drug Sales index includes two items asking respondents whether they sold marijuana or hard drugs such as crack or LSD. The items in each of these indices are presented in Appendix A. In addition to these indices, which are used throughout this book, several other indices of delinquency and drug use are used in specific analyses. These indices and the items contained in them are also presented in Appendix A.

For each of these indices, we calculate a prevalence measure, indicating whether the subject committed any of the offenses on the particular index, and a frequency measure, summing the frequency of all reported offenses across the items in the index. Measures of delinquency and drug use are central variables in our research and extensive documentation on their derivation and validity is available (e.g., Smith and Thornberry, 1995; Thornberry et al., 1994).

In addition to self-report measures of delinquency, official data on involvement with the police were obtained from the records of the Rochester Police Department and the New York State Division of Criminal Justice Services (DCJS). For the juvenile years our data include arrests that were eventually sealed by the juvenile court because we searched the police files on an ongoing basis. Also, because the Rochester Police Department is a central repository for arrest records from other law enforcement agencies in Monroe County, arrests from surrounding communities are included as well. For the adult years the Rochester data include all arrests in Rochester and the surrounding communities. In 1998 we searched the statewide files of DCJS to identify arrests that occurred outside of the Rochester area. Only unsealed records were available in the DCJS files.

To match the self-report data, all arrests were assigned to a particular interview wave. For example, arrests for all offenses occurring between the dates of the person's third interview and his or her fourth interview are assigned to Wave 4 because this interval was also the reference period for the Wave 4 self-reported delinquency questions. As with the self-report data, this procedure allows us to calculate point estimates or cumulative measures.

Other Variables

Throughout this book many variables are used both as predictors of gang membership and as consequences of being a member of a gang. Because the chapter on risk factors (Chapter 4) uses the most inclusive set of variables, we use the categorization of variables employed therein as a framework for describing these measures.

We categorize the risk variables into six domains: area characteristics, family sociodemographic characteristics, parent-child relations, school factors, peer relationships, and individual characteristics. Most of these variables come from parent and youth interviews, but some are drawn from school records, social services records, police records, and census data. Where appropriate, information on scale reliabilities (Cronbach's α) based on the Wave 2 measures is presented. The reliability coefficients for these scales are actually quite constant over time, and there is relatively little difference from wave to wave.

Area Characteristics. Gang research suggests that gang members tend to cluster in high-crime, socially disorganized neighborhoods. We measure seven factors relating to neighborhood or area characteristics. Percentage African American and Percentage in Poverty are standard census measures (taken from the 1980 census) and refer to the census tract the youth lived in at the start of the study. The Community Arrest Rate comes from Rochester police data and refers to the percentage of the total population in the respondent's census tract arrested in 1986. Neighborhood Disorganization is a 17-item scale that measures the parent's perception of crime, dilapidation, and disorganization in his or her neighborhood. Respondents are asked on a scale of 1 to 3 to rate whether the problem is "not a problem," "sort of a problem," or "a big problem." Item responses are averaged, and as with other scale construction, the score is the mean of the items, ranging from 1 to 3. The reliability at Wave 2 is .95. Neighborhood Violence is a 7-item subset of the disorganization scale measuring the extent of violent criminal activity in the neighborhood. Neighborhood Drug Use is a 3-item index of the youth's perception of youth substance use in his or her neighborhood, with a 4-point response scale ranging from "a lot" to "none." Neighborhood Integration is a 7-item scale that indicates the extent to which neighbors interact with one another on a routine basis. The scale reliability at Wave 2 is .85.

Family Sociodemographic Characteristics. Several studies have examined the sociodemographic characteristics of families, such as poverty, race, or family composition, in relation to gang membership. Race/ethnicity was self-reported in the youth interviews. Dichotomous variables for African American and Hispanic adolescents are included in the analysis, with white, non-Hispanic adolescents as the omitted category. Parent Education refers to the highest grade completed by the family's principal wage earner, and ranges from 6 to 13 years. Family Disadvantage is a dichotomous variable indicating whether the family either received welfare, had income below the federally defined poverty level, or had an unemployed principal wage earner (see Farnworth et al., 1994, for descriptions of these indicators). Poverty Level Income is a dichotomous variable indicating whether the family income falls below the federally defined poverty level for a given family size. A dichotomous variable, Lives with Both Biological Parents, indicates whether the adolescent lives with both biological parents or in some other

family constellation.[7] Family Transitions is a dichotomous variable denoting
the parent's report of whether the subject experienced a change in parent
figures between Wave 1 and Wave 2.

Parent-Child Relations. In addition to examining family sociodemographic
composition and structure, many studies have examined parent-child
relations, including family management style, as a risk factor for gang
involvement. Measures we employ include Attachment to Parent, an
11-item adaptation of the Hudson Scale of Attitudes toward Parents
containing questions on the degree of warmth and lack of hostility in
the parent-child relationship (Hudson, 1982). Response choices are
on a 4-point scale ranging from never (1) to often (4). The reliability
for the scale is .87. Attachment to Child is a parallel scale reported by
the parent ($\alpha = .81$). Parental Involvement is an 11-item scale with a
4-point response option measuring how often the parents report being
involved with the subject in a range of prosocial activities. The range
of the scale is 1 to 4, with a reliability of .74. Parental Supervision is a
4-item scale indicating the extent to which the youth feels that his parents
are aware of his whereabouts, friends, and activities. Values on the scale items
range from never (1) to often (4) ($\alpha = .56$). Positive Parenting is a 5-item
scale assessing the degree to which parents reward the child's behavior with
praising, hugging, or similar responses. Item responses range between 1 and
4 ($\alpha = .79$). Report of Child Maltreatment is a dichotomous variable that
indicates whether there is an official report of substantiated maltreatment
of the RYDS subject on file with the Monroe County Department of Social
Services. These incidents are limited to maltreatment that occurred prior
to age 12. Family Hostility is a 3-item index assessing the extent to which
the parent reports a climate of hostility and conflict within the family. Item
responses range from 1 to 4. The derivation, reliability, and validity of these
parenting measures have been reported in several studies (see Krohn et al.,
1992; Smith and Thornberry, 1995; Stern and Smith, 1995).

School Factors. Educational variables have also been examined as risk factors for gang membership. Commitment to School is a 10-item self-report
scale assessing the youth's agreement with questions about the importance
of schoolwork, with four response choices ranging from strongly agree to
strongly disagree. The reliability is .81. Attachment to Teacher is a 5-item
scale that indicates how much the youth likes and respects his teachers,
with response choices ranging from 1 to 4 ($\alpha = .63$). College Aspirations
is a single question with 4 response categories indicating how important

---

[7] We explored other measures of family structure but found this relatively straightforward one
is as predictive as any.

the student thinks it is to attend college, with a higher score indicating greater importance. Subject's College Expectations is a single-item indicator measuring the degree of certainty with which the subject expects to go to college. Parent's College Expectations for Subject measures the parent's assessment of how likely the subject is to attend college. Scores on both of these expectation variables range from 1 to 3. Math Score is a percentile achievement score derived from the California Achievement Test (CAT), administered by the Rochester public schools in 1987 or 1988.[8]

Peer Relationships. Peer relationships are an important source of influence on adolescents' behavior. The measure for Delinquent Peers is based on the subject's report of how many of his or her friends were involved in eight delinquent activities. A 4-point response scale ranging from "none of them" to "most of them" is used ($\alpha = .88$). Early Dating is a dichotomous variable referring to whether the subject has a girlfriend or boyfriend prior to Wave 2 when the average age was 14. Precocious Sexual Activity is also a dichotomous variable indicating whether the subject reports engaging in sexual intercourse prior to his or her 15th birthday. Unsupervised Time with Friends is based on three questions in which the subjects report how often they and their three best friends are unsupervised in the community in situations where criminal activity may occur. A 5-point response choice to each item ranges from "never" to "every day."

Individual Characteristics. A range of individual experiences and attitudes has been linked to gang membership. Negative Life Events measures whether the adolescent experienced eight life stresses, such as breaking up with a boyfriend or girlfriend, being suspended from school, or being seriously ill. Depression is a 14-item self-report scale, derived from a standardized measure (Radloff, 1977) of the frequency of depressive symptoms. Responses to various symptoms range from never (1) to often (4). The reliability is .79. Self-Esteem is a 9-item scale derived from the well-known Rosenberg (1965) measure. The reliability is .78. Externalizing Behaviors is a 24-item scale derived from a short form of the Child Behavior Checklist (CBCL) that includes parent reports of hostility, aggression, and noncompliance with rules (Achenbach and Edelbrock, 1979; Lizotte et al., 1992). For each item, there is a 3-point response choice indicating whether the behavior occurs never, sometimes, or often. The reliability of this short form is .91. The Delinquent Beliefs scale measures how wrong, on a 4-point scale, the subject feels it is to engage in each of eight delinquent acts. Higher

---

[8] In previous work we noted that the math score was somewhat more consistently related to delinquency than was the reading score on the CAT.

scores mean the subject has prodelinquent beliefs. The reliability for this measure is .84.

Life-Course Transitions. We also measure precocious transitions to adult roles in a number of domains. These include high school dropout, early nest leaving, early pregnancy, teenage parenthood, and unstable employment patterns. Descriptive data are presented in Table 2.4, but the measures are defined in Chapter 9, after the conceptual framework for them is introduced.

Summary

Overall, the design of the Rochester Youth Development Study has a number of advantageous features for a study of gang membership. It is based on a sample of urban adolescents that overrepresents youth at high risk for serious delinquency, violence, and gang membership. While overrepresenting high-risk youth, the sample can be weighted to represent the full seventh and eighth grade cohort from which it was drawn. The study site – Rochester, New York – has a diverse population, a relatively high crime rate, and appears to be fairly typical of many midsized cities in this country. As such, it is similar to many other cities that are experiencing gang problems, especially what Spergel and Curry (1990) call newly "emergent" gang cities.

The Rochester study has followed these respondents over a substantial portion of the life course with excellent retention. The full study encompasses 12 interview waves, following the sample from age 13 to age 22. In this book we focus on the data from the first 9 waves – from age 13 to 17.5 – because the prevalence of gang membership drops very substantially at Wave 10. The retention rate at Wave 9 is 88%.

Throughout the study we have relied on a multimethod-multiagent approach to measurement. We have interviewed both the focal adolescent respondent and one of his or her parents. Thus, we have two perspectives on a host of important developmental issues. In addition to these personal interviews, we have collected data from a variety of official agencies – schools, police, courts, and social services. The result is a very broad measurement space depicting the growth and development of these youths. In the following chapters we use this information to compare gang members with adolescents who do not join gangs and to investigate the antecedents and consequences of gang membership.

Characteristics of Gang Members

TO BEGIN our study of gang membership, we examine the prevalence and duration of gang membership for the total sample of the Rochester Youth Development Study and for its major demographic subgroups, compare gang members and nonmembers in terms of delinquent behavior, and then assess the proportionate contribution of gang members to the overall volume of crime.

The Prevalence of Gang Membership

Ever Prevalence

The prevalence of being a gang member at any point up to Wave 9, which essentially covers the high school years, is 30.9% of the total sample (Table 3.1). Thus, although most (69.1%) in this urban sample were not gang members, gang membership is not rare.

This prevalence rate is rather high when comparisons are made with results in other studies. For example, Klein (1971) estimated that in the four geographical areas covered by his study only about 6% of the gang-age youths in those areas were actually gang members. A similar approach, with similar results, has been used by other field researchers – for example, Moore (1978) and Vigil (1988). In a survey of eighth graders in 11 American cities, Esbensen and Winfree (1998) found that 11.8% of the respondents were gang members. Our estimate, based on a measure of lifetime prevalence rather than a point estimate or annual rate, highlights the importance of looking at gang membership as a trajectory that unfolds with age. Youth can enter that trajectory at any point as they move through the adolescent years, and basing estimates of the level of gang membership on annual data

Table 3.1. *Ever Prevalence of Gang Membership, Wave 2 through Wave 9 (%)*

	Nonmembers	Gang Members	n^a
Total Sample	69.1	30.9	848
Gender			
Male	67.6	32.4	630
Female	70.7	29.3	225
Race/Ethnicity			
African American	63.4	36.6*	557
Hispanic	72.8	27.2	139
White	86.7	13.3	152
Race/Ethnicity: Male			
African American	61.9	38.1*	352
Hispanic	59.2	40.8	110
White	84.9	15.1	169
Race/Ethnicity: Female			
African American	64.7	35.3*	170
Hispanic	88.5	11.5	35
White	92.2	7.8	20

^{a}Sample size varies across groups due to the weighting procedure used.
*$p < .05$ (chi-square test).

can seriously underestimate the extent of this phenomenon. Indeed, our annual prevalence rates are quite consistent with Klein's point estimate. On the other hand, our lifetime prevalence rate is higher than those of 15% reported in the Seattle study (Hill et al., 1999) and of 14% in the Denver study (Huizinga, 1997).

Gender

Table 3.1 also presents ever-prevalence rates for various demographic group-ings. Starting with gender, we see that the prevalence of gang membership is approximately equal, and not statistically different, for males and females. One-third of the boys (32.4%) had been gang members at some point as compared with 29.3% of the girls. Put differently, of all the gang members in the Rochester sample, only slightly more than half are males and slightly less than half are females. This relative equality is somewhat at odds with the traditional gang literature that represents the gang world as overwhelm-ingly male. For example, in 1975 Miller suggested that females generally constituted 10% or less of all gang members. In the 1998 National Youth Gang Survey, law enforcement respondents estimated that 92% of gang members were male and only 8% were female (Moore and Cook, 1999). After reviewing the literature on this issue, Esbensen and Winfree recently concluded that "most estimates place the [female prevalence] figure in the single digits and perpetuate the stereotype of girls as auxiliary members" (1998: 507). Spergel aptly summed up the traditional view: "The notion seems to be that female gangs and their members are 'pale imitations' of male gangs" (1995: 90).

Several studies, however, have begun to question this traditional view and present male-female ratios that are closer to those presented in Table 3.1. For example, Klein and Crawford (1967) report that 26% of the gang members in Los Angeles in the 1960s were female, Esbensen and Huizinga (1993) indicate that 21% of the gang members in Denver were females, and Esbensen and Winfree (1998) in a study of gangs in 11 cities found that 38% of the gang members were female. Moore and Hagedorn's (2001) recent review also suggests a higher number of female gang members than that typically portrayed in the literature.

Along with our data, these studies indicate that young girls are more actively involved in street gangs than one would expect based on the traditional gang literature. It is unclear whether this represents a secular change or a shift in research methods and sites. For example, Esbensen and Winfree point out that low estimates of female involvement are typically based on law enforcement or observational data (1998: 508), and these approaches may have very restricted definitions of the gang. In a related vein, Thornberry and Porter (2001) have argued that the picture of gang membership based on the bulk of the gang literature is biased toward traditional gangs found in a few large cities, especially Chicago and Los Angeles. That picture does not appear to apply across the board, especially in smaller, emergent gang cities. In particular, adolescent females appear to be more extensively involved in gangs in cities such as Rochester.

Race/Ethnicity

There is a statistically significant difference in the prevalence of gang membership by race/ethnicity in Rochester. Gang membership is predominantly a minority group phenomenon. Whereas 13.3% of the white respondents report being a gang member, 36.6% of the African American and 27.2% of the Hispanic respondents do. The overrepresentation of minority youths as gang members is generally consistent with the previous literature, although Esbensen and Winfree (1998) caution that estimates based solely on midsized and large cities may overestimate the proportion of gang members drawn from minority groups.

Table 3.2. *Annual Prevalence of Gang Membership (%)*

	Year 1 (n = 913)	Year 2 (n = 906)	Year 3 (n = 872)	Year 4 (n = 862)
Total Sample	22.2	11.5	6.7	5.2
Gender				
Male	19.9	14.6	10.8	8.6
Female	24.5	8.5	2.5	1.8
Race/Ethnicity				
African American	27.5	13.2	6.4	5.5
Hispanic	19.0	10.6	9.8	4.8
White	6.0	6.7	5.2	4.3
Race/Ethnicity: Male				
African American	23.6	17.0	10.8	10.0
Hispanic	26.5	19.6	17.7	9.0
White	8.1	6.8	6.6	5.5
Race/Ethnicity: Female				
African American	30.5	10.4	3.3	2.3
Hispanic	10.7	0.0	0.0	0.0
White	0.0	6.4	0.0	0.0

Note: For Years 1–4, average age is 14.2, 15.2, 16.2, 17.2 and grade is 8–9, 9–10, 10–11, 11–12, respectively.

Race/Ethnicity by Gender

The bottom panels of Table 3.1 present ever-prevalence rates by race/ethnicity for males and females separately. For male subjects, the highest rates are observed for the Hispanic respondents (40.8%) followed closely by the African American respondents (38.1%); the white males have a lower rate, 15.1%. These differences are statistically significant. For females a somewhat different distribution is observed. Only the African American females have an elevated rate of gang membership. Slightly over one-third (35.3%) report being a member of a street gang as compared with 7.8% of the white and 11.5% of the Hispanic females. Again, the chi-square test is significant. The number of Hispanic and white females in the sample, 35 and 20 respectively, is rather low, however, and rates for these groups should be interpreted with caution.

Prevalence by Year

Taking advantage of the longitudinal design of the Rochester study, we can also examine gang membership at specific times or ages. Table 3.2 reports the prevalence of gang membership at four annual periods. Year 1 combines data from the interviews at Waves 2 and 3, Year 2 from Waves 4 and 5, Year 3 from Waves 6 and 7, and Year 4 from Waves 8 and 9. The respondents were on average 14.2 years of age and either 8th or 9th graders during Year 1; by Year 4 they were 17.2 years of age on average and were, or would have been, attending the 11th and 12th grades.

For the total sample the annual prevalence of gang membership declines monotonically across this four-year span. At Year 1, 22.2% of the respondents report being a gang member. This rate drops to 11.5% at Year 2, 6.7% at Year 3, and 5.2% at Year 4. Note that these are annual, not cumulative, rates; thus a respondent who is a gang member at both Year 1 and Year 2 is counted in each of the first two columns in Table 3.2. According to these data it appears that gang membership is largely a phenomenon of early adolescence, at least in Rochester. Whether this is particular to Rochester, a newly emergent gang city, or is more generally true is an issue we return to in the discussion.

Gender

Major differences in the annual prevalence rates are observed for male and female respondents. For the males, there is a more even distribution and a more gradual monotonic decline in gang membership across time. At Year 1, 19.9% of the boys reported being a member of a gang; gang membership drops to 14.6% at Year 2, to 10.8% at Year 3, and to 8.6% at Year 4. For the female respondents, however, the drop off in gang membership is much more precipitous. At Year 1, one-quarter (24.5%) of the girls reported being a member of a gang. By Year 2, however, the rate is 8.5%, and at Years 3 and 4 gang membership for females is quite rare, being 2.5% and 1.8%, respectively.

The clustering of gang involvement during early adolescence for females has been observed in other studies as well. In the Denver Youth Survey, 46% of the gang members were female when the sample was between 11 and 15 years of age, but when the sample was between 15 and 19 the proportion of female gang members dropped to 20% (Esbensen and Huizinga, 1993). Harris (1994) also reports that girls are most active in gangs between the ages of 13 and 16 and then their gang involvement tapers off. Consistent with this finding, Esbensen and Winfree (1998) report one of the highest estimates of female gang membership in the literature, 38%, and their 11-city study is based entirely on eighth graders.

Race/Ethnicity

When the distribution of annual prevalence rates is examined by race/ethnicity (Table 3.2), we see that for all three groups gang membership declines over time. The rates for white respondents are generally lower and very even over time (6.0% at Year 1; 4.3% at Year 4). In contrast, the rates for the African American and Hispanic respondents start off much higher (27.5% and 19.0%, respectively) at Year 1, but by Year 4 are essentially equal to those observed for the white respondents (5.5% and 4.8%, respectively).

Race/Ethnicity by Gender

Finally, the last two panels in Table 3.2 report annual prevalence rates by race/ethnicity separately for males and females. For the male respondents we again see a pattern in which the prevalence of gang membership declines over time for all three groups. Also, at all four years, the white males have lower rates than either the African American or Hispanic males.

For female subjects the pattern of annual prevalence rates by race/ethnicity is quite uneven. For African American females, the rate is very high in Year 1 (30.5%); it then drops sharply to 10.4% at Year 2 and further to 3.3% and 2.3% at Years 3 and 4, respectively. White females only report being gang members at Year 2 (6.4%) and Hispanic females only report being gang members at Year 1 (10.7%). The number of white and Hispanic females in our sample is rather small, however, and because of that, these estimates may not be very stable.[1]

The annual prevalence rates presented thus far are based on the total number of subjects interviewed at each year, regardless of whether they were interviewed in other years. Thus, the number of cases in Table 3.2 varies somewhat from year to year (n = 913 at Year 1; n = 862 at Year 4). We refer to this as the "noncontinuous sample." For many of the longitudinal analyses to follow, however, we restrict the sample to respondents interviewed at every wave, from Wave 2 through Wave 9. There are a total of 796 respondents who meet this condition, representing 80% of the original sample of 1,000 subjects. We refer to this as the "continuous sample" because they are selected only if they were interviewed at all eight waves, from Wave 2 through Wave 9.

In Appendix B (Tables B.1–B.2) we reproduce the relationships already presented in Tables 3.1 and 3.2, based only on the continuous sample. For the continuous sample the prevalence rate for gang membership is somewhat lower (26%), but the pattern of results and the substantive conclusions are virtually identical for the continuous and noncontinuous samples. Because of the similarity of these results, we feel confident that restricting the

---

[1] The annual prevalence rates were created by combining data from two adjacent six-month interviews. Wave-specific prevalence rates, from Wave 2 through Wave 9, were also created. While these half-yearly rates are a little less stable than the annual rates, the substantive conclusions are the same as those drawn from the annualized data presented in Table 3.2.

sample for some of the subsequent analyses to only those respondents who were interviewed at all eight time points does not bias the findings.

Summary

Overall, gang membership is not a particularly rare phenomenon during early adolescence, at least in Rochester; 31% of the respondents reported some gang involvement up to the age of 17. In terms of ever-prevalence rates, males and females were about equally likely to be gang members and adolescents of color were more likely to be gang members than white youth. Also, the annual prevalence of gang membership is clustered at younger ages, and there was a general decline in gang membership over this four-year period.

The results presented so far indicate a major gender difference in the pattern of gang membership over time. Whereas the ever prevalence of gang membership for males and females is about equal, there is a substantial difference in the temporal pattern of gang membership by gender. For female subjects, active membership in street gangs is more typical of earlier rather than later adolescence, and by Year 3 gang membership has become quite uncommon. Because of this pattern, the results in the remainder of this book are presented separately for males and females. Also, because of the low prevalence of gang membership for female respondents after Year 2, some longitudinal analyses can only be conducted for male respondents.

The demographic distribution of gang membership by race/ethnicity also has implications for the design of the analyses to follow. Although examining statistical relationships across the various racial/ethnic groups, especially between minority and nonminority respondents, is theoretically important, the small number of white gang members ($n = 20$) makes this task very difficult. While we appreciate the importance of this issue, we are reluctant to estimate models and relationships without adequate statistical power. Because of this we present comparisons when reasonable (e.g., descriptive univariate results), but, in general, we do not make racial and ethnic comparisons a central theme of these analyses.

Stability of Gang Membership

The previous section adopted a static or cross-sectional perspective on the phenomenon of gang membership. In this section we begin to add a more dynamic or developmental perspective by examining the stability of gang membership over time. Once adolescents join a gang, do they remain members for long periods of time or, like many other aspects of adolescence, is gang membership a fluid and transient phenomenon?

Table 3.3. *Number of Years of Gang Membership (%)*

	Total	African American	Hispanic	White
Males	(n = 152)	(n = 98)	(n = 30)	(n = 24)
One Year Only	50.4	51.0	52.9	44.8
Two Years	28.0	26.6	34.0	26.3
Three Years	14.3	15.1	8.2	18.8
Four Years	7.3	7.3	4.9	10.1
Females		(n = 55)		
One Year Only		66.0		
Two Years		28.1		
Three Years		5.0		
Four Years		0.0		

Note: Results reported for the subsample of gang members who were interviewed at all eight waves (Wave 2 through Wave 9).

Duration of Membership

The basic data pertaining to the duration of gang membership are presented in the top panel of Table 3.3 for male gang members and in the bottom panel for female gang members. Because this analysis is longitudinal and cross-time, the continuous sample is used.

For the males in the Rochester study, gang membership proves to be a rather transient status. Of the 152 male respondents who were ever a gang member, 50.4% reported being a member for one year or less. An additional 28.0% reported being members for two years, 14.3% for three years, and only 7.3% reported being a gang member during all four years.

The distributions are quite similar within racial/ethnic groups. The white males remain in gangs slightly longer than do the African American or Hispanic males; 44.8% of the white males were gang members for one year or less as compared with 51.0% for African American and 52.9% for Hispanic gang members. For all three groups gang membership is more transitory than stable, with relatively few adolescents being active gang members for more than two years.

Data for females can only be reported for the African American respondents because of the lack of temporal variation in gang membership for white and Hispanic females. As the annual prevalence rates reported earlier would suggest, gang membership is even more transitory for the females. For the African American females, two-thirds of them were active members for one year or less, and only 5.0% were active for three years.

Table 3.4. *Pattern of Multiyear Gang Membership, Males Only*

Gang Membership for	Consecutive Years			Nonconsecutive Years		
	Years	%	n	Years	%	n
Two Years (n = 42)	1 & 2	40.5	17	1 & 3	9.5	4
	2 & 3	19.1	8	1 & 4	11.9	5
	3 & 4	7.1	3	2 & 4	11.9	5
	Total	66.7	28		33.3	14
Three Years (n = 24)	1, 2, 3	62.5	15	1, 2, 4	12.5	3
	2, 3, 4	20.8	5	1, 3, 4	4.2	1
	Total	83.3	20		16.7	4

Note: Results reported for the subsample of gang members who were interviewed at all eight waves (Wave 2 through Wave 9).

Intermittency

Another way to examine the stability of gang membership is to see if membership is continuous or intermittent. Do gang members join, leave, and rejoin gangs or do they join a gang, stay a member for some period of time, and then leave the world of active gang membership? The answer depends somewhat on how long a window is opened to measure intermittency, annual periods or semiannual periods. We can start by examining the pattern of membership for those who were involved in gangs for at least two years (Table 3.4).[2]

These results indicate a pattern in which membership is more continuous than intermittent. Of those who were gang members in two different years, 66.7% reported being members in two consecutive years and 33.3% in two nonconsecutive years. Of those who were gang members in three different years, 83.3% were members in three consecutive years and only 16.7% were members in nonconsecutive years. If we combine the multiyear gang members in Table 3.4, ignoring the distinction between two-year and three-year members, we see that 73% (48/66) of them were gang members in consecutive years, whereas only 27% (18/66) were members in nonconsecutive years.

If we look at changes in gang membership status across semiannual intervals, that is, from wave to wave, a somewhat different pattern emerges (Table 3.5). This analysis can only be conducted for up to four waves; after that point, the number of cases is too small for analysis. Slightly less than half (43%) of those who were members in multiple waves were continuous

---

[2] This analysis can be conducted only for male respondents.

Table 3.5. *Pattern of Multiwave Gang Membership, Males Only*

	Consecutive Waves		Nonconsecutive Waves	
Gang Membership for	%	n	%	n
Two Waves	53	18	47	16
Three Waves	43	12	57	16
Four Waves	24	4	76	13
Total	43	34	57	45

Note: Results reported for the subsample of gang members who were interviewed at all eight waves (Wave 2 through Wave 9). After four waves, the number of gang members becomes too small for analysis.

gang members and, of course, slightly more than half (57%) were not. Intermittent patterns increase as the number of waves of membership increases. Thus, of those who report being a member at four different interviews, only 24% were gang members at four consecutive waves and 76% report joining, leaving, and rejoining. At the other extreme, of those who report being members at only two interviews, 53% do so in consecutive waves.

Overall, these results suggest a considerable fluidity to the phenomenon of gang membership during the adolescent years. Most youth who join a gang remain in the gang for less than one year and very few remain for three or four years. Moreover, most multiyear members are members in consecutive years and relatively few leave the gang for as much as a year and then return. In the shorter term, however, there are higher levels of rejoining the gang after a brief hiatus.

In Phase 2 of the Rochester Youth Development Study we conducted annual interviews (Waves 10 to 12) with this sample when the respondents were between the ages of 20 and 22. During this time period, gang membership was quite rare. For example, during the 12 months prior to the Wave 10 interview[3] only 1.6% of the sample (n = 14) reported being in a gang. The prevalence rate did not increase in subsequent years, even though gangs remained active in Rochester at that time, as they do today. Thus, the data presented in this section indicate that the results are not biased by not including data from after age 18 in the estimates. Unless gang membership was to increase substantially again in the mid-20s, which appears rather unlikely, it would seem that the results presented here reflect the career pattern of gang membership in Rochester. Gang membership is more prevalent during earlier rather than later adolescence; it is rather transitory as it lasts for less than a year for most respondents; and, for those who

[3] Wave 10 occurred approximately two and a half years after Wave 9; see Figure 2.1.

remain members for multiple years, they tend to do so during consecutive years.

Gang Membership and Delinquency

We know from much prior research that gang members have higher rates of delinquency as compared to nonmembers (see Chapter 1). In this section we examine this very basic relationship for the Rochester sample. We begin with a global examination, comparing the delinquency and drug use of respondents who were members of a street gang at *any* point during this study period with those who *never* reported being a gang member. The dependent variables are also global measures, cumulating information on the prevalence and frequency of delinquency over eight waves of data (Waves 2–9).[4] In subsequent chapters we present much more refined analyses, relating changes in gang membership status to changing patterns of delinquent behavior to understand better the link between gang membership and delinquency. For the moment, we start with this more global assessment to set the stage for the later work.

Five dependent variables are used in this analysis. Two measure self-reported delinquency: general delinquency and violent delinquency. Two measure involvement in drugs: drug use and drug selling. One measures official delinquency: official contact (juvenile years only) or arrest for any offense recorded by the Rochester Police Department.

For the male respondents, most gang members self-report involvement in general delinquency and violence, whereas significantly smaller proportions of the nonmembers do (Table 3.6). For example, 98.1% of the gang members are involved in general delinquency, whereas 68.4% of the nonmembers are. The difference for involvement in violence is even larger; 90.6% of the gang members report some involvement in violence, as compared with 46.4% of the nonmembers. There are also substantial differences for drug use and drug sales. For example, whereas only 9.5% of the nonmembers ever report involvement in drug sales, 39.5% of the gang members do.

The male gang members are also significantly more likely to be arrested: 54.6% as compared with 31.0% of the nonmembers. Thus, it does not appear that the different offending rates for gang members and nonmembers based on official records (e.g., Huff, 1996; Klein and Maxson, 1989) are solely a

---

[4] The delinquency and drug involvement measures are highly skewed; most respondents commit very few acts, whereas a small number of respondents commit many acts. To reduce the impact of skewness, the natural logarithm of the incidence scores is used in significance testing. In tables presenting frequency scores, however, the actual means (not the log-transformed means) are presented to provide the reader with a better sense of the magnitude of involvement in delinquency and drug use.

Table 3.6. *Ever Prevalence of Delinquency and Drug Use by Ever Prevalence of Gang Membership*

	Nonmembers	Gang Members
Males	(n = 426)	(n = 152)
General Delinquency	68.4	98.1*
Violent Delinquency	46.4	90.6*
Drug Use	23.3	65.1*
Drug Sales	9.5	39.5*
Arrests	31.0	54.6*
Females	(n = 159)	(n = 57)
General Delinquency	56.1	94.4*
Violent Delinquency	39.0	72.2*
Drug Use	30.9	67.8*
Drug Sales	4.7	25.8*
Arrests	19.8	36.7*

Note: Results reported for the subsample of gang members who were interviewed at all eight waves (Wave 2 through Wave 9).
*$p < .05$ (one-tailed t-test).

function of police policy or bias. Importantly, we observe similar differences in Table 3.6 for self-report data and for official data.

A similar pattern of results is observed for the female respondents. Female gang members self-report significantly higher rates of involvement in delinquency and drug use as compared with nonmembers. For example, of the female gang members 94% report involvement in some form of delinquency and 68% some form of drug use, as compared with 56% and 31% of the nonmembers, respectively. Also, female gang members are almost twice as likely to have been arrested as compared to nonmembers.

Comparable results are seen when the frequency of delinquency, drug use, or arrests is used as the dependent variable (Table 3.7). For both male and female respondents, gang members are involved in delinquency and drug use at significantly higher frequencies than are the nonmembers. They are also arrested a significantly greater number of times.

Overall, it is clear that gang members in Rochester are substantially more involved in delinquency and drug use than are the nonmembers. Indeed, female gang members have prevalence and frequency rates that are of the same magnitude as those of male nonmembers. This finding mirrors the one recently reported by Esbensen and Winfree (1998) as well as previous findings using the Rochester data (Bjerregaard and Smith, 1993).

Table 3.7. *Cumulative Frequency of Delinquency and Drug Use by Ever Prevalence of Gang Membership*

	Nonmembers	Gang Members
Males	(n = 426)	(n = 152)
General Delinquency	38.31	139.56*
Violent Delinquency	2.51	14.35*
Drug Use	19.06	62.34*
Drug Sales	6.94	27.83*
Arrests	.91	1.92*
Females	(n = 159)	(n = 57)
General Delinquency	28.86	103.58*
Violent Delinquency	1.59	5.77*
Drug Use	7.75	20.32*
Drug Sales	1.39	6.86*
Arrests	.35	.68*

Note: Results reported for the subsample of gang members who were interviewed at all eight waves (Wave 2 through Wave 9).
*$p < .05$ (one-tailed t-test).

The Impact of the Onset and Duration of Membership on Delinquency

In a previous section we saw that most gang members join gangs at early adolescence and somewhat fewer join at later adolescence. We also saw that the duration of gang membership varied; about half were members for a year or less. In this section we examine whether age at joining (early versus late onset of gang membership) and duration of membership (short-term versus stable) are related to delinquency and drug use. The life-course perspective suggests that they will be. Joining the gang at an early age may indicate antisocial precociousness and hence a more extensive involvement in deviant careers. This prediction is also consistent with recent early starter–late starter models of antisocial behavior (e.g., Moffitt, 1997; Patterson, Reid, and Dishion, 1992). The duration of membership indicates deeper penetration along the trajectory of gang membership and therefore potentially more extensive consequences of membership. For example, more stable members have more exposure to the criminogenic influence of the gang and their longer involvement in the gang may represent greater commitment to the norms of the gang.

Onset of Membership

Onset of membership can be divided into those who joined a gang earlier (Wave 2 or 3) and those who joined later (Waves 4 through 9). As

Table 3.8. *Delinquency and Drug Use by Age of Joining a Gang*

	Prevalence		Frequency	
	Early	Late	Early	Late
Males	(n = 98)	(n = 53)	(n = 98)	(n = 53)
General Delinquency	98.1	98.1	154.05	108.44
Violent Delinquency	90.0	91.5	14.65	13.57
Drug Use	60.9	72.3	72.64	37.94*
Drug Sales	40.7	36.2	34.59	13.68*
Arrests	56.8	49.9	2.10	1.62
Females	(n = 52)	(n = 5)	(n = 52)	(n = 5)
General Delinquency	94.7	90.0	91.31	243.41
Violent Delinquency	73.2	61.6	5.29	11.23
Drug Use	70.8	33.0	17.56	51.79
Drug Sales	25.1	33.0	6.97	5.64
Arrests	33.6	71.4	.59	1.76*

Note: Results reported for the subsample of gang members who were interviewed at all eight waves (Wave 2 through Wave 9).
*$p < .05$ (one-tailed t-test).

can be seen in Table 3.8, there is no strong relationship between onset and any of the self-report measures of delinquency or drugs or the official arrest measures, for either the male or female gang members. None of the 10 comparisons for the prevalence measures is statistically significant, and no clear pattern is evident in the data. Similar results are observed when the frequency measures are used as the dependent variables; 7 of the 10 relationships are not statistically significant (Table 3.8). Overall, therefore, we conclude that, although being a gang member has a strong impact on delinquency and drug use, the age at joining the gang does not have an impact on either the prevalence or frequency of delinquency, at least during the adolescent years that are covered in the Rochester project.

Duration of Membership

Unlike the onset of membership, duration of membership does have an impact on delinquency and drug use (Table 3.9). For the males, stable gang members have higher prevalence rates than short-term (one year or less) members for all the indicators, although not all are statistically significant. The prevalence rates for delinquency – both general delinquency and violence – show that virtually all gang members are involved in some form of delinquent behavior. Because of that, there is little room to observe statistical

Table 3.9. *Delinquency and Drug Use by Duration of Gang Membership*

	Prevalence		Frequency	
	Short-Term	Stable	Short-Term	Stable
Males	(n = 76)	(n = 75)	(n = 76)	(n = 75)
General Delinquency	96.3	100.0*	91.01	185.30*
Violent Delinquency	87.0	94.0	8.55	20.03*
Drug Use	54.2	75.7*	30.41	90.64*
Drug Sales	23.9	54.5*	9.97	44.60*
Arrests	50.2	58.6	1.31	2.55*
Females	(n = 38)	(n = 19)	(n = 38)	(n = 19)
General Delinquency	91.6	100.0*	60.97	190.67*
Violent Delinquency	63.5	90.0*	4.74	7.88
Drug Use	62.6	78.3	14.38	32.46
Drug Sales	18.0	41.6*	6.42	7.75
Arrests	33.2	43.7	.54	.97

Note: Results reported for the subsample of gang members who were interviewed at all eight waves (Wave 2 through Wave 9).
*p < .05 (one-tailed t-test).

significance. Even so, the rate for stable members (100%) is significantly higher than that for short-term members (96.3%). For rates of violence, proportionately more stable members (94.0%) than short-term members (87.0%) self-report violent behavior, but the difference is not statistically significant. For drugs the differences are statistically significant in the expected direction. For example, whereas a quarter (23.9%) of the short-term members self-report drug sales, half (54.5%) of the more stable gang members do. There is no significant difference in the probability of being arrested: 50.2% for the short-term and 58.6% for the stable members.

The muted differences between the short-term and stable gang members in terms of prevalence of involvement in delinquency and drug use is not unexpected given the generally high rates of involvement in these behaviors by all gang members and attendant "ceiling effects." We would expect larger and more systematic differences in terms of frequency measures, however, because there are no ceilings for these open-ended frequency counts. If stable gang members have more exposure to the criminogenic influences of the gang and/or are more committed to the gang, they should exhibit more frequent involvement in delinquency and drugs. The results reported in Table 3.9 are consistent with this prediction.

For the male gang members all the t-tests are statistically significant, and the differences between the means are quite substantial. For example, whereas the mean number of violent offenses reported by the short-term gang members is 8.55, it is 20.03 for the stable gang members. Somewhat larger differences are observed for drug sales – a mean of 9.97 for the short-term gang members versus 44.60 for the more stable members. The frequency with which the respondents were arrested is also statistically different – 1.31 for the short-term members versus 2.55 for the stable members.

For the female members the differences between stable and short-term members are quite consistent. In all cases, the stable members have higher prevalence rates than the short-term members. Three of the comparisons (general delinquency, violence, and drug sales) are statistically significant. For the frequency data, all of the differences are in the expected direction but only one of them, general delinquency, is statistically significant.

Overall, although age at joining a gang is unrelated to either the prevalence or frequency of involvement in delinquency and drugs, duration of membership is related to delinquency and drug use, especially for the male members. Gang members who remain in the gang for more than a year report considerably more involvement in general delinquency, violence, drug use, and drug sales than do the less stable members. They are also more apt to have official police records.

Proportional Contribution to Delinquency

Clearly, gang members in Rochester are significantly more involved in delinquency than are nonmembers. As indicated in the literature review in Chapter 1, prior studies have also demonstrated a strong association between gang membership and delinquency. Despite the uniformity of this finding, we have surprisingly few estimates of the proportion of all delinquent or criminal acts for which gang members are responsible. That is, while we know that gang members have higher *rates* of offending as compared with nonmembers, we do not know what *proportion* of the total amount of crime is attributable to them. This issue is important; if gang members are responsible for a very large proportion of all offenses, effective gang intervention may be a necessary ingredient in efforts to reduce the overall amount of crime in society.

The most straightforward way to examine this issue is to compare the proportion of gang members in the sample with their proportionate share of the total number of crimes reported. For example, if gang members represent 30% of the population we would expect them to be responsible for approximately 30% of the crimes committed, if there were *no relationship* between gang membership and criminal involvement. To the extent that their proportionate share of crimes exceeds 30%, one would conclude that they are disproportionately contributing to the volume of crime in society.

Several recent studies have begun to examine this issue. Fagan (1990) studied a sample of high school students combined with a "snowball" sample of dropouts in San Diego, Los Angeles, and Chicago. He found that gang members constituted only 23% of the sample, but they accounted for 67% of felony assaults, 66% of minor assaults, and 66% of robberies. Fagan reported similar percentages for various forms of theft, ranging from 56% of minor thefts to 72% of felony thefts. Gang members were also disproportionately involved in weapons offenses, illegal services, drug use, and drug sales.

Battin et al. (1996) report a similar pattern of results for gang members in the Seattle Social Development Project. Fifteen percent of the participants in the Seattle sample reported being a gang member at some point between grades 7 and 12. Although constituting only 15% of the total sample, gang members accounted for 85% of the robberies that were committed between grades 7 and 12. They also accounted for at least 50% of all the other forms of delinquency measured in that study. These percentages ranged from 51% for minor assault to 62% for drug selling.

In the Denver Youth Survey 14% of the respondents were gang members at some point between 1988 and 1992 (Huizinga, 1997). During that same period they were responsible for 79% of the acts of serious violence, 71% of serious property offenses, and 87% of drug sales. They were also disproportionately involved in public disorder offenses, alcohol use, and marijuana use.

Finally, Curry (2000) has examined this issue using police data to identify gang members and to measure involvement in offending. Based on a sample of 429 young adolescents in Chicago, he found that 24% of the subjects were identified as gang offenders, but they accounted for 77% of the total offenses.

The results of these studies indicate that gang members, while representing a minority of the overall population, account for the lion's share of all delinquent acts that are reported. Moreover, the proportionate contribution of gang members to delinquency is most pronounced for the more serious forms of delinquency. That is, gang members account for a very large proportion of felony offenses, serious offenses, violent offenses, and drug sales. Their contribution to more minor forms of delinquency, while still large, is somewhat more muted.

In the remainder of this chapter we analyze the contribution of gang members to the overall volume of delinquency for the Rochester sample. We begin by presenting cumulative data that are comparable with those just summarized from the other studies. We then present a more fine-grained temporal analysis in which we identify the proportion of offenses for which *active* gang members are responsible. That is, we examine offenses committed during the same time period as when the gang members were actually involved in the gang.

Table 3.10. *Prevalence of Gang Membership and Percentage of Cumulative Delinquent Acts Attributable to Gang Members*

	Total (n = 848)		Males (n = 630)		Females (n = 225)	
	%	Ratio	%	Ratio	%	Ratio
Gang Membership	30.9		32.4		29.3	
Delinquent Acts						
General	63.3	2.0	63.0	1.9	63.7	2.2
Serious	82.0	2.7	80.3	2.5	87.6	3.0
Moderate	65.3	2.1	70.5	2.2	54.1	1.9
Minor	63.9	2.1	67.2	2.1	58.3	2.0
Violent	69.0	2.1	71.5	2.2	64.1	2.2
Serious Violent	82.4	2.7	80.4	2.5	86.6	3.0
Property	64.7	2.1	68.8	2.1	55.9	1.9
Public Disorder	63.8	2.1	69.2	2.1	49.6	1.7
Drug Sales	69.8	2.3	67.6	2.1	77.3	2.6
Alcohol Use	59.3	1.9	63.2	2.0	49.4	1.7
Drug Use	60.6	2.0	62.9	1.9	53.4	1.8
Arrests	54.4	1.8	56.4	1.7	48.1	1.6

Note: Sample size varies across groups due to the weighting procedure used.

Cumulative Analysis

Table 3.10 compares respondents who were ever a gang member with those who were never a gang member in terms of their proportionate contribution to various types of delinquent behavior. In this case, gang membership includes being a gang member at any point between Waves 2 and 9. The measures of delinquency are cumulated to include all delinquent acts committed during this same time period. A wider array of delinquency indices are used in this analysis; they are described in Appendix A.

The data are displayed in two ways. The first is the percentage of offenses for which the gang members are responsible. This percentage can be compared with the prevalence of gang membership to see if the gang members are responsible for a proportionate or disproportionate share of the volume of delinquency and drug use. The second way is the ratio of these percentages. These ratios provide a summary estimate of the magnitude of the effect.

For the total sample we see that 30.9% of the Rochester sample reported being a member of a street gang prior to the end of high school. Although slightly less than one-third of the population, gang members accounted for about two-thirds (63.3%) of the acts of general delinquency that were self-reported over the four-year period covering the junior high school and high school years. The ratio of these percentages (63.3 to 30.9) is 2.0, indicating that gang members are responsible for twice as many offenses as their share of the population would suggest.

The gang members were also responsible for 82.0% of the acts of delinquency included in the serious delinquency index, which is a combination of serious violent and property crimes. They were also responsible for 69.0% of the acts of violence;[5] when the violent crime measure is restricted to the more serious forms of violence – aggravated assault, robbery, and sexual assault – their proportionate share increases to 82.4%. Also noteworthy is their extensive involvement in drug sales – 69.8% of all those reported. Gang members, as compared with their share in the population, also had much higher rates of moderate and minor delinquency, property offenses, public disorder offenses, alcohol use, and drug use. Overall, the ratios presented for self-reported delinquency and drug use for the total sample range from 1.9 (alcohol use) to 2.7 (serious delinquency and serious violence).

Disproportionate involvement in delinquency is not limited to self-report measures. Gang members account for more than half of all arrests, for a ratio of 1.8 to 1. Overall, gang members demonstrate a somewhat greater disproportionate involvement in self-reported delinquency (ratios between 1.9 and 2.7) than in official delinquency (ratio = 1.8). The results for the official arrests measure suggest that the general relationship found in Table 3.10 (and the next two tables) is not a function of common-method variance produced by using the same reporter – the gang member – for the two variables. When an independent measure of criminal behavior is introduced, the pattern of results remains (see also Curry, 2000).

The same pattern is evident by gender; both male and female gang members have substantially higher rates of involvement in delinquency and substance use than do nonmembers. Although 32.4% of the male respondents report being a gang member at some point, they are responsible for 63.0% of the self-reported acts of general delinquency. They account for 80.3% of the serious acts of delinquency, 71.5% of the violent acts, 80.4% of the serious violent acts, 67.6% of the instances of drug selling, and higher proportions of the other indices of delinquent behavior as well. For the males, the ratios range from 1.9 to 2.5. Male gang members are also disproportionately likely to be arrested.

The disproportionate involvement in delinquency and substance use is, if anything, greater for the females. Although only 29.3% of the girls were gang members during this time period, they accounted for most of the serious delinquencies (87.6%) and substantial proportions of violence (64.1%), drug sales (77.3%), and the other delinquent acts. For the females, the

---

[5] Gang fighting is not included in these measures of violence.

ratio of the proportionate share to the prevalence rate ranges from 1.7 to 3.0. They are also disproportionately likely to be arrested.

These results clearly indicate that, at a general level, gang members disproportionately contribute to the volume of crime in society. While representing a minority of the sample, gang members are responsible for the majority of the offenses committed.

Wave-Specific Analyses

The cumulative results presented here and in prior work (e.g., Battin et al., 1996; Huizinga, 1997), though informative, are not definitive. Because the ever prevalence of gang membership was compared with cumulative measures of delinquency, the time period of gang membership and the period of offending do not necessarily overlap. That is, the offenses for which gang members are responsible, as reported in Table 3.10, could have been committed prior to, during, or subsequent to periods of active gang membership. To provide a more precise assessment of the contribution of gang members to the volume of crime, we repeat the analysis at each wave of data collection. The central question here is, Do gang members disproportionately contribute to the volume of delinquent acts committed during the same time period as when they are active gang members? Because of the truncated temporal distribution of gang membership for females, only gender-specific analyses are presented.

The appropriate data for male respondents are presented in Table 3.11. As expected from previous results (Table 3.2), the prevalence of gang membership declines across time, from 12.6% at Wave 2 to 4.6% at Wave 9. At every wave, however, gang members are disproportionately responsible for the delinquent acts reported by our respondents.

The second row in Table 3.11 presents information on the general delinquency index. At Wave 2, the 12.6% of the male respondents who were gang members accounted for 41.5% of all the delinquent acts self-reported at Wave 2. In other words, gang members are responsible for about 3.3 times as many acts as their share in the sample would suggest. At Wave 9, only 4.6% of the male respondents were gang members, but they reported 23.9% of the delinquent acts, which is 5.2 times that expected. Indeed, at every wave the percentage of delinquent acts reported by gang members far exceeds their proportionate share in the sample. For self-reported general delinquency, the ratios vary from 3.0 at Wave 6 to 5.2 at Wave 9, with a mean ratio of 3.9. In other words, during periods of active gang membership, the gang members were, on average, responsible for four times as many offenses as their share of the population would suggest.

The rest of Table 3.11 presents parallel information for the various indices of delinquency and drug use. The disproportionate involvement of gang

Table 3.11. *Prevalence of Gang Membership and Percentage of Delinquent Acts Attributable to Gang Members by Wave, Males Only*

	Wave 2 (n = 87)		Wave 3 (n = 81)		Wave 4 (n = 69)		Wave 5 (n = 54)		Wave 6 (n = 55)		Wave 7 (n = 39)		Wave 8 (n = 36)		Wave 9 (n = 29)		Mean Ratio
	%	Ratio	%	Ratio	%	Ratio	%	Ratio	%	Ratio	%	Ratio	%	Ratio	%	Ratio	
Gang Membership	12.6		12.1		10.2		8.1		8.4		6.1		5.7		4.6		4.6
Delinquent Acts																	
General	41.5	3.3	55.9	4.6	38.4	3.8	36.4	4.5	25.6	3.0	20.3	3.3	20.7	3.6	23.9	5.2	3.9
Serious	63.0	5.0	83.6	6.9	51.2	5.0	30.3	3.7	53.4	6.4	44.6	7.3	13.3	2.3	29.2	6.3	5.4
Moderate	40.0	3.2	56.6	4.7	42.5	4.2	27.3	3.4	22.9	2.7	27.5	4.5	28.1	4.9	36.1	7.8	4.4
Minor	45.3	3.6	40.8	3.4	18.6	1.8	31.0	3.8	24.6	2.9	10.9	1.8	31.3	5.5	25.1	5.5	3.5
Violent	39.6	3.1	49.2	4.1	39.5	3.9	23.8	2.9	35.2	4.2	32.9	5.4	30.6	5.4	45.4	9.9	4.9
Serious Violent	48.5	3.8	77.6	6.4	63.6	6.2	39.3	4.9	46.5	5.5	45.5	7.5	14.0	2.5	41.4	9.0	5.7
Property	51.7	4.1	50.8	4.2	43.4	4.3	25.0	3.1	30.8	3.7	17.3	2.8	21.2	3.7	20.0	4.3	3.8
Public Disorder	37.7	3.0	59.6	4.9	29.6	2.9	37.9	4.7	17.4	2.1	27.5	4.5	22.9	4.0	31.4	6.8	4.1
Drug Sales	38.5	3.1	59.6	4.9	40.9	4.0	62.7	7.7	22.8	2.7	34.3	5.6	29.1	5.1	16.5	3.6	4.6
Alcohol Use	31.1	2.5	51.0	4.2	44.8	4.4	26.3	3.2	22.5	2.7	17.1	2.8	15.3	2.7	16.2	3.5	3.3
Drug Use	21.6	1.7	58.3	4.8	36.7	3.6	45.6	5.6	19.4	2.3	20.6	3.4	16.2	2.8	29.7	6.5	3.8
Arrests	27.3	2.2	29.5	2.4	17.9	1.8	38.9	4.8	15.9	1.9	18.6	3.0	20.7	3.6	10.7	2.3	2.8

Table 3.12. *Prevalence of Gang Membership and Percentage of Delinquent Acts Attributable to Gang Members by Wave, Females Only*

	Wave 2 (n = 43)		Wave 3 (n = 37)		Wave 4 (n = 19)		Mean Ratio
	%	Ratio	%	Ratio	%	Ratio	
Gang Membership	16.7		14.8		7.7		
Delinquent Acts							
General	47.3	2.8	46.3	3.1	34.7	4.5	3.5
Serious	61.2	3.7	90.0	6.1	85.1	11.1	7.0
Moderate	40.2	2.4	24.9	1.7	41.4	5.4	3.2
Minor	69.8	4.2	13.9	0.9	39.4	5.1	3.4
Violent	40.1	2.4	47.9	3.2	46.6	6.1	3.9
Serious Violent	63.6	3.8	90.0	6.1	77.2	10.0	6.6
Property	52.1	3.1	18.2	1.2	49.0	6.4	3.6
Public Disorder	60.0	3.6	8.9	0.6	38.9	5.1	3.1
Drug Sales	97.9	5.9	79.7	5.4	98.1	12.7	8.0
Alcohol Use	49.8	3.0	27.7	1.9	48.1	6.2	3.7
Drug Use	78.1	4.7	27.2	1.8	32.2	4.2	3.6
Arrests	26.0	1.6	19.5	1.3	15.8	2.1	1.7

members in delinquency is replicated for all of these measures. As in the earlier cumulative analysis, the effect is quite evident for serious forms of delinquency, for violence, and for drug sales. The mean ratio for serious delinquency is 5.4, for serious violence it is 5.7, and for drug sales it is 4.6.

The male gang members are likely to be disproportionately arrested at each of these waves as well. The ratios vary from 1.8 (Wave 4) to 4.8 (Wave 5), with a mean of 2.8. As with the cumulative analysis, we also note in this wave-specific analysis that the disproportionality of gang members' involvement in delinquency is greater for the self-reported than for the official data.

Finally, Table 3.12 presents comparable data for female respondents. Because of the low prevalence of gang membership at later waves, the analysis is only conducted at Waves 2 through 4. Despite this truncation, the disproportionate contribution of gang members to delinquency and drug use is again quite evident, particularly for the more serious types of offenses. For example, while constituting 16.7%, 14.8%, and 7.7% of the sample at these three waves, the female gang members accounted for 40.1%, 47.9%, and 46.6% of the violent delinquent acts and 63.6%, 90.0%, and 77.2% of the serious violent delinquent acts, respectively. The mean ratios range from 3.1 for public disorder offenses to 8.0 for drug sales. The female gang members are also disproportionately arrested.

As these female gang members age, the ratio of gang membership to the proportion of offenses for which they are responsible increases. For example, at Wave 2 they are responsible for 3.8 times the expected rate of serious violent offenses. At Wave 3 they account for 6.1 times the expected amount, and at Wave 4, 10.0 times what one would expect. This pattern is also true for the other more serious offenses. So, although the number of female gang members declines over time, those who remain in gangs appear to become much more active offenders.

Summary

This chapter examined basic, descriptive characteristics of gang members in the Rochester Youth Development Study. Overall, slightly less than one-third of the adolescents report some involvement in street gang activity between the ages of 14 and 17. The prevalence of gang membership is about the same for male and female adolescents but is higher for African American and Hispanic youths as compared with white youths.

Although male and female respondents are about equally likely to join a gang, they have much different temporal patterns of membership. Female membership clusters very heavily in early adolescence and drops off precipitously by midadolescence. For male gang members, however, the early adolescent clustering is somewhat less evident and, while there is still a monotonic decline in membership with age, the decline is less pronounced.

Relying on the longitudinal design of the Rochester Youth Development Study, we also examined the duration and stability of gang membership. As is true of many other aspects of adolescence, involvement with gangs appears to be rather fluid. Most members are members for a year or less and very few are long-term members. Also, although some members leave and rejoin a gang in the short term, when annualized data are used, relatively few members rejoin a gang after having left one.

The findings about the age distribution and duration of membership may be influenced by the fact that Rochester is a newly emergent gang city. Moreover, gangs emerged in Rochester at about the same time that this longitudinal study began. It is impossible to identify the extent to which these results are influenced by that history, or the extent to which they would be replicated in older, established gang cities such as Los Angeles and Chicago. Similar results have been observed in recent longitudinal studies in Denver (Huizinga, 1996) and Seattle (Battin et al., 1998) but, unfortunately, they too occur in newer, rather than older, gang cities. Nevertheless, our results indicate that – at least in this study – gang membership during the adolescent years tends to occur earlier rather than later and to be more short-term than long-term. We analyze some of the implications of these results in later chapters.

In this chapter we also began our investigation of the impact that gang membership has on the life course by examining its link to delinquency and drug use. We first compared gang members and nonmembers in terms of the ever prevalence and frequency of self-reported delinquency and drug use and of official arrest histories. As expected, gang members consistently have higher rates of criminal involvement than nonmembers. Moreover, whereas there are no differences between those who joined a gang early and late, there are substantial differences between short-term and more stable gang members. We continue to examine these differences in later chapters, presenting more refined analyses that take advantage of the longitudinal, repeated-measures design of this project.

We concluded with a very straightforward descriptive issue: for what proportion of the overall volume of crime are gang members responsible? It is clear that gang members are responsible for substantially more of the total volume of crimes that are committed than their share of the population would suggest. This conclusion holds for the cumulative and wave-specific analyses, for every type of delinquency and drug use investigated, for self-reported and official measures, and for males and females.

Substantively, this finding highlights the importance of understanding the role of gang membership in the lives of adolescents if we are to design effective programs to reduce delinquency and violence. For it is not simply the case that gang members are somewhat more delinquent than nonmembers. They are, in fact, responsible for a huge proportion of the crime, especially the serious and violent crime that occurs. The fact that these differences were consistently greater for self-reported than for official delinquency suggests that this is not simply a product of police decisions to target gang members. It also means that gang members are efficient criminals. They produce many times more criminal activity for their numbers than they do arrests. This is especially true for the female gang members. Given this disproportionality, failure to change the behavior patterns of gang members successfully, or to reduce the number of gangs and gang members, probably means that we will also fail to reduce the crime rate substantially. This conclusion should follow unless we assume that the gang members would still be responsible for this volume of crime, even if they never joined a gang. We investigate this central issue in Chapter 6 of this book. First, however, we roll the clock backward a bit and examine the antecedents of gang membership.

The Antecedents of Gang Membership

HAVING PROVIDED a description of gang members by examining their demographic characteristics, we now extend this description considerably by identifying risk factors for gang membership. After examining how antecedent characteristics and attributes affect the likelihood that an individual will join a gang, we examine the ability of these same risk factors to distinguish transient from stable gang members. Following these bivariate analyses, we turn to multivariate models and examine how experiencing multiple risk affects the odds of joining a street gang.

A Risk Factor Approach

Risk factors are "individual or environmental hazards that increase an individual's vulnerability to negative developmental outcomes" (Small and Luster, 1994: 182; see also Farrington, 2000; Werner and Smith, 1982). Consistent with the multidimensionality of the life-course approach, risk factor models assume that there are multiple, and often overlapping, risk factors in an individual's background that lead to adverse outcomes. In the terms of developmental psychopathology, outcomes are characterized by equifinality, or multiple pathways to the same outcome (Cicchetti and Rogosch, 1996). Furthermore, this approach assumes that *cumulative* risk, that is, risk that occurs in many different life domains, is most strongly related to adversity (Werner and Smith, 1982).

Identifying risk factors, especially those that occur early in the life course, has several theoretical and practical advantages (Farrington, 2000). Theoretically, identifying factors that increase risk suggests fruitful areas for exploration in more formal causal analyses. It also helps in isolating variables that mediate or translate increased vulnerability into actually experiencing the outcome. Practically, knowledge of risk factors helps structure the design of intervention programs by identifying "at-risk" youth for whom prevention and treatment efforts are most warranted. Also, the identification of the most salient risk factors suggests substantive areas for intervention efforts. Alleviating antecedent variables that are associated with increased risk for a particular outcome may also reduce the probability that the person will experience the outcome. Moreover, identifying the cluster or constellation of risk factors associated with a particular outcome is helpful to clinicians because they deal with the entire individual and all of his or her presenting problems.

Despite these advantages, there have been surprisingly few examinations of risk factors for gang membership. Prior studies in this area are primarily correlational in design and compare gang members to nonmembers in terms of attributes measured during periods of active gang membership. In these studies temporal order is not established and it is therefore not clear whether the factors identified are antecedent risk factors for gang membership, co-occurring problems, or consequences of being in a gang. Because most prior studies do not establish proper temporal order, they suggest, rather than identify, risk factors for gang membership. In this section we first review the results of these studies and then review in more detail the few studies that more properly assess risk factors for gang membership.

Correlational Studies

Consistent with the basic tenet of a risk factor approach – that there are likely to be multiple rather than single pathways to adverse outcomes – prior research has examined correlates of gang membership in a variety of domains. Howell (1997: 124) has categorized risk factors into five groups: community, family, school, peer, and individual characteristics. We further divide Howell's category of individual characteristics into a prior problem behavior category and other individual characteristics. We also subdivide the family category into family sociodemographic characteristics and parent-child relationship factors.

Area Characteristics

Several studies have found that living in socially disorganized areas is related to gang membership (Bowker and Klein, 1983; Curry and Spergel, 1992; Moore, 1978, 1991; Short, 1990). These findings are consistent with the general observation that gangs themselves tend to cluster in high-crime, socially disorganized neighborhoods (e.g., Fagan, 1996; Short and Strodtbeck, 1965; Vigil, 1988). Not surprisingly, youths who reside in those same neighborhoods are at increased risk for gang membership. These findings are also consistent with research results that suggest that the availability of drugs (Curry and Spergel, 1992; Hill et al., 1995) and the presence of gangs (Curry and Spergel, 1992; Nirdorf, 1988) in the neighborhood also increase the risk for gang membership.

Other studies, however, do not link area characteristics with an increased risk of gang membership. For example, in a study by Bjerregaard and Smith (1993) using the Rochester data, social disorganization and neighborhood poverty are not significantly related to the risk of gang membership. Fagan (1990) also found no significant association between gang membership and social integration, neighborhood integration, or neighborhood violence. Similarly, Winfree, Backstrom, and Mays (1994) found that urban residence does not differentiate gang members from nonmembers.

Family Sociodemographic Characteristics

Several studies have examined sociodemographic characteristics as risk factors for gang membership. Very little research in the gang literature examines race or ethnicity as a predictor of gang membership, because most studies are conducted within racially homogeneous gangs. Among the studies that do exist, the comparison is generally between white subjects and either African American or Hispanic youths. By and large, Hispanic and African American subjects are more likely to be gang members than are white subjects (Esbensen and Huizinga, 1993; Hill et al., 1999; Schwartz, 1989; Winfree et al., 1994), an outcome consistent with our data presented in Chapter 3.

Some studies have found that low family socioeconomic status or poverty is related to gang membership (Bowker and Klein, 1983; Moore, 1991; Schwartz, 1989). Structural characteristics of families have also been examined with varying results. Bowker and Klein (1983) and Vigil (1988) found that coming from single-parent families increases the risk of joining gangs, whereas LeBlanc and Lanctôt (1998), in a study comparing gang members and nonmembers in a Quebec sample restricted to adjudicated boys, did not.

Parent-Child Relations

In addition to concerns about family structure, many studies have examined family processes and parent-child relationships as risk factors for gang involvement. In general, poor family management strategies increase the risk for gang membership by adolescents (LeBlanc and Lanctôt, 1998; Moore, 1991; Vigil, 1988). More specifically, low family involvement (Friedman, Mann, and Friedman, 1975; LeBlanc and Lanctôt, 1998), inappropriate parental discipline (Winfree et al., 1994), low parental control or monitoring (Bowker and Klein, 1983; Campbell, 1990; LeBlanc and Lanctôt, 1998; Moore, 1991), poor affective relationships between parent and child (Campbell, 1990; Moore, 1991), and parental conflict (LeBlanc and Lanctôt, 1998) put youths at risk for becoming gang members. These family-based risk factors are quite consistent with those generally observed as increasing risk for involvement in delinquency (see Hawkins, Catalano, and Miller, 1992; Loeber and Stouthamer-Loeber, 1986).

School Factors

Failure in the educational arena can also be a major source of risk for gang membership. Bowker and Klein (1983) reported that female students who have low educational expectations are at increased risk for gang membership, a finding also observed by Bjerregaard and Smith (1993) for females but not males. Gang membership is more likely among adolescents whose parents have low educational expectations for them (Schwartz, 1989). Poor school performance and low commitment to and involvement in school are correlated with gang membership (LeBlanc and Lanctôt, 1998). In a related vein, gang membership is associated with educational frustration (Curry and Spergel, 1992) and stress (LeBlanc and Lanctôt, 1998).

Teachers also play a role in predicting the likelihood of gang membership. Gang members, as compared with nonmembers, are more likely to experience negative labeling by teachers (Esbensen, Huizinga, and Weiher, 1993) and are less likely to have a teacher as a positive role model (Schwartz, 1989; Wang, 1994), although LeBlanc and Lanctôt (1998) did not find low attachment to teachers to be related to gang membership.

Low school self-esteem (Curry and Spergel, 1992; Schwartz, 1989) and educational marginality (Bjerregaard and Smith, 1993) increase the risk for gang membership. Two studies have suggested that school stress resulting from factors such as getting into trouble in school or getting poor grades is related to gang membership (Cohen et al., 1994; Shelden, Snodgrass, and Snodgrass, 1992).

Peer Relationships

Several studies have found that adolescents who associate with deviant peers are more likely to join gangs, especially peers who are themselves gang members (Curry and Spergel, 1992; Nirdorf, 1988; Winfree et al., 1994). Gang membership has been shown to be related to precocious sexual activity (Bjerregaard and Smith, 1993; LeBlanc and Lanctôt, 1998) and also, in the case of young women, dating older males, especially older gang males who are involved in deviant activity (Bowker and Klein, 1983).

Having friends who are involved in delinquency is strongly related to being a gang member (Bjerregaard and Lizotte, 1995; Bjerregaard and Smith, 1993; Bowker and Klein, 1983; Curry and Spergel, 1992; Esbensen et al., 1993; Fagan, 1990; LeBlanc and Lanctôt, 1998; Nirdorf, 1988; Winfree et al.,

1994). The relationship between deviant peers and gang membership is perhaps the strongest one observed in this literature. Because delinquent gangs are in many ways a specific version of a delinquent peer group, the finding is not surprising. Relatedly, loitering or "hanging out" with peers in unsupervised peer groups is also related to gang membership (LeBlanc and Lanctôt, 1998).

Individual Characteristics

Gang members have been characterized as being personally maladjusted, although findings in this area are rather inconsistent (see Bjerregaard and Smith, 1993, for a review). With regard to self-esteem, a number of studies found that low self-esteem increases the likelihood of gang membership (Cartwright, Tomson, and Schwartz, 1975; Rice, 1963; Schwartz, 1989; Wang, 1994). In contrast, Bjerregaard and Smith (1993), Bowker and Klein (1983), and Esbensen et al. (1993) did not find self-esteem to be related to gang membership. We have little information on the effect of stressful or negative life events as a risk factor for joining a gang except for the studies cited earlier relating to school stress and family stress.

The individual's attitudes also play a role in increasing the risk of gang membership. Winfree et al. (1994) found that progang attitudes are associated with gang membership and Esbensen et al. (1993) found that gang members have a higher tolerance for deviance and higher levels of normlessness (see also Fagan, 1990). LeBlanc and Lanctôt (1998) reported that deviant beliefs and techniques of neutralization are related to gang membership and also that gang members have significantly poorer scores than nonmembers on 10 of their 13 personality scales, including orientation to tough and adult-type behaviors, aggression, repression, denial, neuroticism, and extraversion.

Prior Deviance

Finally, several studies have found that adolescents who are already involved in deviant and problem behaviors are more likely to join gangs than are adolescents who are not involved in those behaviors. For example, gang membership has been shown to be related to alcohol and drug use (Bjerregaard and Smith, 1993; Cohen et al., 1994; LeBlanc and Lanctôt, 1998; Thornberry, Krohn, et al., 1993), violence (Friedman et al., 1975; LeBlanc and Lanctôt, 1998), being an illegal gun owner (Bjerregaard and Lizotte, 1995), and general delinquency (Curry and Spergel, 1992; Esbensen and Huizinga, 1993; LeBlanc and Lanctôt, 1998; Nirdorf, 1988). In addition, official contact with the juvenile justice system has been shown to be related to gang membership (Cohen et al., 1994; LeBlanc and Lanctôt, 1998).

Risk Factor Studies

Recently a few longitudinal studies have begun to investigate the impact of *prior* attributes and characteristics that may increase the risk of subsequent gang membership. That is, they have begun to assess more properly a risk factor model for gang membership.

Using data from the Seattle Social Development Project, Hill et al. (1999) examined risk factors measured at ages 10–12 as predictors of gang membership between ages 13 and 18. Risk factors were drawn from five domains: neighborhood, family, school, peers, and individual characteristics. They found that "[21] of the 25 constructs measured at ages 10–12 predicted joining a gang at ages 13 to 18. Predictors of gang membership were found in all of the measured domains" (Hill et al., 1999: 308). Within each of these domains the most potent risk factors are neighborhood youth in trouble and availability of marijuana; family structure, especially living with one parent and other adults or with no parents; low achievement in elementary school or being identified as learning disabled; association with deviant peers; prior involvement in marijuana use or violence; and externalizing problem behaviors. Hill et al. also found that having multiple risk factors greatly increases the chances of joining a gang.

Bjerregaard and Lizotte (1995) used the Rochester data to look specifically at the impact of earlier delinquency and gun ownership on the likelihood of being a gang member. They found that prior involvement in serious delinquency and street delinquency, but not more general forms of delinquency, increases the likelihood of later gang membership. They also found that owning guns for protection, but not for sporting purposes, increases the chances of joining a gang.

Lahey et al. (1999) examined predictors of first gang entry for the males in the Pittsburgh Youth Study. Their study was restricted to African American males because of the small number of white male gang members available for analysis. In bivariate relationships, gang membership is predicted by prior conduct disorder behaviors, self-reported delinquency, and associations with delinquent peers. Gang membership is not bivariately related to household income, household structure, neighborhood crime level, or parental supervision, however.

Summary

Overall, we have a good deal of information from prior studies that can inform a risk factor model. It appears that gang membership is a product of numerous risk factors from multiple developmental domains and that gang members are likely to have serious deficits in many developmental areas. Because of the cross-sectional nature of most of these studies, however, we do not have a clear, well-replicated understanding of which *antecedent* conditions increase risk for *later* gang membership. In addition, a risk factor model requires a general, representative sample that includes both individuals who experience the outcome (i.e., gang membership) and those who do not experience it. Unfortunately, there are relatively few gang studies (e.g., Hill et al., 1999; Lahey et al., 1999) that have both of these design features – that is, a representative sample that follows both gang members and comparison nonmembers across time. We now capitalize on the longitudinal design of the Rochester study to help fill this gap in our knowledge.

Measurement

The key variable in this analysis is gang membership. As indicated in Chapter 2, gang membership is measured by a self-report item contained in our interviews. Unfortunately for this analysis, at Wave 2 we asked the respondents if they had *ever* been a gang member, but not the age at which they joined the gang. Thus, for subjects who were in a gang at Wave 2 proper temporal order cannot be established between Wave 1 risk factors and *later* gang membership. We therefore limit this analysis to respondents who joined a gang at Wave 3 or after. Starting at the Wave 3 interview, we asked the respondents whether they were a gang member at any time during the six-month interval since the previous interview. Because of this, we can establish proper temporal order between earlier risk factors, measured at either Wave 2 or prior to Wave 2, and later gang membership. Thus, the primary dependent variable in this chapter is joining a gang at any time between Waves 3 and 9.

Based on the domains previously identified, and consistent with a general ecological framework (Bronfenbrenner, 1979), risk factors for gang membership are grouped into seven domains: area characteristics, family sociodemographic characteristics, parent-child relations, school factors, peer relationships, individual characteristics, and early delinquency. More comprehensive descriptions of the measures within each domain were presented in Chapter 2. Briefly, area risk factors include racial composition, census-tract-level poverty, and arrest rate, as well as family perceptions of neighborhood disorganization and violence. Sociodemographic characteristics of families include economic disadvantage, race/ethnicity, and the composition of households. Measures of parent-child relations include attachment, involvement, supervision, positive parenting, child maltreatment, and family hostility. School factors include lack of school commitment, aspirations and achievement, and lack of attachment to teachers. Peer risk factors include peer delinquency, early dating, precocious sexual activity, and unsupervised time with friends. Individual factors include stressful or negative life events and various indicators of psychopathology such as high levels of externalizing behavior, low self-esteem, depressive symptoms, and delinquent beliefs. Prior delinquency includes early general delinquency, violent delinquency, drug use, and age of onset of delinquency.

Because of the nature of the analysis to follow, especially the examination of cumulative risk, we dichotomize all the risk factor variables. Many are already dichotomies, for example, race/ethnicity and whether or not there is a history of child maltreatment. Continuous variables were divided at their median, so variables such as attachment to parents or commitment to school represent respondents who are above or below the midway point on the variable. Dichotomizing all the variables creates a common metric for the logistic regressions reported here and provides a rather intuitive interpretation for the odds ratios that are presented. Also, dichotomies are helpful in determining whether a respondent has a particular risk factor, a necessary step in assessing cumulative risk. Table 4.1 presents means for these dichotomous variables for male and female respondents separately.

Results

Bivariate Analysis

The first step in the analysis is an examination of bivariate relationships between early risk factors and subsequent gang membership. Because gang membership is a dichotomous variable, we use odds ratios from bivariate logistic regressions to estimate the strength of the associations. Odds ratios of less than 1 indicate that the risk factor is associated with a *reduced* likelihood of gang membership, whereas odds ratios greater than 1 indicate that the likelihood of gang membership is *increased* when this factor is present. For example, an odds ratio of .8 indicates that respondents who possess the particular attribute indicated by the predictor variable have a likelihood of gang membership that is 80% of that of those who do not have the attribute. On the other hand, an odds ratio of 1.3 indicates that those with the risk factor have a likelihood of gang membership that is 30% higher than those without the risk factor. An odds ratio of 2.0 indicates that the likelihood of gang membership is 100% higher or, in other words, is twice as high. An odds ratio of 1 indicates no relationship between the two variables. To examine whether the same risk factors predict gang membership for boys and girls, we do separate analyses by gender (see Table 4.2).

Male Gang Membership

For males, 25 of the 40 Wave 2 risk factors are significantly related to subsequent gang membership in the expected direction. Each domain contains a number of significant relationships indicating that diverse areas of the lives of these adolescents have the potential to put a youth at risk for joining a gang.

Table 4.1. *Means for Dichotomous Risk Factors*

	Males	Females
Area Characteristics		
Percentage African American	.50	.51
Percentage in Poverty	.47	.53
Community Arrest Rate	.49	.53
Neighborhood Disorganization	.53	.51
Neighborhood Violence	.45	.47
Neighborhood Drug Use	.33	.50
Neighborhood Integration	.59	.61
Family Sociodemographic Characteristics		
African American	.55	.71
Hispanic	.16	.18
Parent Education	.60	.54
Family Disadvantage	.56	.62
Poverty Level Income	.30	.38
Lives with Both Biological Parents	.33	.19
Family Transitions	.22	.17
Parent-Child Relations		
Attachment to Parent (Subject Report)	.45	.45
Attachment to Child (Parent Report)	.56	.57
Parental Involvement (Parent Report)	.51	.57
Parental Supervision (Subject Report)	.55	.70
Positive Parenting (Parent Report)	.35	.44
Report of Child Maltreatment	.12	.14
Family Hostility	.57	.49
School Factors		
Commitment to School	.48	.56
Attachment to Teacher	.49	.60
College Aspirations	.69	.73
Subject's College Expectations	.77	.80
Parent's College Expectations for Subject	.53	.68
Math Score	.57	.54
Peer Relationships		
Delinquent Peers	.33	.45
Early Dating	.41	.43
Precocious Sexual Activity	.29	.26
Unsupervised Time with Friends	.49	.40
Individual Characteristics		
Negative Life Events	.31	.40
Depression	.47	.62
Self-Esteem	.52	.49
Externalizing Behaviors	.46	.40
Delinquent Beliefs	.65	.62

Table 4.1. (*cont.*)

	Males	Females
Early Delinquency		
General Delinquency	.47	.41
Violent Delinquency	.27	.26
Drug Use	.07	.09
Age of Onset of General Delinquency	.26	.18

Note: To preserve temporal order, risk factors are measured either at Wave 2 or prior to Wave 2. Because of missing data, the n's vary across these measures, ranging from 488 to 534 for the males and from 169 to 183 for the females. The only exception is age of onset, which can only be calculated for offenders (n = 340 for males and n = 96 for females).

The objective indicators of area characteristics are more important predictors of gang membership than are the subjective perceptions of what neighborhoods are like. Respondents who live in neighborhoods that have a higher proportion of African Americans, poorer residents, and a higher arrest rate are more likely to become gang members. On the other hand, among indicators based on parental perceptions of problems in the neighborhood, only neighborhood drug use significantly increases the likelihood of males becoming gang members.

The risk of joining a gang is significantly related to four demographic characteristics. Being African American, having a parent with less education, living in a family with an income below the poverty level, and living in homes where both biological parents are not present increase the risk of joining a gang. The combined results from the area and family domains confirm the results of many previous gang studies and indicate that socioeconomic disadvantage is an important risk factor for gang membership.

The quality of the relationship between parents and children also contributes to the risk of joining a gang. In families where parents are less attached to their sons and do not supervise them very well, the odds that the child will become a gang member increase. Also, if there is an official record of child maltreatment, the boy's chances of being a gang member are increased.

Both objective and subjective measures of school problems significantly increase the risk that males will join gangs. Low commitment to school, weak attachment to teacher, and lower parental expectations that their son will go to college are significantly related to gang membership. Those respondents who scored lower on a standardized math test also are significantly more likely to join a gang.

Table 4.2. *Bivariate Odds Ratios between Risk Factors and Joining a Gang between Waves 3 and 9*

	Males	Females
Area Characteristics		
Percentage African American	1.59*	.81
Percentage in Poverty	1.88**	1.40
Community Arrest Rate	1.79**	1.14
Neighborhood Disorganization	.95	2.56*
Neighborhood Violence	.86	1.64
Neighborhood Drug Use	1.51*	1.87
Neighborhood Integration	.71	1.97
Family Sociodemographic Characteristics		
African American	2.28**	2.06
Hispanic	1.19	.50
Parent Education	.53**	.96
Family Disadvantage	1.39	1.90
Poverty Level Income	1.91**	1.40
Lives with Both Biological Parents	.47**	.50
Family Transitions	1.42	1.46
Parent-Child Relations		
Attachment to Parent	1.02	.80
Attachment to Child	.69*	1.36
Parental Involvement	.94	1.29
Parental Supervision	.53**	1.01
Positive Parenting	1.10	3.07
Report of Child Maltreatment	1.78*	1.77
Family Hostility	.77	1.21
School Factors		
Commitment to School	.64*	.80
Attachment to Teacher	.48**	.24**
College Aspirations	1.09	.30**
Subject's College Expectations	.70	.12**
Parent's College Expectations for Subject	.64*	.43*
Math Score	.41**	.65
Peer Relationships		
Delinquent Peers	1.97**	2.02
Early Dating	2.82**	2.91*
Precocious Sexual Activity	1.58*	1.66
Unsupervised Time with Friends	1.41	1.35
Individual Characteristics		
Negative Life Events	3.25**	1.28
Depression	1.71**	1.13
Self-Esteem	.82	.93

Table 4.2. (*cont.*)

	Males	Females
Externalizing Behaviors	1.98**	2.24*
Delinquent Beliefs	2.15**	4.27**
Early Delinquency		
General Delinquency	3.26**	2.82*
Violent Delinquency	4.19**	1.44
Drug Use	2.49**	2.57
Age of Onset of General Delinquency	.78	.35

Note: To preserve temporal order, risk factors are measured either at Wave 2 or prior to Wave 2. Because of missing data, the n's vary across these measures, ranging from 488 to 534 for the males and from 169 to 183 for the females. The only exception is age of onset, which can only be calculated for offenders (n = 340 for males and n = 96 for females).
*p < .05 (one-tailed test). **p < .01 (one-tailed test).

Three of the four measures in the peer domain significantly increase the risk that youth will join gangs. Having friends who are involved in delinquent behavior increases the risk for gang membership. Also, males who are involved in precocious sexual activity and who begin dating at an early age are more likely to become gang members.

Among the individual characteristics, experiencing negative life events has a substantial impact on the risk of gang membership, increasing the odds of joining a gang threefold. Mental health problems such as having depressive symptoms and externalizing problem behaviors also play an important role. Attitudes that are favorable to delinquent behavior increase the odds that males will become gang members. Only self-esteem is not significantly related to gang membership.

Finally, involvement in prior illegal activity increases the likelihood of later gang membership. As might be expected, this is particularly true for violence; those who self-report violence above the median value at Wave 1 are four times as likely to become gang members as are those who self-report less violence. Early age of onset of delinquency is not significantly related to gang membership, however.

In summary, a wide band of factors from different domains of the adolescent's life appear to come together to influence the chances of becoming a gang member for these young males. These range from the contextual impact of poor neighborhoods and family hardship to the more personally experienced stress of negative life events and proximity to deviant peers.

Although many risk factors are significantly related to later gang membership, fewer factors appear to have a strong effect based on the size of the odds ratios (OR) presented in Table 4.2. The following variables at least double (OR > 2.0) or cut in half (OR < .50) the odds of being a gang member: being African American; not living with both parents; low attachment to teachers; low math scores; early dating; experiencing negative life events; delinquent beliefs; and prior delinquency, violence, and drug use.

Female Gang Membership

As indicated in Chapter 3, the temporal distribution of gang membership is highly skewed for the female respondents; most joined a gang by Wave 2 and only 18 joined at Wave 3 or after. Consequently, the number of female gang members available for this analysis is quite low and that reduces statistical power. Hence, we can expect fewer risk factors to be significant predictors of gang membership for females as compared with males. Indeed, only 9 of the 40 potential risk factors are statistically significant.

For the females, none of the objective neighborhood characteristics is statistically significant, which is in direct contrast to what we found for males. Of the perceptual measures, only parental perception of neighborhood disorganization significantly increases the odds of females becoming gang members.

Among the sociodemographic characteristics, none of the measures is statistically significant. The size and direction of most of the coefficients are, however, consistent with what was found for males. It would appear that coming from a disadvantaged family background increases the odds of gang membership for females, as it did for males.

The odds of joining a gang are not significantly affected by any of the parent-child relations variables, although several of these variables were important for the males.

School variables appear to be the most important domain for predicting female gang membership. In particular, being attached to teachers and having aspirations to attend college decrease the odds of females joining gangs. Relatedly, both the parent's and the adolescent's lowered expectations about attending college are significantly related to increasing the odds of gang membership.

Early dating is the only peer variable that significantly increases the odds of joining a gang for the females; females who begin dating boys at an early age are more likely to be gang members than those who wait till an older age. Although the odds ratios are not statistically significant for precocious sexual activity and having delinquent peers, they are in the expected direction and of approximately the same magnitude as those observed for the males.

Among the individual characteristics, only externalizing behaviors and delinquent beliefs are statistically significant. Perhaps most surprising is the relatively small effect that experiencing negative life events has in increasing the odds of female gang membership. Negative life events are very important for males but appear to have little impact for females, a finding that is consistent with the general literature on gender differences in the effects of childhood and adolescent stress (e.g., Bolger et al., 1995; Emery and O'Leary, 1982).

Interestingly, prior participation in violence and drug use does not significantly increase the odds of joining a gang, perhaps because of the lower rate of female involvement in violence and drug use at these ages. The significant effect for general delinquency indicates that participation in any type of delinquency is important in predicting female gang membership rather than participation in a particular type.

Statements concerning the effect of risk factors on female gang membership cannot be as definitive as they were for males because of the smaller number of females in our sample and especially the smaller number of female gang members in this analysis. However, living in a socially disorganized neighborhood, school-related variables, early dating, externalizing behaviors, having delinquent beliefs, and prior general delinquency appear to be important factors in increasing the odds that females will join gangs. Although not as clear-cut as the situation for males, it also appears that female gang members have multiple risk factors in multiple domains, an analytic issue we return to later in this chapter.

Predicting Stable Gang Membership

Up to this point we have concentrated on identifying risk factors for gang membership. In Chapter 3 we saw that the duration of gang membership, at least for the males, varies considerably; about half of the gang members were in a gang for a year or less (short-term members) and about half remained active for more than a year (stable members). Moreover, stable gang members have significantly higher rates of self-reported and official delinquency than short-term members. Do the risk factors that predict gang membership also predict the stability of gang membership?

To answer this question, we present bivariate odds ratios between each of the risk factors and the stability of gang membership for the 166 male gang members.[1] Because the outcome variable – the duration of gang membership – unfolds over the course of adolescence, we include all male

[1] There are not enough female gang members, especially those who were stable gang members, for this analysis.

gang members in this analysis, not just those who joined at Wave 3 or after. Doing so preserves proper temporal order between the risk factors and the outcome and maximizes the sample size. All other analyses in this chapter include only those who joined a gang between Waves 3 and 9.

The results (Table 4.3) suggest that two clusters of variables increase the risk of stable gang membership. The first concerns structural disadvantage: gang members who come from poor or disadvantaged families, whose parents have lower than average levels of education, and who experience changes in family structure are more apt to remain gang members for longer periods. The second area concerns early adolescent risky behaviors: early dating and early drug use significantly increase the odds of becoming a stable gang member.

Overall, although early risk factors do an effective job of discriminating between gang members and nonmembers, they do not do an equally effective job of discriminating within the gang member population. This result is consistent with examinations of delinquent behavior conducted from a criminal career perspective (e.g., Blumstein et al., 1986), which show that the predictors of the prevalence of offending are often not very effective predictors of individual offending rates among active offenders. Presumably, the homogeneity of the onset groups – either the offenders or, in our case, the gang members – reduces the explanatory power of the antecedent variables. It would appear that developmental variables that unfold during the period of gang membership may be more predictive of the duration of membership. Given the pattern of these bivariate results, the multivariate models that follow only examine risk factors for gang membership, not the duration of membership.

Cumulative Risk

One of the basic premises of a life-course approach is that risk accumulates, and, as a consequence, exposure to risk in multiple domains of development greatly increases the person's vulnerability to adverse outcomes (see Garmezy, 1995; Rutter, 1987; Werner and Smith, 1992). In other words, while experiencing risk in one domain (e.g., family *or* school) increases the odds of adverse outcomes, experiencing risk in multiple domains (e.g., family *and* school) should have an even larger impact on behavior. To test this hypothesis we examine two models of cumulative risk, a variable-based model and a domain-based model.

Variable-Based Model

In the variable-based model we simply count the number of risk factors that each person experienced at Wave 2. The risk factors are those listed

Table 4.3. *Bivariate Odds Ratios between Risk Factors and Stability of Gang Membership, Males Only (n = 166)*

Area Characteristics		School Factors	
Percentage African		Commitment to	
American	.99	School	1.15
Percentage in		Attachment to	
Poverty	1.46	Teacher	1.72
Community Arrest Rate	.85	College Aspirations	1.12
Neighborhood		Subject's College	
Disorganization	.48	Expectations	.61
Neighborhood Violence	.55	Parent's College Expectations	
Neighborhood Drug Use	1.05	for Subject	.69
Neighborhood Integration	1.69	Math Score	1.00
Family Sociodemographic		*Peer Relationships*	
Characteristics		Delinquent Peers	.97
African American	.90	Early Dating	2.26**
Hispanic	.93	Precocious Sexual	
Parent Education	.39**	Activity	1.11
Family Disadvantage	2.09*	Unsupervised Time	
Poverty Level Income	1.99*	with Friends	1.67
Lives with Both		*Individual Characteristics*	
Biological Parents	.80	Negative Life Events	1.39
Family Transitions	2.91**	Depression	1.55
Parent-Child Relations		Self-Esteem	.72
Attachment to Parent	1.48	Externalizing Behaviors	.94
Attachment to Child	.89	Delinquent Beliefs	1.54
Parental Involvement	1.45	*Early Delinquency*	
Parental Supervision	.93	General Delinquency	.82
Positive Parenting	1.26	Violent Delinquency	.78
Report of Child		Drug Use	2.14*
Maltreatment	.84	Age of Onset of	
Family Hostility	1.41	General Delinquency	1.88

Note: To preserve temporal order, risk factors are measured either at Wave 2 or prior to Wave 2.
*p < .05 (one-tailed test). **p < .01 (one-tailed test).

in the bivariate table (Table 4.2). In this analysis some of the variables are reverse coded so that a score of 1 always indicates risk. For example, coding for commitment to school is reversed, with those scoring below the median (i.e., having low commitment) receiving a score of one. Overall, scores could range from 0 to 40. For this analysis the respondents are grouped into four categories, those experiencing 10 or fewer risk factors, 11–15 risk factors,

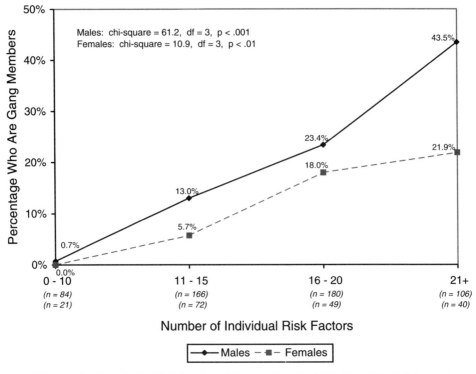

Figure 4.1. Cumulative Risk for Gang Membership, Variable-Based Model (top n is for males, bottom n is for females)

16–20 risk factors, and 21 or more.[2] The results are presented in Figure 4.1, for males and females separately. Recall that to preserve temporal order, this analysis is limited to those who first joined a gang at Wave 3 or after. The total prevalence of gang membership at these waves is 19.7% for the males and 11.9% for the females.

There is a strong positive relationship between experiencing multiple risks and the chances of becoming a gang member. For the male subjects, only 1 (0.7%) of those with 10 or fewer risk factors joined a gang. For those with 11–15 risk factors in their background 13.0% were gang members, and that percentage increased to 23.4% for those with 16–20 risk factors and to 43.5% for those with 21 or more risk factors. Clearly, a strong relationship exists between accumulated risk and the likelihood of joining a gang.

---

[2] Without grouping, the substantive results are the same but the pattern is not as smooth because of the uneven number of cases across the distribution.

The data for the female respondents paint much the same picture. None of the females with fewer than 10 risk factors reported being a gang member. As risk accumulates, however, the prevalence of gang membership increases to 5.7%, to 18.0%, and finally to 21.9% for those with 21 or more risk factors.

These patterns suggest that youths can experience some degree of risk – here fewer than 10 risk factors – and still be quite resilient to the lure of gang membership. As risk accumulates, however, the chances of joining a gang increase sharply. Youths experiencing many risk factors are far more likely to join a gang than are their counterparts.[3]

Domain-Based Model

The results in Figure 4.1 suggest that youths experiencing risk in multiple developmental domains are at increased risk for gang membership. Because the model is variable-based, however, it is possible that risk only accumulated in a few domains and not across multiple domains. For example, under the scoring procedure in Figure 4.1, a respondent who was a very poor student could receive a score of six, without experiencing risk in any other domain. This possibility, generated by the richness of measurement that is available, is not very consistent with the notion of multidimensionality, which is concerned with the consequences of different pathways or arenas of development on producing different outcomes. To examine the issue of multidimensionality more exactly, we now switch to a domain-based model of risk.

The domain-based measure is created in a two-step process. We first de-termined if the respondent experienced higher than average risk in each domain – for example, area characteristics or family sociodemographic characteristics. To do so, we calculated the median number of risk factors experienced by the subjects in each domain and then classified each sub-ject as being above or below the median in that domain. Second, we then counted the number of domains in which the respondent was above the median. With seven domains, scores could range from 0 to 7 (see Table 4.2). The results are presented in Figure 4.2 for male and female respondents separately.

Here we see an even stronger relationship between cumulative risk and the chances of becoming a gang member. Of the males who did not

---

[3] The analysis just presented counts all the risk factors listed in Table 4.2, including those that are statistically significantly related to gang membership and those that are not. The inclusion of the nonsignificant variables may mute the impact of cumulative risk. We therefore repeated the analysis, including only the significant variables. The pattern is identical to that in Figure 4.1. For example, of the males in the highest category, 16–21 significant risk factors, 43% were gang members.

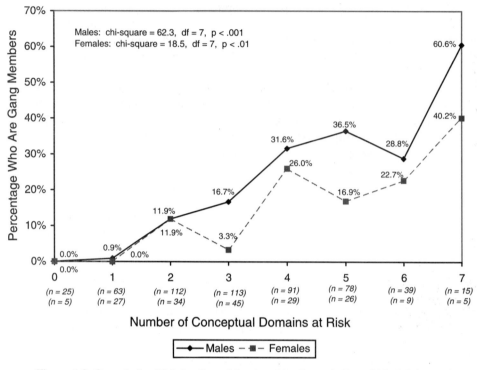

Figure 4.2. Cumulative Risk for Gang Membership, Domain-Based Model (top n is for males, bottom n is for females)

experience risk in any of these seven domains, none became a gang member. Of those who experienced risk in only one domain, only 0.9% joined a gang. After that point the prevalence of gang membership increases rather steadily from 11.9% of those who were above average on two domains to 36.5% of those experiencing risk in five of the seven domains. There is then a slight decrease – to 28.8% – for those experiencing risk in six of the seven domains. For the 15 youths who were above average in all seven domains, however, the prevalence of gang membership reaches a peak at 60.6%, a high rate compared with a total prevalence of gang membership (at Waves 3 to 9) of about 20% for the males.

The pattern of results for female respondents is similar, although somewhat more erratic because of the smaller sample sizes. None of the young girls who avoid risk or have risk in a single domain becomes a gang member. Risk in a few domains increases the chances of gang membership and the prevalence of gang membership increases to about 20% for those who experience risk in between four and six domains. At the end of the distribution, of those experiencing risk in all seven domains, 40.2% report being a gang member.

Summary

Overall, the results for the cumulative risk analysis are quite consistent with the basic hypothesis of the multidimensionality of risk. As risk accumulates, the chances of gang membership increase dramatically. Youth are quite resilient – at least in terms of the chances of joining a gang – in light of low levels of risk. As risk accumulates, however, the likelihood of joining a gang increases substantially, a pattern observed for both males and females. For example, 43.5% of the male and 21.9% of the female respondents were gang members if they experienced 21 or more risk factors, as compared with average rates of gang membership of 19.7% for the males and 11.9% for the females. In the domain-based approach, 60.6% of the male and 40.2% of the female respondents were gang members if they experienced risk in all seven domains.

Substantively, it is interesting that the impact of cumulative risk is stronger in the domain-based approach. Consistent with a life-course model, it indicates that nonredundant disadvantages that cumulate across different domains or ecological contexts appear to generate a greater chance of adverse outcomes than do more redundant disadvantages, accumulated in one or two domains. This finding also highlights the difficulties we face in trying to intervene with individual gang members, because they are likely to experience disadvantage in multiple developmental domains.

Conclusion

The results of our examination of risk factors for gang membership are quite consistent with the multidimensionality of a life-course perspective. It does not appear that gang membership is associated with a single developmental domain; on the contrary, gang members have multiple disadvantages in multiple domains of their development. Whereas the impact of individual risk factors is rather modest, their cumulative impact is quite large. It appears that youth can tolerate lower levels of risk, or risk in a few domains, and still avoid an increased likelihood of joining a gang. As risk increases, however, so too does the likelihood of joining a gang. Indeed, in the highest category of cumulative risk the chances of joining a gang are generally more than twice as high as the mean prevalence at these ages.

In terms of individual risk factors, we saw that many more individual variables are significant for the males than for the females. This difference may be an artifact of the smaller number of female gang members and attenuated statistical power, a possibility supported in the cumulative risk factor analysis where sample size is less important. In that case, the results are quite similar for both the males and the females. Overall, the results suggest that social disadvantage, poor performance in school, early dating, externalizing behaviors, prior delinquency, and delinquent beliefs increase the chances of a youth subsequently joining a gang. These findings, based on analyses where proper temporal order is preserved, are consistent with those from prior cross-sectional research.

Although accumulated disadvantage in these areas increases the chances of later gang membership, it does not guarantee it. Indeed, even at the highest level of risk (see Figures 4.1 and 4.2), many adolescents are *not* gang members. Despite the accumulated level of disadvantage in their backgrounds, there appear to be protective processes that help them avoid this outcome. Identifying the processes that do so is a significant challenge for future research as that information could be particularly helpful to intervention efforts.

The Origins of Gang Membership

THE RESULTS OF the risk factor analyses are descriptively informative, but they are also theoretically limited. A risk factor approach provides a somewhat atomized view of gang members that is focused on individual variables; it fails to identify the causal processes by which more distal variables lead to more proximal variables and how they, in turn, lead to outcomes of interest. Indeed, as Farrington has noted, "a major problem with the risk factor prevention paradigm is to determine which risk factors are causes and which are merely markers or correlated with causes. It is also important to establish processes or developmental pathways that intervene between risk factors and outcomes, and to bridge the gap between risk factor research and more complex explanatory theories" (2000: 7). In this chapter we begin to address the general topic of identifying the causes of gang membership. The central question is, Why do some youths join street gangs while others manage to avoid the lure of the gang?

We address this question using two complementary approaches. The first approach is more qualitative and is based on the perceptions of the gang members. We asked them why they joined the gang and these open-ended responses provide information on their perceptions of the more immediate influences that led to their decision. The second approach is based in the tradition of causal modeling. We develop a path model of the origins of gang membership derived from the premises of interactional theory (Thornberry, 1987; Thornberry and Krohn, 2001) and test it using the longitudinal panel data of the Rochester study.

The Perceptions of Gang Members

What do gang members say about their motivation for joining a gang? To gauge their perceptions we simply asked them why they joined and recorded

77

their responses. As expected, various answers were provided but they tend to cluster along several major dimensions. We have collapsed them into four general categories.

The first, Family/Friends, indicated that they joined because family members – usually siblings or cousins – or friends were already members of the gang and encouraged them to join. We recognize that finer distinctions in this and other categories would be helpful, but the number of cases becomes quite small when they are subdivided. It is particularly hard to subdivide this category because many respondents combined them on their actual answers, for example, "my cousins and friends were in the gang," or "my sister and friends from school asked me to." In any event, the first category indicates that access to a gang via primary group relations with a friend or family member led the youth to join the gang. Illustrations of some of the actual responses, for this and the other categories, are presented in Figure 5.1.

Family/Friends
    Brothers and guys at center in it
    Friends were in it and wanted to be part of it
    My brother was in the posse
    My boyfriend is a g-boy

Protection
    For protection and the "in" thing to do
    Protection of friends' joint
    So gang members wouldn't bother me

Fun/Action
    A lot of fun
    Something to do
    There was nothing else to do – I was bored

Other Reasons
    Just to be in it
    Felt like it
    For what they believed in

Figure 5.1. Illustrative Reasons for Joining a Gang

Table 5.1. *Reasons for Joining a Gang, by Gender*

	Males		Females		Total	
	%	n	%	n	%	n
Family/Friends	49.3	65	59.7	71	54.2	137
Protection	20.1	27	16.7	20	18.5	47
Fun/Action	17.6	23	11.8	14	14.8	37
Other	13.0	17	11.8	14	12.4	31
Total	100.0	133	100.0	119	100.0	252

$X^2 = 3.17$; df $= 3$; p $= .37$.

The second cluster of reasons is labeled Protection. Some youth joined because the gang was perceived to provide protection from a hostile world, typified, for example, by rival gangs or crime in their neighborhood or at school.

The third cluster, Fun/Action, is reminiscent of Thrasher's (1927) gang world and some of Miller's (1958) focal concerns. Adolescents report joining the gang for the excitement, fun, and adventure associated with gang life. In brief, they think it is where the action is. Finally, a catchall Other category combines a number of low frequency, more idiosyncratic responses.

We classified each gang member according to the primary reason he or she gave for joining the gang. Table 5.1 separates the basic data for males and females. Of the total sample, about half (54%) cited Family/Friends – they joined the gang because other family members or friends were in the gang and encouraged them to do so. The next most popular response, provided by 19% of the sample, was for Protection. A slightly smaller proportion, 15%, said they joined for the Fun/Action of gang life. Finally, 12% of the respondents were placed in the Other category.

Slight gender differences are evident in the distributions (Table 5.1). Females are more apt to be classified in the Family/Friends category than are the males (60% vs. 49%). In contrast, males are slightly more apt to report that they joined the gang for Protection (20% vs. 17%) or for Fun/Action (18% vs. 12%). Although these differences are evident, they are rather modest (and not significantly different), again reminding us of the general similarity of male and female gang members.

While the reasons for joining a gang differ only marginally by gender, there are more pronounced and statistically significant differences by race/ethnicity (Table 5.2). Compared with the other groups, the African American gang members are more apt to join a gang because of the influences of Family/Friends (59%) and for Protection (19%). The white respondents are most likely to join because of Family/Friends (63%) and for

Table 5.2. *Reasons for Joining a Gang, by Race/Ethnicity*

	African American		Hispanic		White		Total	
	%	n	%	n	%	n	%	n
Family/Friends	58.7	114	26.3	10	63.4	12	54.2	137
Protection	19.4	38	22.1	8	2.1	0[a]	18.5	47
Fun/Action	11.4	22	37.1	14	5.3	1	14.8	37
Other	10.4	20	14.6	6	29.2	6	12.4	31
Total	100.0	195	100.0	38	100.0	19	100.0	252

[a] Due to the weighting procedure used, the one subject in this category is weighted such that it rounds to 0.

$X^2 = 30.06$; df = 6; p < .01.

Table 5.3. *Reasons for Joining a Gang, by Onset of Gang Membership and Duration of Gang Membership, Males Only*

	Early Onset		Late Onset		Stable Duration		Short-Term Duration	
	%	n	%	n	%	n	%	n
Family/Friends	40.6	45	62.7	31	46.8	41	48.2	35
Protection	26.3	29	10.6	5	20.6	18	22.5	16
Fun/Action	20.3	22	13.4	7	21.8	19	13.8	10
Other	12.8	14	13.3	7	10.9	10	15.5	11
Total	100.0	110	100.0	49	100.0	88	100.0	72

Onset: $X^2 = 8.30$; df = 3; p < .05. Duration: $X^2 = 2.11$; df = 3; p = .5.

other, more idiosyncratic, reasons (29%).[1] In contrast, for the Hispanic gang members, Family/Friends play a smaller role in why they join gangs (26%); they are more likely than the other groups to join a gang for Fun/Action (37%) and for Protection (22%).

Finally, we examine whether the reasons for joining a gang that are provided by the adolescent boys differ by onset or duration of membership (Table 5.3).[2] Boys with an earlier onset (who joined by Wave 3) are more likely than those with a later onset to join for Protection (26% vs. 11%) and less likely to join because of influence from Family/Friends (41% vs. 63%).

[1] There are only six subjects in this category and they provided five different reasons.
[2] There are too few female gang members to conduct this analysis by gender. Also, the number of male subjects differs between Tables 5.1 and 5.3 because of the weighting procedures used to return to a random sample.

This relationship is statistically significant ($p < .05$). The enhanced importance of Protection for the younger subjects is reasonable since younger adolescents are more prone to victimization by older adolescents. There is no significant association between duration of membership and the reasons for joining, however. The distributions for short-term members and for stable members are very similar.

Summary

Overall, these findings suggest two strong themes in the reasons that gang members provide for joining a gang. The first is to be involved in a social network already populated with close friends and relatives that is centered around the excitement and action they expect to be associated with street gangs. The second is to be involved in a group that can provide protection and security from the type of hostile environment that is often associated with growing up under conditions of structural disadvantage. While these perceptions differ somewhat by gender, race/ethnicity, and age of onset of gang membership, these dominant themes emerge across the various groupings. Indeed, with the exception of Hispanic males, the role of joining up with family and friends is the predominant reason provided by these gang members.

The reasons given by the Rochester gang members are similar to those provided by a sample of gang members in St. Louis who were also interviewed during early adolescence (Decker and Curry, 2000). In that study the influence of family members and friends was also evident, as were the search for protection and for fun and excitement. There was a stronger theme of neighborhood influences in the St. Louis data – a response that was typically assigned to either the peer or protection categories in the Rochester data. Finally, Decker and Curry report that about one-fifth of the respondents indicated that they joined either to meet or to impress girls.

The reasons that are *not* frequently mentioned by these gang members, either in Rochester or St. Louis, are also informative. Relatively few instrumental reasons, including drug selling, are given. The absence of these responses is not consistent with what Decker and Curry (2000) call the instrumental-rational view of the gang as presented by such scholars as Skolnick, Correl, and Rabb (1988) or Jankowski (1991), which sees the gang as a well-organized, disciplined, profit-making group. In contrast, the pattern of these responses is much more consistent with the informal-individual view of the gang as presented by Decker and Van Winkle (1996), Hagedorn (1998), Klein (1995), and others. This view sees the gang as a poorly organized collection of youths who have difficulty achieving either the consensus or discipline needed to generate profit.

In general, the adolescent gang members in Rochester focus on rather immediate, situational reasons for joining a gang, for example, encouragement or invitations from close friends. Their responses are understandably less reflective of more distal, structural reasons, for example, the consequences of structural adversity or family disruption. To examine the role of these broader influences, we turn now to the presentation and testing of a causal model that traces the influence of more distal factors through the influence of more immediate ones to help explain the origins of gang membership.

A Causal Model of Gang Membership

Several theories of juvenile gangs provide explanations for why gangs form and why some adolescents join them. Most of the traditional theories have a strong structural orientation – that is, they argue that gang behavior is an adolescent response to structural disadvantage, minority status, and exclusion from mainstream opportunities. This approach is strongly influenced by the general image of gang members as overwhelmingly urban, lower-class, minority males.

There are several variants of this general approach. For example, Cohen (1955) and Cloward and Ohlin (1960) adopt a strain theory orientation arguing that barriers in the social structure limit the ability of lower-class youths to attain the American dream. The power and universality of the dominant success goals, coupled with limited opportunities, create an inherently frustrating situation that leads to subcultural (i.e., gang) adaptations. Miller (1958) adopts a model more consistent with culture conflict theory (Sellin, 1938). Gangs and gang behavior are seen as natural offshoots of lower-class culture, "a long-established, distinctively patterned tradition with an integrity of its own" (Miller, 1958: 5). In adhering to the norms and focal concerns of that culture, youths often run afoul of the law, not because of a desire to achieve middle-class goals but because of a conflict between the norms of the lower-class culture and the dominant middle-class culture.

More recent explanations of gangs and gang behavior continue to emphasize structural explanations. Klein discusses the influence of "poverty, inadequate educational processes, population shifts, and ethnic segregation" (1995: 137). He also discusses individual characteristics, such as the need for identity and status, but there is a strong structural theme throughout his discussion. Hagedorn's (1998) model emphasizes the impact of the current political-economic environment in this process. Not only are gang members influenced by traditional problems of limited opportunities, but those opportunities are further eroded by current societal changes. Notable among them is the de-industrialization impacting American society, especially the industrial infrastructure of large, rust-belt cities. In a related statement, Decker and Van Winkle (1996) emphasize the twin processes of de-industrialization and the flight of middle-class and working-class families from urban America. De-industrialization, coupled with increasing racial segregation and the concentration of poverty, further alienates poor adolescents from the mainstream and enhances the lure of the gang. All of these more recent models are influenced by Wilson's (1987) classic work on the emerging and entrenched underclass population in American cities.

These theories provide a rich description of the contributions of structural conditions to the formation of gangs and to some of the factors that lead to gang membership. Nevertheless, various theoretical issues have not been fully addressed in these traditional theories. For example, our understanding of the role of social-psychological processes such as parenting behaviors, social bonding, and peer relationships – fundamental causal influences in many theories of delinquency and antisocial behavior – is not very fully developed in theories of gangs. Moreover, many of the traditional gang theories focus more on explaining why gangs emerge and why certain types of gangs emerge in certain types of areas (e.g., Cloward and Ohlin, 1960) than on accounting for why particular adolescents join gangs while other similarly situated youths do not. In order to expand our understanding of the causal processes associated with gang membership, therefore, we present a model derived from interactional theory (Thornberry, 1987; Thornberry and Krohn, 2001). This approach includes both structural conditions and social-psychological processes in its causal framework.

Interactional Theory

Interactional theory was originally developed to explain adolescent delinquency, especially prolonged involvement in serious delinquency. More recently, Thornberry and Krohn (2001) have presented a life-course extension of this model to examine antisocial behavior across the life-span, from toddlerhood to adulthood. Three fundamental premises form the structure of interactional theory. First, interactional theory adopts a developmental or life-course perspective, assuming that the causes of behavior are not set or determined in childhood. Behavior patterns continue to unfold and change across the person's life, in part because of the consequences of earlier patterns of behavior. Second, interactional theory emphasizes behavioral interactions and bidirectional causality. For example, it does not assume that if peer associations influence antisocial behavior that antisocial behavior cannot also causally influence the selection of peers. Quite the contrary, the model assumes that these and other process variables reciprocally influence one another over time. Third, interactional theory incorporates the impact of social structural influences in explaining the development of individual delinquent careers. In particular, conditions of structural disadvantage

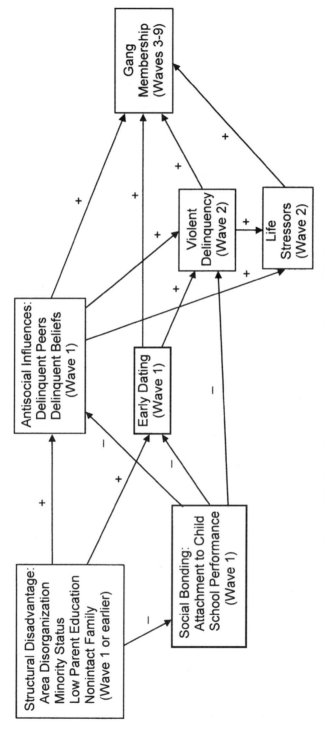

Figure 5.2. Causal Processes Associated with Gang Membership

should increase the number and level of risk factors that youth are exposed to and, via that elevated risk, the severity of the outcomes.

Interactional theory posits that a weakening of bonds to conventional society is needed before serious delinquency is likely to occur. Weak bonds are not, in and of themselves, sufficient to bring about delinquency, however. A learning environment that provides normative support for delinquency, and in which delinquency is reinforced, is also necessary. All of these conditions are more likely to emerge for youth who grow up under conditions of structural disadvantage – for example, in poor families and in areas of concentrated poverty. Finally, the strong bidirectional emphasis of interactional theory leads to the hypothesis that the bonding, associational, and behavioral variables are likely to become mutually reinforcing over time.

In Figure 5.2 we present a causal model of gang membership derived from interactional theory. The causal process that ultimately leads to gang membership starts with structural position. Consistent with the premises of interactional theory and with traditional theories of gang behavior, gang members are more likely than nonmembers to come from disadvantaged backgrounds. Specifically, they are likely to be members of minority groups, to come from disorganized neighborhoods, and from nonintact families with lower levels of parental education.

These structural variables are not expected to directly lead to gang membership, however. Structural position is expected to lead to a number of indirect paths, starting with a reduction in bonds to conventional sources of social control. In particular, the stress associated with living under conditions of structural disadvantage should lead to a deterioration in family processes – for example, the attachment relationship between parent and child – and to a reduction in the child's performance in school. These hypotheses are consistent with previous gang theories and the results of observational studies of gang members. In her observations of two generations of gang members and their families, Moore (1991) has documented how economic pressures adversely affect family life resulting in a high incidence of family problems among gang members. Vigil (1988) has suggested that the gang may act as a surrogate family in light of the disruption in the family of origin. Moore (1991), Curry and Decker (1998), and others have pointed out that gang members experience more problems in school and have a higher dropout rate.

Both structural position and attenuated prosocial bonds should increase antisocial influences such as association with delinquent peers and holding delinquent beliefs, as well as early dating. Growing up in poor neighborhoods and families, having weaker attachment to parents, and having attenuated commitment to school should all increase exposure to deviant networks and, via those networks, lead to delinquent belief systems. From a life-course perspective, off-time or early patterns of dating can be considered an indicator of entry into problematic peer networks, for example, by increasing the exposure of younger adolescents to deviant networks and to risky behaviors associated with older dating partners. These behavior patterns should be more likely for youths from disadvantaged backgrounds and with lower prosocial bonding.

The consequences of structural disadvantage, including reductions in prosocial bonds and enhancements in antisocial influences, are likely to disrupt the normal course of adolescent development. If so, this ought to lead to increased levels of acting out, for example, involvement in antisocial behavior. It should also lead to increased levels of stress, a prediction consistent with traditional theories of gang behavior, especially those derived from a strain or opportunity structure perspective.

Finally, antisocial influences, delinquent behavior, and life stresses are all expected to have a direct impact on the chances of becoming a gang member. Being involved in deviant networks and routines, and experiencing high levels of stress should increase the chances that the excitement, fun, and activity of the gang will be viewed as a viable means of adjustment to the adolescent's somewhat bleak world. The direct effects on gang membership that are posited in the model are consistent with the gang members' stated reasons for joining presented earlier. They focused on the influence of family and friends, including boyfriends and girlfriends, as well as the search for fun, excitement, and protection.

In brief, our model derived from interactional theory posits that structural disadvantage leads to a reduction in prosocial bonds, and both of these lead to an enhancement in antisocial influences. In turn, these earlier factors increase involvement in delinquency and violence, as well as levels of stress, all of which increase the likelihood of a youth joining a gang.

Methods

To test the model presented in Figure 5.2 we estimated a set of reduced-form equations using logistic regression. The more familiar path-analytic approach is not used since the endogenous variable of interest – gang membership – is dichotomous. Thus, ordinary least squares (OLS) estimates are not appropriate for the final equation and indirect effects leading to the endogenous variable cannot be estimated. All the variables are dichotomized (as was done in Table 4.2), and variables in each of the conceptual areas in Figure 5.2 are stepped into the equation in blocks. In all the equations the dependent variable is gang membership.

By examining when the magnitudes of the odds ratios for the more distal variables increase, diminish, or become nonsignificant, patterns of indirect effects can be determined. To help interpret the mediational effect of the more proximal variables, we include several columns in Table 5.4 that are

Table 5.4. Estimating the Causal Model: Reduced-Form Equations Predicting Gang Membership, Males Only

	Equation 1	Equation 2		Equation 3		Equation 4		Equation 5		Cumulative
	OR	OR	Percent Change	OR	Percent Change	OR	Percent Change	OR	Percent Change	Percent Change
Structural Variables										
Area Disorganization	1.23	1.23		1.28		1.37		1.38		
African American	2.76**	2.55**	−12	2.06*	−32	1.83	a	1.79		−55
Hispanic	2.63**	2.31*	−20	2.21*	−8	2.08*	−11	2.27*	+18	−22
Parent Education	.63*	.69	a	.69	−8	.68		.68		−8
Both Biological Parents	.63*	.58*	+8	.58*	0	.60*	−3	.56*	+7	+11
Social Bonding										
Attachment to Child		.90		.92		.88		.90		
School Performance		.48**		.44**	+8	.46**	−5	.47**	−2	+2
Antisocial Influences										
Early Dating				2.56**		2.55**	−1	2.37**	−12	−12
Delinquent Peers				1.46		1.00		.93		
Delinquent Beliefs				2.10**		1.84*	−24	1.77*	−8	−30
Earlier Deviance										
Violent Delinquency						3.09**		2.73**	−17	−17
Stress										
Life Stressors								1.91**		
Model Improvement X^2	28.66+	10.38+		29.38+		17.33+		5.87+		
	(n = 488)	(n = 488)		(n = 488)		(n = 488)		(n = 488)		

a Odds ratio is not significant.

* p < .05 (one-tailed). ** p < .01 (one-tailed). + p < .05.

labeled "Percent Change." For the ones associated with Equations 2 through 5, the percent change indicates the change, either the increase or the decrease, in that variable's impact on gang membership when the *new* variables are added to the equation. If the new variables are, in fact, intervening or mediating variables the percent change indicator will be either positive or negative. Because we are presenting odds ratios where 1.0 equals no effect, it is important to bear in mind that odds ratios moving closer to 1.0 from *either* direction indicate a declining effect. For odds ratios greater than 1.0 a declining effect means the absolute value becomes smaller; for odds ratios less than 1.0 a declining effect means the absolute value becomes larger (e.g., an odds ratio moving from .50 to .60 actually indicates a declining impact). In both cases this is indicated by a negative percent change. Positive changes in odds ratios show strengthening relationships due to the added variables. This also indicates an indirect effect.

The percent change values associated with Equations 2 through 5 indicate only the change in the variable's impact from the immediately preceding equation to the current one (e.g., from Equation 1 to 2 or from Equation 3 to 4). The final column, "Cumulative Percent Change," reflects the extent to which all of the later variables mediate that variable's impact on gang membership. In this case it reflects the change in the variable's odds ratio between the first equation in which the variable appears and Equation 5. For example, for the variable Delinquent Beliefs, it is the change between Equation 3 (OR = 2.10) and Equation 5 (OR = 1.77), or −30%.

Three criteria were used in selecting the particular measures that are used as indicators of each of these constructs. First, the measure represents a core aspect of the theoretical concept. Second, when multiple measures are available, we tried to select ones that were shown to be strongly related to gang membership in the risk factor analysis (Chapter 4). Third, we selected measures to minimize problems of multicollinearity.

Two cautionary notes about the analysis should be offered. First, we can establish temporal order between the explanatory variables and gang membership because all the explanatory variables in the causal model are measured at Waves 1 or 2 and the dependent variable is joining a gang at Wave 3 or after. It is harder to establish temporal order among all the explanatory variables, such as the social bonding and antisocial influences variables, however, as they are measured at the same wave. Thus the path from the former to the latter can only be evaluated cross-sectionally. Second, for the same reasons noted with the earlier multivariate risk factor analyses in Chapter 4, these equations can only be estimated for the male respondents. The results are presented in a series of logistic regression equations in Table 5.4.

Results

The model improvement chi-square statistics are statistically significant for each of the equations reported here. This indicates that the variables that are added to the equations at each subsequent step significantly add to the fit of the model to the data.

Equation 1

The first equation in Table 5.4 examines the relationship between gang membership and the indicators of structural position. As hypothesized, they have sizable effects on the odds of joining a gang. The largest odds ratios are associated with race/ethnicity: African American males are 2.8 times as likely to be gang members as white males, and Hispanic males are 2.6 times as likely. In addition, the odds of joining a gang for youths living with both biological parents is 63% of that for youths living in other types of families. The level of parental education also alters the chances of joining a gang (OR = .63); adolescents whose parents have not graduated from high school are more apt to become gang members. The only structural variable not related to gang membership is area disorganization. In general, minority youths who come from nonintact families where there is a lower level of parental education are more likely to join a gang than are their counterparts.

Equation 2

The second equation adds the two social bonding variables: parental attachment to the adolescent and the adolescent's school performance as indicated by the California Achievement Test (CAT) math scores. Based on interactional theory we hypothesize that both will reduce the odds of joining a gang and that they will mediate part of the impact of the structural variables. If the second hypothesis is supported, the odds ratios of the distal variables in the model should diminish in size – that is, move closer to 1.0 – as the more proximal variables are entered at each step.

Of the two indicators of prosocial bonding, the level of parental attachment is unrelated to the outcome. School performance is significantly related to gang membership, however. Performing above the median on the math component of the CAT approximately halves the chances of gang membership (OR = .48). The strong impact of school performance is consistent with the earlier risk factor analyses, which indicated that a number of school variables are significantly related to later gang membership. It is also consistent with traditional gang theories (e.g., Cohen, 1955; Klein, 1995) that emphasize the failure of the educational system to prepare lower-class youths for success, which leads to stress and frustration, making the gang world an appealing source of adjustment.

School performance also mediates a substantial part of the racial/ethnic effects evident in Equation 1.[3] For the African American males, for example, the odds ratio drops from 2.76 to 2.55 when school performance is taken into account, a 12% decline in its effect. That is, 12% of the initial impact of being African American on gang membership is due to indirect effects operating via school performance. School performance also reduces the impact of being Hispanic by 20%. It also partly mediates the impact of family structure, strengthening its impact by 8%. School performance has a major impact on mediating the impact of parental education on gang membership. Indeed, when it is entered into the equation, the odds ratio associated with this variable becomes indistinguishable from 1, that is, not statistically significant.

Overall, we see that poor performance in school has a sizable impact on gang membership. It directly increases the odds of joining a gang and helps explain why poor, minority youths are more apt to join a gang than are wealthier, white adolescents.

Equation 3

In Equation 3 we enter the variables associated with delinquent networks, delinquent beliefs, and early dating. Two are significantly related to gang membership: early dating more than doubles the odds of gang membership (OR = 2.56), and delinquent beliefs increases them by a factor of two (OR = 2.10). When these variables are taken into account, however, associating with delinquent peers is not significantly related to later gang membership.

The impacts of early dating and of delinquent beliefs suggest that the search for excitement and adventure described by Thrasher (1927) and Miller (1958) may be a particularly powerful pull for potential gang members. It is also very consistent with the perceptions of our gang members. Perhaps youths who are sexually active and who begin dating at an early age, and who have antisocial belief systems, find the gang a particularly hospitable social network for their life-style. Precocious involvement in adultlike behaviors (Moffitt, 1997) makes the gang an attractive arena for enacting those behaviors.

These variables further diminish the impact of minority group status, especially being African American. When these variables are included, the

---

[3] We focus on school performance as the source of the mediating effect because parental attachment is not significantly related to the outcome and cannot therefore be an important mediator.

odds ratio associated with being African American drops by an additional 32% and with being Hispanic by 8%.[4] Delinquent beliefs and early dating mediate none of the family structure effect. Finally, when they are explicitly considered, the impact of school performance on gang membership actually increases by 8%, because the odds ratio changes from .48 to .44.

To this point it appears that the process variables of prosocial bonding (especially in the school arena) and antisocial influences help explain, in large part, why structural conditions lead to gang membership. As predicted by interactional theory, youth from disadvantaged backgrounds have higher levels of the risk factors that lead to this outcome.

Equation 4

In the next equation (Equation 4) we add self-reported involvement in earlier violence, measured at Wave 2. This variable more than triples the odds of joining a gang (OR = 3.09). Youths who are already involved in violence are more likely than those who are not to seek out or to be recruited by gangs.

In addition, earlier involvement in violence plays a major mediating role, dropping the impact of being African American to statistical insignificance and diminishing the impact of being Hispanic by an additional 11%. Involvement in violence is also a major pathway by which delinquent beliefs impact gang membership. The odds ratio associated with delinquent beliefs drops by 24% when violent behavior is explicitly considered. Involvement in violence has a smaller impact in mediating the family structure effect (3%), school performance (5%), and early dating (1%).

Equation 5

The final equation in Table 5.4 adds recent life stressors to the mix. This variable almost doubles the odds of a young man joining a gang (OR = 1.91). Youths, who feel stressed perhaps because of limited opportunities or failure in school, are more apt to join a street gang than youths who experience lower levels of stress. Life stressors also mediate the impact of early dating (12%), delinquent beliefs (8%), and violence (17%). Finally, when this variable is included in the equation, the impacts of family structure (7%) and of being Hispanic (18%) increase somewhat.

The odds ratios presented in Equation 5 also provide an indication of the direct causal paths that lead to gang membership. The only structural variables that significantly affect gang membership are being Hispanic (positive

---

[4] The percent change statistic refers to changes in the odds ratios in adjacent equations. The final column in Table 5.4 is the only cumulative one.

effect) and having an intact family (negative effect). The other structural variables only have indirect effects. Of the social bonding variables, parental attachment is not directly related to gang membership but school performance is. Early dating, delinquent beliefs, earlier violence, and life stressors (but not earlier associations with delinquent peers) are all related in the expected direction to gang membership.

To provide a sense of the mediating pathways that lead to gang membership, the final column in Table 5.4 provides the cumulative change in the odds ratios for each of the more distal variables. For each variable this is the change between its odds ratio in the first equation in which it is statistically significant and the odds ratio in Equation 5.

A sizable part of the impact of being African American and Hispanic, 55% and 22% respectively, is mediated by more proximal variables. Put differently, in large part, the reason African American and Hispanic youths are more likely than white youths to join gangs is because of their lower performance in school, their greater involvement with antisocial influences and their earlier involvement in violent behavior, and their higher level of life stressors.

In addition to minority status, the effect of parental education is also mediated by later variables in the causal model, as its effect becomes nonsignificant. The impact of delinquent beliefs is also substantially mediated by later variables. Indeed, 30% of its initial effect on gang membership can be attributed to indirect effects.

The impacts of the other variables are also mediated by later variables but to a lesser extent. Of the initial impact of earlier violence, 17% is due to indirect effects; 12%, for early dating; and 11%, for family structure. Only the adolescent's school performance remains largely unmediated. Its initial direct effect on gang membership is sizable (OR = .48), and only 2% of this is attributable to indirect effects.

Conclusion

This chapter opened two windows into the causal processes that lead to gang membership. The first is based on the perceptions of the gang members themselves and describes their reasons for joining the gang. The second is based on the interrelations among the explanatory variables collected across time in this long-term study of antisocial behavior.

The first approach highlights the more immediate, situational factors that lead to gang membership. As with many aspects of adolescent life, peer and primary-group relationships play a major role. The cluster of reasons most often mentioned by the gang members centers around the influence of friends and family members. Many youths join gangs to associate with friends, girlfriends or boyfriends, siblings, and cousins who are already members. The formation of social networks around deviant behaviors has been noted before (Hawkins and Fraser, 1985; Kandel, 1978; Kandel and Davies, 1991; Krohn, Massey, and Zielinski, 1988; Krohn and Thornberry, 1993; Wister and Avison, 1982) and juvenile street gangs appear to be another venue in which this takes place.

Consistent with the emphasis on peer and family relations is the role played by the fun, action, and excitement that this particular network provides. While gangs can be a violent and volatile environment, they are also a source of adolescent pleasure. The gang is often where the action is, a ready source of drugs, parties, dating and sexual partners, and risk-taking behaviors. These themes abound in the gang literature, from Thrasher (1927) to Miller (1958), Short and Strodtbeck (1965), and Vigil (1988), and it appears that gang members are also well aware of them. Wanting to be with friends and family members in that type of exciting environment is foremost in the minds of these gang members when they reflect on why they joined the gang.

The other factor consistently mentioned is for protection. Gangs in Rochester, as elsewhere, are largely territorial: many of the gang names in Rochester refer to areas or locales in the more socially disorganized areas of the city. The areas in which gang members live are often violent and dangerous. Moreover, gang members often move through other territories on the way to and from school, work, shopping malls, and the like. Membership in one's own gang is seen as offering some degree of protection from an often hostile world.

While these perceptions offer valuable insights into the attributions gang members offer for their decision to join a gang, they are rather silent about broader social, structural, and developmental influences. Not surprisingly, the gang members' accounts are focused on positive features of gang life – friendship, fun, and protection – rather than on developmental deficits that may also drive them toward gang membership. To examine these processes, we constructed and tested a causal model incorporating both structural and process variables based on the premises of interactional theory.

We found that structural disadvantage increases the likelihood of gang membership. A large part of the initial effects of the structural variables is indirect, however, flowing through the later process variables. In particular, the impact is mediated by school performance and antisocial influences.

Youths who do poorly in school are more apt to join gangs than are youths who do well in school. The strong effect of school failure has long been noted in the gang literature (e.g., Cohen, 1955; Klein, 1995) and is echoed in our longitudinal analysis. While educational performance has a sizable impact on gang membership (see also the risk factor analysis in Chapter 4), family bonding does not. This is not simply a function of the indicator we use, parent attachment to child; other indicators produce similar results. Although this finding is not consistent with some previous models of gang membership (e.g. Vigil, 1988), it is consistent with some developmental models of delinquency (e.g., Jang, 1999; Thornberry, 1987), which argue that family effects fade as youths enter adolescence, while school and peer effects increase in magnitude. Our results also suggest that family influences on gang membership are more strongly associated with structural characteristics – for example, parent education and family structure – than with the processes within the family.

The results of the causal model also point to the strong influence that precocious or early dating has on the likelihood of joining a gang. Young males who begin dating at an early age are more apt to seek out or be recruited by the gang. These adolescents may be akin to Cloward and Ohlin's (1960) retreatists; already sexually active, they view the gang's life-style as a source of partying, dating partners, and excitement. Many of the early adolescent gang members in St. Louis indicated that they joined gangs to either meet or impress girls (Decker and Curry, 2000), and both Bowker and Klein (1983) and LeBlanc and Lanctôt (1998) have identified precocious sexual behavior and early dating as risk factors for gang membership. The impact of early dating is also consistent with the perceptions of many gang members who reported that they joined the gang for fun and excitement.

The strong impact of dating behaviors on the decision to join a gang may be a precursor to one of the consequences of gang membership. In an earlier examination of risk factors for teenage fatherhood (Thornberry, Smith, and Howard, 1997), we showed that the interaction of gang membership and heavy drug use raised the likelihood of becoming a teen father to near certainty. Similarly, Moore (1991) found that one of the reasons girls leave the gang, typically at earlier ages than boys, is because they become pregnant. Overall these results suggest that human sexuality may play a larger role in the social forces associated with street gangs than previously thought. It is certainly a topic worth investigation, especially for gang membership during younger adolescence.

Two other processes have direct effects on gang membership. Adolescents who are already involved in violence are more apt to join a gang than are other youth. That is hardly surprising given the criminal and often violent nature of the gang. The role of earlier deviance is one focus of Chapter 6 so we defer further discussion of it until a fuller examination of its role is offered. The final variable related to gang membership is experiencing higher than average levels of stress. Given the accumulation of risk in their backgrounds, it is not surprising that these youths report more negative life experiences than their counterparts. Also, given their generally positive expectations about the gang – as a source of fun and excitement, for example – many adolescents may join the gang as a way of alleviating this level of stress.

Overall, the results of the causal model analysis point to a set of structural and developmental deficits that increase the likelihood of an adolescent male joining a gang. Youths experiencing structural adversity, who are doing poorly in school, who are involved in antisocial networks and behaviors, and who have higher than average levels of stress are more likely to succumb to the lure of the gang.

The gang members' own perceptions are less deficit-laden, however. They point to the positive features of the gang. The gang is where one's friends are, where the action is, and where one can find protection from a hostile world. The two stories are, of course, not inconsistent: youths may well see the gang as an oasis of relief from the consequences of these disadvantaged, urban settings. And the gang may well be that oasis to some degree. If it is, the difficulty of preventing youths from joining the gang and of suppressing gang activity is all the harder.

Gangs as a Facilitating Context for Delinquent Behavior

UP TO THIS POINT the analysis has focused on the antecedents of gang membership, examining risk factors for and causal processes associated with joining a gang. Now we examine whether membership in a juvenile street gang alters the short-term behavior patterns and the long-term life-course development of gang members. The first set of issues we address concerns the extent to which the gang actually facilitates various forms of deviant behavior.

In Chapter 3 we demonstrated that gang members in Rochester have significantly higher rates of delinquency than nonmembers. This finding confirms results from earlier observational studies (Hagedorn, 1998; Klein, 1971; Miller, 1966; Moore, 1978; Taylor, 1990), from studies using official data (Cohen, 1969; Klein et al., 1986; Maxson and Klein, 1990), and from those using survey techniques (Fagan, 1989, 1990; Fagan et al., 1986; Short and Strodtbeck, 1965; Tracy, 1979). We also demonstrated that gang members account for a disproportionate share of the crime problem relative to their representation in the general population. Because gangs clearly connote groups that have a deviant or criminal orientation, a strong relationship between gang membership and high rates of involvement in delinquency and drug use is hardly surprising. What these studies do not identify, however, are the social processes that bring about the association between gang membership and higher rates of delinquency. As Fagan has noted, "it is uncertain whether the differences reflect the positive correlation between group crime and violence, features of the gang itself, or the state of social controls in the inner cities where gangs are most evident" (1990: 186).

In earlier work (Thornberry, 1998; Thornberry, Krohn, et al., 1993) we identified three competing models that could account for the strong relationship between gang membership and delinquency: selection, facilitation, and a mixed model that combines both selection and facilitation effects.

Theoretical Models

Selection

A selection or "kind of person" model posits that gangs recruit their members from adolescents who have a high propensity for delinquency and who will engage in delinquency and drug use regardless of their membership in gangs. Gangs do not cause their members to be delinquent; they recruit or attract people who are already delinquent. This view is consistent with a social control perspective (e.g., Hirschi, 1969) and especially Gottfredson and Hirschi's propensity theory of crime (1990). In this view the gang attracts adolescents who lack self-control and, therefore, are already likely to be involved in delinquency.

If a selection or "kind of person" model is accurate we would expect to observe first that gang members have higher rates of delinquency than nonmembers and, second, that this difference would hold across time – before, during, and after their membership in the gang. That is, if gang members are truly different kinds of people – those with high propensities toward deviance – they are likely to act on those propensities regardless of their gang membership status at any particular time. Indeed, in a pure version of the selection model the gang becomes epiphenomenal, as Gottfredson and Hirschi argue:

> Given the large numbers of adolescents with relatively low self-control living in close proximity and given the relatively low level of supervision exercised over them, it is inevitable that from time to time they will congregate in the streets of U.S. cities. Given these facts, it is also inevitable that the "gang" will occasionally engage in delinquent and criminal activities, ranging from shoplifting cigarettes and intimidating the elderly to using heavy drugs and participating in drive-by shootings directed at no one in particular. (1990: 209)

In this model, the gang itself, however, has no causal impact on these behaviors.

A selection model is also consistent with the view that "the gang is an aggregate of individuals with 'shared incapacities'" (Spergel, 1990: 230). Such a perspective is seen in the work of Yablonsky (1962), Gerrard (1964), and others, especially those approaching gang research from a psychiatric or clinical perspective (see Spergel, 1990: 229–231).

Facilitation

In contrast, a facilitation or "kind of group" model posits that gang members are not intrinsically different from nonmembers in terms of delinquency or drug use. They do not have a stronger propensity toward these behaviors and, left to their own devices, are no more likely to engage in delinquency or drug use than are nonmembers. Upon joining a gang, however, the normative structure and group processes of the gang are likely to bring about high rates of delinquency and drug use. Gang membership is thus viewed as a major cause of deviant behavior.

If the facilitation model is accurate, gang members will differ from nonmembers in terms of delinquency and drug use only when they are active members of a gang. Before and after membership they should not differ substantially from nonmembers because they are, after all, not different "kinds of people." While members of a gang, however, they should have higher rates of delinquency and drug use because of the normative climate of the gang and because of the influence of group processes on the behavior of gang members.

Gangs provide strong normative support for a variety of delinquent and deviant behaviors. Indeed, Cohen (1955) and Cloward and Ohlin (1960) argue that gang norms arise in reaction to middle-class values and for that very reason support deviant behavior. Short and Strodtbeck (1965) provide empirical support consistent with this assertion. In their study in Chicago they found that gang members are more likely to grant legitimacy to deviant values than are nonmembers. More recently, Deschenes and Esbensen (1999), in a survey of eighth graders in 11 American cities, reported that gang members feel significantly less guilty than nonmembers about committing violent crimes and are more supportive of proviolence values. Indeed, "the differences between gang and non-gang members were striking – virtually all gang members, both male and female, indicated approval of physical violence" (1999: 86).

In their study of female gang members, Miller and Decker (2001) found additional evidence for the view that the gang normatively supports violent behavior. Although female gang members were not as heavily involved in violent crime as were the male gang members, they expressed strong normative support for gang violence and accorded enhanced status to male gang members "who 'did dirt' for the gang by committing gang-motivated assaults and by confronting rivals" (2001: 127).

Short and Strodtbeck (1965) also described a number of group processes that bring about high rates of delinquency for active gang members. When the status of gang leaders is threatened, the leaders often resort to out-group aggression "because of the limited resources they have for internal control of the group" (1965: 185). More generally, threats to the status of gangs and gang members are likely to lead to delinquent behavior, especially violent behavior, as a way of regaining status: "Specifically, it is our hypothesis that much of what has previously been described as short-run hedonism may, under closer scrutiny, be revealed to be a rational balancing from the actor's perspective, of the near certainty of *immediate* loss of status in the group against the remote possibility of punishment by the larger society *if* the most serious outcome eventuates" (1965: 250). Other gang researchers have also pointed to group processes that are likely to increase delinquency by active gang members. Klein (1971) has reported that enhanced group cohesion increases levels of delinquency. In a similar vein, Miller, Geertz, and Cutter (1961) reported that aggression is important for creating and maintaining group cohesion, and Jansyn (1966) reported that delinquency is often a response to threats to the gang's solidarity. Decker (1996) has presented a seven-step model in which external threats increase group identification and cohesion, which, in turn, lead to violence.

More recently, Rosenfeld, Bray, and Egley (1999) have pointed to two gang processes that may facilitate gang violence. The first is that the routine activities of gang members "may facilitate access to risky situations such as drug markets" and the second is the "public and participatory nature of gang violence," such as gang fights and retaliatory assaults (Rosenfeld et al., 1999: 514). In a parallel vein, Miller and Brunson (2000) found that male gang members attribute many violent victimizations to being in risky situations and to being targets of rival gangs.

In sum, prior gang studies suggest that group norms and group processes revolving around dimensions such as status, solidarity, and cohesion, as well as exposure to risky and violent situations, are likely to increase the level of delinquency for gang members. Because these are properties of the group, however, they should have no impact on delinquent behavior either before or after the person is a gang member.

Enhancement

The third model identified by Thornberry, Krohn, et al. (1993) is a mixed or enhancement model that combines the other two. It suggests that both selection and facilitation effects operate to account for the high levels of delinquency and violence observed for gang members. That is, gangs recruit or attract adolescents who have already shown a propensity for delinquent behavior but, once in the gang, the norms and group processes enhance their involvement in delinquency. A mixed model, therefore, predicts that even when they are not active members, gang members will have significantly higher rates of delinquency than nonmembers; *and* delinquency rates will be particularly high when they are active gang members.

In sum, three plausible models could account for the well-established relationship between gang membership and delinquency. There is little empirical information about the relative validity of these competing models, however.

Prior Research

In an earlier analysis of the Rochester data, Thornberry, Krohn, et al. (1993) tested these competing models. After comparing male gang members with nonmembers, they reported strong support for the facilitation model and virtually no support for the selection model:

> Perhaps the strongest support for the social facilitation model is found in the analysis of the type of behavior most often associated with gangs – crimes against the person.... Gang members have higher rates of person offenses only when they are active gang members. Of particular interest is the drop-off in the rate of person crimes once boys leave the gang. The means for crimes against the person for boys when they are active members of the gang are, by and large, at least twice as high as when they are not. Clearly, being in the gang is generative of violent behavior among these boys. (1993: 80–81)

A gang facilitation effect was also observed for general delinquency, drug sales, and, to a somewhat lesser extent, drug use. It was not observed for property offenses.

Subsequent to the publication of these findings, other longitudinal studies have examined the processes associated with the relationship between gang membership and delinquency. Results from the Denver Youth Survey are consistent with the mixed or enhancement model. Esbensen and Huizinga (1993) reported that there is some elevation in the prevalence of delinquency by future gang members in the year prior to joining a gang. Prevalence rates, however, are highest during the year that the gang members are in the gang.

Hill et al. (1996), using data from the Seattle Social Development Project, reported findings that are consistent with those reported by Thornberry, Krohn, et al. (1993). Violent delinquency is only slightly elevated in the year prior to joining a gang, increases substantially during active membership, and is lower in the years following active gang membership. Hill et al. (1996) reported that drug sales do not follow this pattern, however; the prevalence of drug sales is very high during periods of active membership and stays high after the individual leaves the gang. Subsequent research using the Rochester Youth Development Study data support this finding on drug sales (Bjerregaard and Lizotte, 1995; Lizotte et al., 1997).

This issue has also been examined with data collected on 1,034 boys drawn from 53 low socioeconomic status schools in Montreal (Tremblay et al., 1994). The initial results based on the Montreal gang data were reported in Thornberry (1998), and more recent results have been presented by Gatti et al. (2002). Overall, the Montreal results replicated Thornberry, Krohn, et al.'s results (1993), finding that the facilitation model best describes the pattern of results for general delinquency, property crimes, and violence. They also found that drug sales increase during periods of gang membership and remain high even after the adolescent leaves the gang. Unlike prior studies of the facilitation effect that have been conducted in American cities using predominately African American or Hispanic gang members, the Montreal results are based on a predominately white, French-speaking sample in a large Canadian city. The similarity of the findings suggests that gang processes in fairly diverse settings may be similar.

Overall, results from these studies provide rather consistent support for the gang facilitation effect described by Thornberry, Krohn, et al. (1993) and little, if any, support for a pure selection model. Rates of delinquency, especially violent delinquency and drug sales, increase substantially once an adolescent becomes an active gang member. With the exception of drug sales, there is also a general drop-off in delinquency following periods of gang membership. While there is little evidence to support a social selection model, there is some evidence, especially in the Denver study (Esbensen and Huizinga, 1993), to support the mixed or enhancement model. Support for a mixed model, however, is both less powerful and less consistent across studies than is the facilitation effect.

The Current Study

In this chapter, we extend our examination of the processes that lead to higher rates of delinquent behavior among gang members in two important ways. First, prior research, including our own, has only examined rates of delinquency at three points in time. Here we extend the data analysis to a fourth year. Doing so provides additional data points for comparing pre- and postgang effects and allows us to examine whether the temporal patterns observed in the earlier studies are seen for gang members who remain in the gang over a more extended period of time.

Second, we examine more explicitly whether gang members have higher rates of delinquency and violence, not because of a gang facilitation effect, but because of the accumulation of other deficits in their backgrounds. In the tabular analyses reported to date (e.g., Esbensen and Huizinga, 1993; Thornberry, Krohn, et al., 1993), each individual serves as his own control because we are comparing changes in the individual's delinquency over time as a function of his changing status as a gang member. LeBlanc and Lanctôt (1998: 25) suggest, however, that "to thoroughly verify the nature of the causal role of the gang, longitudinal data sets should be reanalyzed controlling self and social control characteristics of individuals." To address this issue, we use two different statistical approaches. In the first we statistically hold major risk factors for delinquency and gang membership constant while examining the impact of selection and facilitation effects on delinquency. In the second we estimate a "random effects model" (Nagin and Farrington, 1992; Nagin and Paternoster, 1991), which allows us to

Table 6.1. *Number and Percentage of Subjects in
Various Groupings of Gang Membership, Males Only*

Group	Gang Member in	Subjects %	n
1	(Nonmember)	75.3	426
2	Year 1 only	7.4	42
3	Year 2 only	2.5	14
4	Year 3 only	1.8	10
5	Year 4 only	1.8	10
6	Year 1 & 2	3.0	17
7	Year 1–3	3.5	20
8	Year 2–3 or 2–4	2.8	16
9	Year 1–4	1.9	11
Total		100.0	566

control unmeasured population heterogeneity as well as the measured risk
factors.

Methods

In this analysis, we again group data from Waves 2 through 9 into four annual
time periods. Data from Waves 2 and 3 are combined to form Year 1, data
from Waves 4 and 5 form Year 2, Waves 6 and 7 form Year 3, and Waves 8
and 9 form Year 4. Because of the limited number of female gang members,
especially after Wave 4, this analysis is conducted only for males.

To make the necessary comparisons between gang members and nonmembers, and between gang members before, during, and after gang membership, respondents are divided into nine groups (Table 6.1). Group 1, the
largest group with 75.3% of the respondents, includes the adolescents who
never reported being a member of a gang throughout the data collection
period. Groups 2 through 5 represent gang members who were in a gang
during only one annual time period and were not in a gang during the other
three annual periods. Thus, Group 2 includes respondents who were in the
gang *only* during Year 1; Group 3 include respondents who were members
only during Year 2, and so on. By grouping respondents in this manner, we
are able to compare their delinquency rates before, during, and after gang
membership.

Groups 6 through 9 include more stable gang members – those respondents who were in a gang at more than one time period. We were not able
to include all the possible combinations because the number of cases for
some categories is too low. Group 6 includes respondents who were in a

gang in Years 1 and 2, but not 3 and 4. Group 7 includes those who were members during the first three years, but not the last year. Group 8 includes respondents who did not join until Year 2 but remained in the gang for at least one additional year. Some were members in Years 2 and 3 and some in Years 2, 3, and 4. Though not ideal, this grouping is necessitated by the low frequencies. Finally, Group 9 contains the adolescents, only 1.9% of the sample, who were gang members at all four years.

Because membership is a low-frequency status even in this high-risk urban sample, the number of cases in each of the gang groupings is fairly small. The low number of cases makes it more difficult to obtain statistically significant findings; hence, the following analysis represents a conservative test of our hypotheses.

All of the variables used in this chapter have been described in Chapter 2. Measures of delinquency include the general delinquency and violent delinquency indices (without gang fighting), drug use, and drug sales. Risk factors from major developmental domains – family poverty level, parental supervision, commitment to school, association with delinquent peers, negative life events, and prior involvement in delinquency – are also included in this analysis.

Hypotheses

In empirically contrasting the facilitation and selection models, two types of comparisons can be made: *cross-group* comparisons between gang members and nonmembers and *cross-time* comparisons within group, comparing rates of delinquency before, during, and after periods of gang membership. In Table 6.2 we indicate the pattern of results that would be expected in a pure facilitation model and in a pure selection model. We label the delinquency rate of the nonmembers as "average," reflecting the general age-specific rates of delinquency for each time period. The label "high" indicates delinquency rates that are hypothesized to be significantly higher than the corresponding rate for the nonmembers at that same time point, and significantly higher than the "average" rates for that same group at different time points. Delinquency rates that occur during time periods of active gang membership are placed in boxes in Table 6.2. Thus, only the Year 1 delinquency rate for Year-1-only gang members is in a box; the Year 1 and 2 delinquency rates are placed in a box for adolescents who were gang members in Years 1 and 2 only, and so forth. We do not expect significant differences in delinquency rates across time for the nonmembers. That is, during this four-year period we do not necessarily anticipate sizable age effects.

Panel A of Table 6.2 presents the expected pattern of delinquency rates if a pure facilitation model is operating. In this case the only time periods in which delinquency is elevated for gang members are during the time

Table 6.2. *Hypothetical Relationships Expected under the Facilitation and Selection Models*

Gang Member in	Year 1	Year 2	Year 3	Year 4
(Nonmember)	Average	Average	Average	Average
A. Facilitation Model				
Year 1 only	High	Average	Average	Average
Year 2 only	Average	High	Average	Average
Year 3 only	Average	Average	High	Average
Year 4 only	Average	Average	Average	High
Year 1 & 2	High	High	Average	Average
Year 1–3	High	High	High	Average
Year 2–3 or 2–4	Average	High	High	High
B. Selection Model				
Year 1 only	High			
Year 2 only	High	High		
Year 3 only	High	High	High	
Year 4 only	High	High	High	High
Year 1 & 2	High	High		
Year 1–3	High	High	High	
Year 2–3 or 2–4	High	High	High	High

periods of active gang membership. Graphically, that means that there is a perfect overlap between the labels of "high" and the boxes indicating being a member of a gang. Two specific predictions follow: gang members will have significantly higher rates of delinquency than the nonmembers only in those time periods when they are actively involved in the gang; and for the various groups of gang members, rates of delinquency will be higher during periods of active gang membership than either before or after those periods.

Panel B of Table 6.2 presents the expected pattern of relationships if a selection model is operating. In this case gang members have higher rates of delinquency both prior to joining *and* during periods of active gang membership. That is, gangs attract or recruit adolescents *already* highly involved in delinquency, and their high delinquency involvement continues once they are in a gang; the gang, however, has no causal impact on delinquency. In this case we make no predictions about the rate of delinquency following involvement in the gang because the expectations are ambiguous. On the one hand, a pure version of a selection model, such as that offered by Gottfredson and Hirschi (1990), would predict that the rates of delinquency for the gang members would always be "high." That is, if the association between gang membership and delinquency is truly spurious – both being produced by a common prior cause such as low self-control – then these adolescents will always have higher rates of delinquency than nonmembers and those rates will not fluctuate as a function of entering or leaving a gang. On the other hand, higher rates of delinquency following a period of gang membership may reflect learning processes and opportunity structures provided by the gang, not selection effects. In this case, the gang plays a causal role in bringing about delinquent behavior, but once initiated by the gang the behavior continues after the person leaves the gang. Because of these varying possibilities, we focus on the rates of delinquency prior to and during periods of active membership to assess the selection model.

Finally, in a mixed or enhancement model (not represented graphically) both selection and facilitation effects are hypothesized to operate. First, the selection effect predicts that prior to joining the gang, gang members have significantly higher rates of delinquency than the nonmembers. Second, the facilitation effect predicts that those rates then increase significantly once the youth joins the gang.

The design outlined in Table 6.2 has a number of positive features for comparing these conceptual models. First, as mentioned earlier, because we are comparing the behavior of the same individual before, during, and after he becomes a gang member, each respondent acts as his own control. Thus, time-stable covariates are controlled by design. Second, because the gang members join and leave gangs at different ages (Year-1-only members are 14 years old; Year-4-only members are 17), we can see if the effect of gang membership runs counter to the general age-trend for the various measures of delinquency. For example, if there is a decreasing trend with age (represented by the delinquency rates for the adolescents who were never gang members) but, regardless of that trend, delinquency always increases when the person joins the gang, that would further support the notion that the gang facilitates delinquent behavior. In contrast, if the changing patterns of delinquency for the gang members merely reflect the underlying age trend, it would weaken the argument for a facilitation effect.

Results

Results are presented in three sections. We first look at temporal patterns of involvement in delinquency and drug use to see if they conform to the patterns expected under the facilitation, selection, or mixed model. We then examine multivariate models to see if the gang effect remains once major time-varying risk factors are controlled. Finally, we examine random effects models that test for unmeasured heterogeneity.

Patterns of Delinquency

We begin with an examination of the omnibus index of general delinquency (Table 6.3). For the nonmembers there is an upward trend in the incidence

Table 6.3. *Relationship between General Delinquency and Periods of Active Gang Membership, Males Only*

Gang Member in	Year 1	Year 2	Year 3	Year 4
(Nonmember)	7.00[c,d]	11.86	13.59	20.38
Year 1 only	40.12[a]	19.63	25.76	23.25
Year 2 only	15.71[b,c]	34.82[a]	51.95[a]	53.22
Year 3 only	15.49	34.41[a]	50.14	22.95
Year 4 only	10.32[d]	31.20[d]	35.07[d]	144.49[a]
Year 1 & 2	80.76[a]	112.81[a,c]	37.97[a]	48.58
Year 1–3	84.38[a]	71.82[a]	66.00[a]	44.34
Year 2–3 or 2–4	12.26[c]	25.77[a]	53.52[a]	57.18
Year 1–4	123.93[a]	47.51[a]	74.26[a]	143.03[a]

[a] $p < .05$ (one-tailed t-test) compared with nonmembers.
[b] $p < .05$ (one-tailed t-test) compared with Year 2.
[c] $p < .05$ (one-tailed t-test) compared with Year 3.
[d] $p < .05$ (one-tailed t-test) compared with Year 4.

of general delinquency across these four years. The mean incidence scores increase from 7.00 at Year 1 to 20.38 at Year 4 and the means at Years 3 and 4 are significantly higher than the Year 1 mean.

There appears to be a substantial "main effect" of gang membership. That is, the means in the lower two sections of Table 6.3, for both the short-term and the more stable gang members, are generally higher than those for the nonmembers. This observation essentially replicates the basic association between gang membership and delinquency that we saw in Chapter 3. The issue now is: are the delinquency rates of gang members particularly high, relative to those of nonmembers, during their periods of active membership?

Recall from Table 6.2 that the facilitation effect predicts a perfect overlap between periods of active gang membership and the location of significant group differences. Thus, the gang members should exhibit significantly higher rates of delinquency *only* during the year(s) in which they are active gang members. With few exceptions, that is what we observe in Table 6.3. Of the 16 delinquency means appearing in boxes (indicating periods of active gang membership), 14 are statistically significantly higher than the mean for the nonmembers at the same year. For example, the mean at Year 1 for the Year-1-only gang members is 40.12, compared with a mean of 7.00 for the nonmembers in that same year. In contrast, of the 16 delinquency means not appearing in boxes, 13 are not statistically different from the delinquency means for the nonmembers at the same year. Thus, for the cross-group comparisons the results are quite consistent with a facilitation effect. Gang members self-report significantly more delinquency than nonmembers when they are in a gang; they do not report significantly higher rates of delinquency either before or after they are in a gang.

The within-group temporal patterns are also consistent with the facilitation model. With only a few exceptions, the mean delinquency scores that appear in the boxes are higher than those not in the boxes. For the Year-1-only gang members, for example, the mean at Year 1 is 40.12 and that drops to 19.63 at Year 2, after these subjects leave the gang, and continues at about that level through Year 4. For the Year 1 and 2 gang members the means while they are in the gang are 80.76 and 112.81; after they leave the gang the means are 37.97 and 48.58. It is important to note that this postgang decline runs counter to the general, increasing age trend reflected in the data for the nonmembers.

A few general comments about the cross-time comparisons in Table 6.3 can be made. First, while the direction of the cross-time comparisons is consistent with a facilitation effect, only some of the comparisons attain statistical significance. This may be due to the relatively small sample sizes, which range from 10 to 42, for these within-group comparisons. Nevertheless, the mean delinquency scores for the year immediately prior to joining the gang are *always* lower than those observed in the first (or only) year of gang membership. Moreover, except for the Year-2-only gang members, the mean delinquency scores for the year immediately after leaving the gang are always lower than those observed for the last (or only) year of gang membership. Therefore, general delinquency tends to increase upon joining a gang and to decrease upon leaving.

In Table 6.4 we present results for violent delinquency. For the nonmembers there is a downward drift in the frequency scores over these four years. At Year 1 the mean is .88 and that drops to .39 at Year 4. Again, we see a rather substantial "main effect" of gang membership. Overall, the violent delinquency means observed for the gang members are larger than those observed for the nonmembers.

The cross-group comparisons between the nonmembers and the gang members are quite consistent with predictions based on the facilitation model. Of the 16 comparisons between active gang members and nonmembers, 14 are statistically significant in the expected direction; of the 16 comparisons made either before or after periods of active membership, only 3 are statistically significant. As was the case with general delinquency, therefore, gang members have significantly higher frequency scores on violent delinquency than nonmembers only during periods when they are active members of the gang.

The cross-time comparisons for each of the groupings reveal that in all but one instance the rates of violent delinquency are higher during periods

Table 6.4. *Relationship between Violent Delinquency and Periods of Active Gang Membership, Males Only*

Gang Member in	Year 1	Year 2	Year 3	Year 4
(Nonmember)	.88[c,d]	.74[c,d]	.50[d]	.39
Year 1 only	3.52[a,b,c,d]	.68	.79	.56
Year 2 only	4.11	5.50	1.26	2.27
Year 3 only	2.53	1.46	2.97[a]	1.19
Year 4 only	4.10	2.56[a]	3.42	5.41[a]
Year 1 & 2	10.08[a,c]	5.07[a,c]	1.67	5.90
Year 1–3	7.97[a]	3.60[a]	4.86[a]	2.80[a]
Year 2–3 or 2–4	2.19[a]	3.92[a]	3.71	2.33[a]
Year 1–4	13.04[a]	3.52[a]	3.30[a]	5.29[a]

[a] $p < .05$ (one-tailed t-test) compared with nonmembers.
[b] $p < .05$ (one-tailed t-test) compared with Year 2.
[c] $p < .05$ (one-tailed t-test) compared with Year 3.
[d] $p < .05$ (one-tailed t-test) compared with Year 4.

of gang membership than either before or after, although these differences are seldom statistically significant. Differences in the comparisons between the year prior to joining a gang and the first (or only) year of membership are more muted here than was the case for general delinquency. Although in every case there is an increase in violent delinquency across these adjacent years, none of the differences is statistically significant. The differences are more pronounced for the postgang year. After adolescents leave the gang, they generally exhibit substantial reductions in their level of violent offending. Indeed, for all groups except the Year 1–3 members, the mean in the year after the last (or only) year of gang membership is less than half of the mean in the preceding year.

Summary

Overall, it would appear that there is a strong facilitation effect of gang membership on general delinquency and on violent delinquency for the male gang members in the Rochester Youth Development Study. The highest rates of delinquency and violence are exhibited during periods of active gang membership. With very few exceptions, only at these times are the gang members significantly different from the nonmembers. Also, across time, the highest rates are observed during, as compared with either before or after, periods of gang membership. It is important to note that these differences apply regardless of the underlying age trend indicated by the nonmembers. All of these results suggest a strong facilitating effect of gang

Table 6.5. *Relationship between Drug Use and Periods of Active Gang Membership, Males Only*

Gang Member in	Year 1	Year 2	Year 3	Year 4
(Nonmember)	$2.40^{c,d}$	$3.61^{c,d}$	4.28^{d}	8.76
Year 1 only	6.92	6.85	3.82^{d}	13.52
Year 2 only	$.39^{d}$	6.26	4.33	15.55
Year 3 only	2.36	2.47	16.93	29.76
Year 4 only	.39	.00	.00	10.62
Year 1 & 2	7.59^{b}	$75.28^{a,c}$	5.09^{d}	35.04
Year 1–3	27.08^{a}	8.07	36.22^{a}	25.97
Year 2–3 or 2–4	.30	1.73	1.47	57.40^{a}
Year 1–4	3.74^{d}	16.06^{d}	16.38^{d}	83.11^{a}

[a] p < .05 (one-tailed t-test) compared with nonmembers.
[b] p < .05 (one-tailed t-test) compared with Year 2.
[c] p < .05 (one-tailed t-test) compared with Year 3.
[d] p < .05 (one-tailed t-test) compared with Year 4.

membership on delinquency. Put simply, when gang members join gangs their behavior worsens; when they leave gangs their behavior improves.

At the same time there also appear to be some selection effects at play. Although rarely statistically significant, gang members, as compared with nonmembers, do exhibit higher rates of delinquency and violence in the year prior to joining the gang. This observation, combined with the main effect of gang membership on rates of delinquency, suggests that gang members are recruited from adolescents who are somewhat predisposed to delinquency. Once in the gang, however, involvement in delinquency increases further and then decreases once they leave the gang. Overall, it would appear that these data on general delinquency and on violent delinquency are most consistent with a strong facilitation effect with an overlap of a weaker and less consistent selection effect.

Patterns of Drug Involvement

In this section we examine the impact of gang membership on the use of drugs and on the selling of drugs. We begin with the former behavior, which, at these ages, refers primarily to marijuana use.

As expected from the general literature on the age distribution of drug use, there is an increase in drug use across the ages represented by these four years (Table 6.5). For the nonmembers drug use more than triples from a mean frequency of 2.40 at Year 1 to a mean frequency of 8.76 at Year 4. The increase is particularly pronounced from Year 3 to Year 4.

Table 6.6. *Relationship between Drug Sales and Periods of Active Gang Membership, Males Only*

Gang Member in	Year 1	Year 2	Year 3	Year 4
(Nonmember)	.61[c,d]	1.08[c,d]	1.21	4.04
Year 1 only	2.48	.36	1.61	2.62
Year 2 only	.00	2.60	6.32	18.90
Year 3 only	.00	.07	2.82	4.08
Year 4 only	.00	.00	.00	.96
Year 1 & 2	7.08[b]	37.92[a]	11.80	11.40
Year 1–3	4.33	4.13	11.82	18.77
Year 2–3 or 2–4	.00	1.45	7.00	8.31
Year 1–4	2.66	6.84	14.11	65.36[a]

[a] $p < .05$ (one-tailed t-test) compared with nonmembers.
[b] $p < .05$ (one-tailed t-test) compared with Year 2.
[c] $p < .05$ (one-tailed t-test) compared with Year 3.
[d] $p < .05$ (one-tailed t-test) compared with Year 4.

The evidence of a gang effect on drug use is somewhat ambiguous. On the one hand, gang members, when they are actively involved in the gang, do have higher rates of drug use than the nonmembers. For example, among the short-term members, the rates along the main diagonal in Table 6.5 are consistently higher than the rates for the nonmembers at the same time period. On the other hand, few of these differences are statistically significant. Indeed, in only 5 of the 16 comparisons between active gang members and nonmembers do the results attain statistical significance.

The cross-time comparisons for the gang members are also somewhat ambiguous. Gang members do exhibit an increase in drug use from the year prior to joining the gang to the first (or only) year of gang membership. For example, for the Year-2-only gang members, their drug use increases from .39 at Year 1 to 6.26 at Year 2, when they join the gang; for the Year-4-only gang members the increase is from 0 to 10.62. Even though these increases are large, the differences are not statistically significant. Finally, after leaving the gang, levels of drug use generally decline but the pattern is somewhat erratic.

The last form of deviant behavior we examine is selling drugs (Table 6.6). The mean frequencies for the nonmembers increase with age, from .61 at Year 1 to 4.04 at Year 4. The means at the earlier years are significantly lower than those at the later years.

Relatively few statistically significant differences are reported in Table 6.6; this may be due to the combination of low n's and the somewhat low prevalence of drug selling at these ages. Nevertheless, the pattern of results is generally consistent with a facilitation effect. The most compelling evidence comes from the observation that it is extremely rare for gang members to become involved in drug sales prior to joining a gang. For gang members from Year 2 only, Year 4 only, and Years 2–3 or 2–4, there is *no* involvement in drug sales in the years prior to joining a gang; for the Year-3-only gang members, there is no involvement in drug sales at Year 1 and minimal involvement at Year 2 (mean = .07). In contrast, drug sales increase substantially during the first year of gang membership. Active gang members generally exhibit rates of drug sales that are higher than those of nonmembers, even though the differences are seldom statistically significant.

Some evidence from recent studies suggests that involvement in drug sales remains high for gang members after they leave the gang (Hill et al., 1996; Lizotte et al., 1997). The data in Table 6.6 are fairly consistent with this finding. The postgang means for those who were in a gang in Year 2 only, Years 1 and 2, and Years 1–3 are considerably higher than those observed for the nonmembers at the same time periods. The only exception concerns the Year-1-only gang members; for them the postgang means are generally lower than those of the nonmembers.

Overall, there appears to be a rather pronounced effect of gang membership on the frequency of drug sales. Prior to joining a gang, gang members have virtually no involvement in selling drugs, but once in a gang their rates increase substantially. There also appears to be an increasing involvement in drug sales the longer one stays in the gang. Indeed, the highest rates are observed for the stable gang members, at the end of their period of gang involvement.

Summary

In assessing the impact of gang membership on involvement in drug use and drug sales for male adolescents, three general conclusions seem warranted. First, there is virtually no support for a social selection model. Prior to joining the gang, gang members do not have particularly elevated rates of drug use and they have virtually no involvement in drug sales.

Second, there is some support for a gang facilitation effect. For drug use, the support is modest; drug use does increase when adolescents join gangs, and the drug use of gang members is higher than that of nonmembers during periods of active membership. Few of the expected differences are statistically significant, however. For drug sales, there appears to be a more powerful gang facilitation effect. For the gang members, involvement in drug sales is virtually nonexistent prior to becoming a gang member. Drug selling increases after joining the gang and remains high after the gang members leave the gang.

There are several possible explanations for the postgang maintenance of drug selling. One is that the gang is a gateway to drug dealing for some gang members but, once introduced to drug markets and suppliers by the gang, the individual does not require the gang to continue in this line of behavior. Second, there is growing evidence that gang members or cliques within the gang are involved in selling drugs, but not the gang itself (Decker, 2000; Decker and Van Winkle, 1996; Fagan, 1989; Hagedorn, 1998; Maxson, Klein, and Cunningham, 1991). The structure of the gang is too disorganized and volatile to support this profit-making behavior in the long run. One consequence of this may be to force drug dealers to leave the gang, for business purposes if you will, if they plan on continuing to sell drugs.[1] In general, it appears that street gangs facilitate drug dealing by their members, but once the individual members have learned this behavior and acquired access to its opportunity structure, the behavior can continue without the support of the gang.

Third, gang membership appears to have a more consistent and powerful impact on general delinquency and on violence than on either drug sales or drug use. That is, delinquency and violence appear to increase and decrease more precisely as a function of gang membership and there are consistently more significant differences between gang members and nonmembers for these behaviors. Drug involvement exhibits similar patterns but they are not as crisp and there are fewer significant differences.

Multivariate Models

In the previous analysis we examined the temporal patterning of delinquency and drug use in relation to periods of active gang membership in order to assess the competing models that may explain why gang membership is so strongly related to delinquent behavior. In that analysis each individual acts as his own control because we are examining changing patterns of behavior for the same individual as that person enters and leaves gangs. Doing so helps control the impact of a number of possible covariates.

An alternate strategy is to control explicitly for the impact of major risk factors for both gang membership and delinquency in multivariate equations. Doing so allows us to assess whether gang membership still has an impact on delinquency and drug involvement after the impact of those risk factors is held constant. The literature on risk factors for gang membership (see Chapter 4; see also Hill et al., 1999) and for delinquency and violence (e.g., Farrington, 1987; Hawkins et al., 1998) suggests that risk is generated in multiple domains. These include social class position, family, school, peers, individual characteristics, and prior deviant behavior. We include one central indicator from each of these domains in this analysis:[2] family

---

[1] We thank Malcolm Klein for suggesting these hypotheses.
[2] Multiple indicators from each domain often generate problems of multicollinearity.

poverty level, parental supervision, commitment to school, association with delinquent peers, negative life events, and prior deviant behavior. The particular indicator of prior deviance that is included in each equation varies to match the dependent variable. The risk factors are measured in the year immediately prior to the measurement of the dependent variable. Also, the dependent variable is logged because of the skewness of self-reported delinquency data.

To assess the relative impact of selection versus facilitation effects, we estimate separate regression equations at each of the four annual observation points. In each equation, two dummy variables are incorporated to examine the role of gang membership. The first, "current gang member," includes all respondents who were gang members during the year in which the dependent variable was measured. The second, "not current gang member," includes all respondents who were gang members in some other year but who are not currently a gang member. Some of them were gang members in prior years, some will be in future years, or both. In all cases, the omitted category is "never gang member."

A pure facilitation effect would be indicated by finding a significant impact only for the variable signifying current gang membership. That is, net of other risk factors, deviance would be elevated only during periods of active gang membership, but one's status as either a past or future gang member would have no significant impact on current levels of deviance. In contrast, a selection effect would be consistent with the additional finding that the impact of the variable representing gang members who are not currently active is significant and of a similar magnitude. This would indicate that gang members in general, whether they are active or not, have higher rates of delinquency than youth who never join gangs.

OLS Models

In Table 6.7 we present the results for general delinquency for Years 1 through 4. At each of the four years the coefficient for "current gang member" is positive and significant. These coefficients are of the same magnitude as or larger than the coefficients for association with delinquent peers and prior delinquency, typically two of the strongest predictors of delinquent behavior. Active gang membership facilitates involvement in delinquency even when family poverty level, parental supervision, commitment to school, association with delinquent peers, negative life events, and prior general delinquency are held constant.

If there were a strong selection effect, the coefficients for "not current gang member" would be statistically significant and of approximately the same magnitude as the coefficients observed for "current gang member." The coefficients for "not current gang member" are significant at three

Table 6.7. *The Impact of Gang Membership Status on Self-Reported General Delinquency, OLS Estimates, Males Only (standardized regression coefficients)*

	Self-Reported General Delinquency (logged)			
	Year 1[a]	Year 2[b]	Year 3[c]	Year 4[d]
Gang Membership Status				
Current Gang Member	.26**	.29**	.27**	.22**
Not Current				
Gang Member	.10**	.12**	.13**	.02
Risk Factors				
Family Poverty Level	.02	.00	−.04	−.02
Parental Supervision	−.07*	−.01	−.01	−.10*
Commitment to School	−.12**	−.15**	−.22**	−.04
Association with				
Delinquent Peers	.31**	.10**	.15**	.22**
Negative Life Events	.17**	.14**	.18**	.16**
Prior General				
Delinquency	.23**	.16**	.14**	.13**
Adjusted R^2	.56	.34	.37	.26
	(n = 518)	(n = 525)	(n = 480)	(n = 428)

[a]Year 1 general delinquency combines data from Waves 2 and 3; risk factors are from Wave 2.
[b]Year 2 general delinquency combines data from Waves 4 and 5; risk factors are from Wave 3.
[c]Year 3 general delinquency combines data from Waves 6 and 7; risk factors are from Wave 5.
[d]Year 4 general delinquency combines data from Waves 8 and 9; risk factors are from Wave 7.
*p < .05. **p < .01.

of the four years but these coefficients are less than half the size of those observed for "current gang member."

Table 6.8 presents parallel results for violent delinquency. Current gang membership exerts a strong, positive influence on violent delinquency; indeed, in three of the four years it has the largest coefficient of any variable in the equation. The coefficients for the other central variable, "not current gang member," while statistically significant, are of smaller magnitude, usually about a third of the size of the coefficients for "current gang member." These effects are observed, net of the control variables.

These results, in which major risk factors for both gang membership and delinquency are controlled, are quite similar to those observed in the earlier

Table 6.8. *The Impact of Gang Membership Status on Self-Reported Violent Delinquency, OLS Estimates, Males Only (standardized regression coefficients)*

	Self-Reported Violent Delinquency (logged)			
	Year 1[a]	Year 2[b]	Year 3[c]	Year 4[d]
Gang Membership Status				
Current Gang Member	.26**	.35**	.33**	.33**
Not Current Gang Member	.13**	.08*	.10**	.12**
Risk Factors				
Family Poverty Level	.02	−.05	.04	.03
Parental Supervision	−.05	−.08*	−.01	−.04
Commitment to School	−.04	−.03	.01	−.03
Association with				
Delinquent Peers	.32**	.08*	.13**	.24**
Negative Life Events	.14**	.15**	.20**	.02
Prior Violent Delinquency	.15**	.10*	.12**	.09*
Adjusted R^2	.42	.28	.27	.26
	(n = 518)	(n = 525)	(n = 480)	(n = 428)

[a]Year 1 violence combines data from Waves 2 and 3; risk factors are from Wave 2.
[b]Year 2 violence combines data from Waves 4 and 5; risk factors are from Wave 3.
[c]Year 3 violence combines data from Waves 6 and 7; risk factors are from Wave 5.
[d]Year 4 violence combines data from Waves 8 and 9; risk factors are from Wave 7.
*p < .05. **p < .01.

tabular analysis. There appears to be a substantial facilitation effect of gang membership on delinquency (represented here by the variable "current gang member") and a smaller selection effect (represented here by the variable "not current gang member").

Tables 6.9 and 6.10 present the results for drug use and for drug sales, respectively. Here the evidence for a gang facilitation effect is clearer. When risk factors from the major adolescent life domains of social class, family, school, peers, individual characteristics, and prior deviance are held constant, current gang membership exerts a strong positive impact both on drug use (Table 6.9) and on drug sales (Table 6.10) in all four years. In contrast, in the equations for drug use, only the coefficient for "not current gang member" at Year 4 attains statistical significance. In the four equations for drug sales, none of the coefficients for "not current gang member" attains statistical significance.[3]

---

[3] The "not current gang member" group can be subdivided into "past gang member," those who previously had been a member of a gang but are not currently, and "future gang member," those who will join a gang but have not done so yet. When this is done, the results are the

Table 6.9. *The Impact of Gang Membership Status on Self-Reported Drug Use, OLS Estimates, Males Only (standardized regression coefficients)*

	Self-Reported Drug Use (logged)			
	Year 1[a]	Year 2[b]	Year 3[c]	Year 4[d]
Gang Membership Status				
Current Gang Member	.14**	.23**	.18**	.23**
Not Current Gang Member	.03	.01	−.05	.09*
Risk Factors				
Family Poverty Level	.01	.07*	.00	−.02
Parental Supervision	−.04	−.01	−.01	−.00
Commitment to School	−.03	−.04	−.13**	−.12**
Association with Delinquent Peers	.36**	.16**	.17**	.09*
Negative Life Events	−.02	.04	.03	.12**
Prior Drug Use	.05	.28**	.28**	.30**
Adjusted R^2	.19	.22	.22	.24
	(n = 518)	(n = 525)	(n = 480)	(n = 428)

[a]Year 1 drug use combines data from Waves 2 and 3; risk factors are from Wave 2.
[b]Year 2 drug use combines data from Waves 4 and 5; risk factors are from Wave 3.
[c]Year 3 drug use combines data from Waves 6 and 7; risk factors are from Wave 5.
[d]Year 4 drug use combines data from Waves 8 and 9; risk factors are from Wave 7.
*p < .05. **p < .01.

Random Effects Models

Finally, we reestimate the impact of gang membership on involvement in delinquency and drugs using a random effects model. This type of model represents the most stringent test of the facilitation model as it controls for unmeasured heterogeneity in the population, as well as measured risk factors, while examining the impact of gang membership status on delinquency. Population heterogeneity refers to time-stable individual differences, such as criminal propensity, that can produce varying rates of crime across individuals that are not a function of changing states, such as movement into and out of gangs, but are really a function of the individual's stable underlying propensity. Ordinary least squares (OLS) regression ignores this possibility by assuming (somewhat questionably) that the error terms vary independently over time for a given individual.

same as those reported here. There is a large effect for "current gang member" but smaller, and less consistently significant, effects for past and future gang members. The appropriate tables are presented in Appendix C.

Table 6.10. *The Impact of Gang Membership Status on Self-Reported Drug Sales, OLS Estimates, Males Only (standardized regression coefficients)*

	Self-Reported Drug Sales (logged)			
	Year 1[a]	Year 2[b]	Year 3[c]	Year 4[d]
Gang Membership Status				
Current Gang Member	.23**	.34**	.23**	.15**
Not Current Gang Member	.00	−.02	−.01	−.01
Risk Factors				
Family Poverty Level	.00	.11**	.01	−.04
Parental Supervision	.04	−.03	−.01	.00
Commitment to School	−.02	.07	−.05	.03
Association with Delinquent Peers	.17**	.21**	.17**	.22**
Negative Life Events	−.03	.02	.04	.08*
Prior Drug Sales	.36**	−.01	.06	.31**
Adjusted R^2	.27	.21	.11	.21
	(n = 518)	(n = 525)	(n = 480)	(n = 428)

[a]Year 1 drug sales combine data from Waves 2 and 3; risk factors are from Wave 2.
[b]Year 2 drug sales combine data from Waves 4 and 5; risk factors are from Wave 3.
[c]Year 3 drug sales combine data from Waves 6 and 7; risk factors are from Wave 5.
[d]Year 4 drug sales combine data from Waves 8 and 9; risk factors are from Wave 7.
*p < .05. **p < .01.

Random effects models correct for this by dividing the error term into two components. The first is an individual-specific part that does not vary over time; that is, it is time-stable. "This component of the error structure captures the influence of any enduring but unmeasured individual (e.g., impulsivity) or environmental (e.g., persistent poverty) characteristics affecting potential to offend" (Nagin and Farrington, 1992: 240). The second part of the error term is assumed to vary across time and population. This decomposition of the error term allows one to control for persistent unmeasured heterogeneity, and to measure its magnitude by the coefficient ρ. A random effects model offers a strong test of the gang facilitation hypothesis because both measured risk factors and unmeasured, enduring characteristics are controlled when we examine the impact of gang membership status on delinquency.[4]

---

[4] We recognize that there are advantages to estimating "fixed effects" as opposed to "random effects" models. Unfortunately, fixed effects models cannot estimate coefficients for variables that are constant within persons. For example, one cannot estimate a coefficient for gender in a fixed effects model, because each person is either male or female over all waves. In

Table 6.11. *The Impact of Gang Membership Status on Involvement in Delinquency and Drugs, Random Effects Models, Males Only (unstandardized coefficients)*

	General Delinquency	Violent Delinquency	Drug Use	Drug Sales
Gang Member Status				
Current Gang Member	1.49**	.72**	.70**	.57**
Not Current Gang Member	.61**	.26**	.20**	.07
Risk Factors				
Family Poverty Level	−.03	.01	.05	.00
Parental Supervision	−.17	−.03	−.01	.00
Commitment to School	−.46**	−.05	−.17**	.01
Association with Delinquent Peers	.56**	.23**	.29**	.27**
Negative Life Events	.83**	.38**	.03	−.03*
Prior Deviance[a]	.01**	.01**	.02**	.01
Control Variables				
Year 2	.10	.12**	.05	.06
Year 3	.20**	−.16**	.14**	.13*
Year 4	.31**	−.18**	.32**	.19**
ρ	.26	.17	.34	.18

[a]The measure of prior deviance matches the dependent variable.
*p < .05. **p < .01.

Results are presented in Table 6.11. One equation is estimated for each dependent variable because in these models the effects of independent variables are assumed to be stable over time. We also include dummy variables for different years, which controls for maturation effects.

By and large, the results here replicate the earlier ones based on the OLS estimates. For all four dependent variables the coefficient for "current gang member" is statistically significant and sizable. For general delinquency, violence, and drug use, but not drug sales, the coefficient for the variable "not current gang member" is statistically significant. These coefficients,

other words, fixed effects models allow estimates only for variables that change over time. This leads to an interesting difficulty in the current case. Gang membership is divided into three dummy variables: never gang member, not current gang member, and current gang member. A fixed effects model cannot estimate a coefficient for the first variable, because it is constant within persons. A fixed effects model can estimate effects for the other two variables, because their values change within people. *But*, within person, "current gang member" and "not current gang member" are perfectly collinear. So, as a practical matter, only one effect can be estimated. As that does not allow for a test of our core hypothesis, we have opted to estimate random effects models, which do.

however, are substantially smaller in size. For general delinquency, for example, the coefficient for being a "current gang member" is 1.49, 2.5 times as large as the coefficient of .61 for "not current gang member." The coefficient for "current gang member" is 2.8 times larger for violence, 3.5 times larger for drug use, and 8.1 times larger for drug sales than the respective coefficient for "not current gang member." The other variables in the equations, the measured risk factors, behave in approximately the same ways they did in the OLS equations.

Summary

In this section we adopted a multivariate approach to assessing possible gang facilitation and selection effects, by estimating two types of regression models. The OLS regressions, estimated at each year, explicitly control for a number of important risk factors both for gang membership and for deviance, while assessing the impact of gang membership status on involvement in delinquency and drugs. The random effects model additionally controlled for enduring unmeasured characteristics of the individual. Recall that this analysis is limited to male respondents because of the temporal distribution of female gang membership in the Rochester sample.

Net of the impact of family poverty, parental supervision, commitment to school, association with delinquent peers, negative life events, prior deviance, and unobserved population heterogeneity, the coefficients associated with "current gang member" are sizable and statistically significant in predicting general delinquency, violence, drug use, and drug sales in all the equations. The coefficients associated with "not current gang member" are of smaller magnitude and are less consistently significant, however. In general, the pattern of these results is quite consistent with the one derived from the earlier, tabular analysis: there seems to be a strong facilitation effect and a rather modest selection effect.

Discussion

Gang members have higher rates of delinquency than do nonmembers and gang members are responsible for a very substantial proportion of all offenses that are reported. In this chapter we identified and tested three competing processes that could account for this behavior pattern for male gang members. The selection model adopts a "kind of person" perspective, whereas the facilitation model adopts a "kind of group" perspective. The enhancement model is a mixed approach, combining aspects of both selection and facilitation effects.

These models, especially the two pure types, offer fundamentally different perspectives on the motivation for delinquency and on the way in which gang membership affects delinquency. The selection model offers a static orientation (Nagin and Paternoster, 1991) in which the causes of delinquency are set early in life and are carried by the individual to different situations (see Gottfredson and Hirschi, 1990). Changing social environments, such as joining and leaving street gangs, have relatively little, if any, causal impact on behavior. Indeed, in a pure selection model the relationship between gang members and delinquency is spurious.

The facilitation model offers a more dynamic perspective consistent with a life-course orientation (Nagin and Paternoster, 1991) in which delinquency is viewed as a product of both enduring characteristics of the person *and* changing social environments. From this theoretical orientation, changing life-course circumstances – such as changing family and peer relationships or status transitions like marriage and employment – can have causal impacts on behavior (see Sampson and Laub, 1993; Thornberry and Krohn, 2001). So too, can gang membership. Delinquent careers are not predetermined but are malleable, changing as the person's life course unfolds.

To assess the empirical validity of these two perspectives, we examined changing patterns of delinquency for male members of the Rochester Youth Development Study as they moved into and out of active participation in gangs. Two analytic strategies were adopted. The first looked to see if involvement in general delinquency, violence, drug use, and drug selling co-occurred with periods of active gang membership. This approach focused on within-individual change. The second strategy explicitly controlled for the effect of major risk factors for both gang membership and delinquency and for unobserved population heterogeneity in a series of multivariate regression equations. The risk factors included family poverty, parental supervision, commitment to school, association with delinquent peers, negative life events, and prior deviance.

These results, as well as those reported by Esbensen and Huizinga (1993), Hill et al. (1996), and Gatti et al. (2002), indicate that there is a strong, consistent gang facilitation effect. When male adolescents join gangs their behavior changes; delinquency, violence, drug selling, and – to a lesser extent – drug use increase. When they leave the gang, their behavior changes again; involvement in deviant behavior decreases, with the exception of involvement in drug selling.

In contrast, there is very little convincing evidence for a selection model. Gang members do not have consistently higher rates of delinquency than nonmembers either before or after the time periods they are in the gang. Indeed, the most consistent finding in this chapter is that gang members do *not* have significantly higher rates of general delinquency, violence, drug use, and drug selling than the nonmembers unless they are actively involved in the gang. We do not know how well these findings would apply to female adolescents.

Finally, we note that in some ways these results can be interpreted as being consistent with a mixed or enhancement model. Gang members generally have higher rates of delinquency than nonmembers, what we referred to earlier as a "main effect"; but they have statistically significantly higher rates only when they are in the gang. If the mixed model is the appropriate one, it comprises a large facilitation effect and a small selection effect.

At a more general level, these findings are consistent with recent research on a life-course approach to understanding delinquent and criminal careers that indicates a substantial dynamic component to offending (Bushway, Brame, and Paternoster, 1999). Although static, enduring attributes of the person are important, so too are dynamic components and changing life circumstances. This research suggests that membership in street gangs may be one of the more important social environments for explaining patterns of adolescent delinquency. As indicated by the earlier work of Short and Strodtbeck (1965), Klein (1971), and Miller et al. (1961), the normative climate and the group processes associated with American street gangs provide a fertile ground for eliciting delinquent behavior, especially violent behavior.

Gangs, Guns, and Crime

THE PREVIOUS ANALYSIS indicates that gang membership facilitates a broad range of delinquent behaviors including violence, drug use, and drug sales. When boys join gangs their delinquency increases and when they leave gangs their delinquency decreases. Here we focus on a related form of illegal behavior: owning and carrying illegal firearms.[1] In particular, we are interested in the interplay between gang membership and patterns of owning and carrying guns. There are three general analytic questions. First, do gangs recruit those who carry illegal guns prior to gang membership, does gang membership enhance gun carrying, or are both processes at work? Second, do former gang members continue carrying guns as a result of their gang experience? Finally, what is the joint impact of gang membership and gun involvement on delinquency, drug use, and drug sales? Because research has shown that illegal gun carriers are more active in criminal activity (Lizotte et al., 2000) and that gang members show higher levels of criminal activity (Chapter 6), we hypothesize that gang members who also carry guns will have higher levels of criminal activity than one would predict from either factor alone. We conduct all these analyses for two types of illegal gun carriers: those who carry illegal guns but do not own them, and those who carry illegal guns that they own. The distinction is important, especially at these ages and especially for gang members. Gang members associate with others who have guns and the gang becomes an environment in which guns can be borrowed or rented. Thus, gang members need not own a gun to have access to one for use in crime.

---

[1] As in the previous chapter we only include males in this analysis because of the low frequencies of gang membership and gun ownership among the female respondents.

Gangs and Guns

Strong and consistent evidence from decades of research shows that gang members are frequently armed with guns (Bjerregaard and Lizotte, 1995; Decker and Van Winkle, 1996; Newton and Zimring, 1969; Sheley and Wright, 1993, 1995; Strodtbeck and Short, 1964). For example, in surveys of juveniles in correctional facilities and inner-city high schools, Sheley and Wright (1993, 1995) found that 59% of inmates and 23% of high school students were members of a gang or "quasi-gang." In both samples gang members were more likely to possess guns than were the nonmembers. Sixty-five percent of inmate gang members and 30% of high school gang members owned a revolver compared with 47% of nongang inmates and 11% of nongang students (1995: 100). Similarly, in a field study of 99 gang members in St. Louis, Decker and Van Winkle (1996: 177) found that 81% owned guns. On average, they owned more than four guns. Using data from the Rochester Youth Development Study, Bjerregaard and Lizotte (1995) reported that at about age 18, male gang members are more than twice as likely to own guns for "protection" than are nonmembers. However, gang members are neither more nor less likely than nonmembers to own legal guns for sporting purposes. Thus, it is crucial to be able to measure both the type of gun *and* the reason for having it – sport versus protection – in this research area.

Not only are gang members more likely than their counterparts to own guns, they are also more likely to carry illegal guns on the street (Bjerregaard and Lizotte, 1995; Lizotte et al., 2000). Given this, it is no surprise that gang members are also more likely to use guns to commit crimes (Bjerregaard and Lizotte, 1995: 49). For example, Klein, Maxson, and Cunningham (1991) found that gang homicides are significantly more likely than nongang homicides to involve guns (91% vs. 64%). Similarly, Decker and Van Winkle (1996: 177) reported that two-thirds of gang members have used their guns in crime, usually in gang fights. However, they also reported the use of guns in drive-by shootings, attacks on strangers, and other such incidents. Gang members are also much more likely than nonmembers to have peers who own illegal guns for protection (Bjerregaard and Lizotte, 1995: 49). Given the interplay between gang membership and guns, and the increased severity of crimes committed with the aid of guns, it is particularly important to understand more about how these strands of deviant behavior become intertwined over the life course.

The Selection of Gang Members and the Facilitation of Illegal Gun Carrying

Several reasons may account for why gang members are likely to carry guns. One concerns their routine activities. They often travel in a dangerous world where their peers carry guns and they often need protection from others like themselves (Horowitz, 1983; Lizotte et al., 2000; Wright and Rossi, 1986: 139). "[T]he rationale [for carrying weapons] appears to arise from widespread fear that sudden violence may be perpetuated – almost any time – and that the police will not be effective to stop it" (Strodtbeck and Short, 1964: 134).

Another reason stems from their ease of access to guns from other members of their gang. This access includes not only buying but also borrowing or renting guns from fellow gang members. Although they did not present the results by gang membership, Sheley and Wright (1995) reported that 45% of teenage inmates say that they could borrow a gun to commit a crime, a situation that may be facilitated by gang membership. If gang members can easily borrow, rent, or otherwise obtain guns from other members, one gun can become an instrument for many criminal players, across many different situations, and for many crimes. Interdicting a "gang gun" would also cut its usage by many individuals, for potentially different types of crime, involving many separate incidents.

It is not clear from prior research if gangs recruit members who carry guns before becoming gang members. In one study using the Rochester data, Bjerregaard and Lizotte (1995) found that future gang members are not significantly more likely than nonmembers to own illegal guns. If there were an impact of prior gun carrying on the likelihood of joining a gang, it would be similar to the selection or "kind of person" model discussed in Chapter 6. There we found some evidence that gangs may select members who are already involved in general and violent delinquency but not those involved in drug use and drug sales.

An individual who joins a gang because he owns a gun can then facilitate the gun use of other gang members by renting, selling, or loaning the gun to them. Similarly, an individual who does not own a gun can have his future illegal gun use facilitated by joining a gang whose other members already have guns. If guns get handed around but are not necessarily owned by those who use them, it could explain why there is relatively rapid turnover in gun carrying from wave to wave in our Rochester data. For example, throughout their adolescence more than 50% of the boys who carry illegal guns do so for six months or less, while nearly 75% carry at no more than two (not necessarily consecutive) six-month intervals (Lizotte et al., 1997). Cook, Molliconi, and Cole (1995) also found that adolescents cycle in and out of gun possession rather quickly. This pattern, of course, is consistent with the short-term, episodic character of gang membership that we observed in Chapter 3.

Gangs can facilitate the ownership and use of guns in several ways. First, the gang may be a source of illegal firearms for members who wish to buy them. Also, because gangs are involved in a variety of illegal markets (e.g., drug dealing and fencing), that may also enhance a gang member's access to illegal gun markets. Second, as a central repository, the gang allows one illegal gun to suit the needs of many clients, whether or not those individuals actually steal or purchase and own the gun. If this is true, other things being equal, we might expect gang membership to enhance the probability of members *owning* illegal guns. However, we would also expect gang members to have a substantially elevated likelihood of *carrying* illegal guns, whether or not they own them. One thing is certain for any particular criminal incident in which an illegal gun is involved: whether the offender owns or just borrows the gun has no bearing on its efficacy.

The Joint Impact of Gang Membership and Gun Possession on Illegal Behavior

As we have shown in Chapter 3, gang members have dramatically elevated levels of offending for a variety of offenses. There are a variety of processes that can bring this about, including the normative climate of gangs, group processes associated with gangs, the protection of turf and leadership status, and so forth.

There is also some evidence that adolescent gun ownership and gun carrying facilitates involvement in a variety of crime types, not just gun crimes (Lizotte et al., forthcoming). With a gun in his pocket a boy may feel equipped to take advantage of criminal situations for which the gun is not initially necessary. In other words, guns that are carried do not need to be used (in terms of firing, pointing, brandishing, or even referring to them) for the boy to feel prepared for criminal activity. Similarly, adolescent males who have easy access to guns, even if they are not carrying them at the moment, may feel emboldened to initiate criminal acts they may otherwise avoid. If illegal gun users have been characterized as *the* crime problem in the United States (Wright and Rossi, 1986), then gang members with guns may be at the very core of the crime problem, especially the problem of youth violence.

The Measurement of Illegal Gun Carrying

The distinction between illegal gun carrying, when the gun is not owned, on the one hand, and illegal gun ownership *and* carrying on the other, has important measurement and analytic implications. If we only ask respondents about illegal gun *ownership* and use, we are likely to miss a substantial amount of actual illegal gun use. As noted, this may be particularly true for gang members because of access to guns that the gang can provide. If one believes, as we do, that gun-carrying gang members are particularly high-rate offenders, measuring the impact of the interaction of gang membership and the carrying of guns that they also own would miss many gun-carrying gang members who do not happen to own the guns they use. This would have the effect of minimizing the impact of the gang-gun interaction on crime because the gang members who carry guns that they do not own would be mistakenly categorized as simply gang members and not also as gun carriers.

In this chapter, therefore, we measure gun use in two ways: carrying a gun that is not owned, and owning and carrying a gun. We predict both kinds of gun use from future, current, and past gang membership, controlling for other variables. By predicting usage for three one-year time periods to assess the changing impact of the relationship over adolescence,[2] we can measure the possibly changing effects of gang selection and facilitation for both types of gun carrying.

Next we assess the impact of the interaction of gang membership and each measure of gun carrying on the commission of general and violent delinquency and on drug use and drug sales. We expect the interaction of gang membership and gun carrying to have a strong impact on the commission of crime, an effect that is above and beyond the main effects of gang membership or gun carrying individually. Furthermore, we expect that the impact of the interaction of gang membership with the carrying of a gun that is not owned will be weaker in predicting offending than is the interaction of gang membership and owning and carrying a gun. This is because once a boy owns a gun he no longer needs the gang to obtain a gun to commit crime, whereas for boys without guns the gang facilitates only temporary use of a gun for criminal purposes, making the gun less available for general use.

Owning and Carrying a Gun

In measuring gun ownership, one way of categorizing owners would be as those who own a gun legally (e.g., with a license) and those who own a gun illegally (e.g., a stolen gun). Although important for studies of adults, that distinction is not particularly helpful in our case; in New York State virtually all ownership of guns by adolescents is illegal. Handguns require a special permit, which must be signed by a judge, and in Monroe County the judge responsible for permits would sign only rarely for adolescents during the period of the Rochester study. Therefore, if a respondent reports owning a handgun, it is either owned illegally or some adult (e.g., his parent) owns the gun but the subject thinks of it as his own. For example, the parent could buy the gun and the boy could "possess" it.

Because of this we use the person's reason or motivation for obtaining the gun as a proxy to zero in on illegal gun owners. In particular, we ask the

---

[2] These relationships are only examined at Years 2, 3, and 4, because the variables are not available for Year 1.

boys if they own a gun for sporting purposes or if they own it for protection.[3] If they report owning for protection, we consider them to be the equivalent of illegal gun owners. In this case they do not own the gun for sport (e.g., for hunting, target practice, or collecting), and more legitimate notions of protection, such as protecting one's home or business, do not readily apply to 15- and 16-year-olds. The "protection" most likely applies to protection from risky situations and environments (Wright and Rossi, 1986: 122). If boys who report owning guns for protection are akin to illegal owners as we hypothesize, one would expect them to be more likely to own handguns and sawed-off rifles and shotguns. Conversely, those who report owning guns for sport should be more likely to own unadulterated long guns. This is precisely what we find. For example, at Wave 4, of the 30 boys who own guns for protection, 28 own handguns and 22 own long guns. However, over half (12) of the long guns are sawed off. In contrast, the 27 boys who own guns for sport own a total of 30 guns. More than two-thirds of these (21) are rifles and shotguns (only 1 of which was sawed off), and 9 are handguns.[4] These results suggest that the protection gun ownership variable is a reasonable measure of illegal gun ownership for adolescents. If the respondent reported owning a gun for protection, we asked if he had carried it on the street in the past six months. For this analysis, if the boy reports carrying the protection gun on the street, he is categorized as carrying an illegal gun that he owns with two exceptions.

First, a few boys report gun owning for both reasons (sport and protection). Because we cannot distinguish their carrying illegally from carrying for sport, they are not categorized as owning and carrying in this analysis. Second, if a boy reports owning and carrying a protection gun but does not report carrying a gun in the self-reported delinquency battery (see the next section), he is not categorized as owning and carrying for protection.

Carrying Other Guns

Our second measure, carrying a gun that is not owned, comes from the self-reported delinquency battery. At each interview we ask the boys whether they carried a hidden weapon since the time of the last interview; if they did, we asked if it was a gun. This item is likely to tap illegal gun carrying, as opposed to carrying for sporting purposes, for several reasons. First, we ask the question near the end of a long inventory of other self-reported delinquencies. Second, the screening question asks about hidden weapon carrying in general, before asking if the weapon is a firearm. We do this because other studies have asked if respondents carried a gun, counting

---

[3] In Waves 5 and 6 we ask if anyone in the household owns a gun for protection.
[4] The pattern is the same in the other waves as well.

Table 7.1. *Percentage of Gang Members and*
Nonmembers Who Carry Guns and Who Own and
Carry Guns, Males Only

	Gang Members		Nonmembers	
	%	n	%	n
Gun Carriers				
Year 2	35.7	25	3.5	17
Year 3	31.0	18	3.8	19
Year 4	32.4	12	5.4	28
Gun Owners				
Year 2	20.0	15	2.3	11
Year 3	18.5	12	3.3	16
Year 4	25.6	10	4.1	21

any carrying as illegal. This artificially inflates the reporting of illegal gun carrying because not all gun carrying is illegal or undesirable. For example, one could legally carry a gun from the car to the house after going target shooting. This wording also eliminates toy guns, caulking guns, and the like. If the respondent reports carrying an illegal hidden weapon and reports that the weapon is a firearm, he is coded as an illegal gun carrier. On this measure, if the subject owns and carries the firearm, as is the case on the previous measure, he is not coded as a carrier here. As a result, this is different from the ownership measure discussed earlier. It only measures carriers who do *not* own the gun that they carry.

Results

Predicting Gun Carrying

We begin by analyzing the relationship between gang membership and the percentage of boys in each of the years who carry guns, referred to as "Carriers," and then those who both own and carry hidden guns, referred to as "Owners" (Table 7.1). As one would expect, higher percentages of gang members carry guns (between 31.0% and 35.7%) as compared with non-members (between 3.5% and 5.4%). For example, in Year 2 the percentage of boys not in gangs who carry guns is only about one-tenth that of gang members (3.5% compared with 35.7%). The percentage of nonmembers who carry guns climbs as the boys get older. By Year 4 about 5.4% of non-members carry guns.

Turning to the issue of youth who both own and carry guns – gun owners in Table 7.1 – we see that, depending upon the year, between 18.5% and

25.6% of boys in gangs own guns.[5] By comparison, 2.3% of boys not in gangs own in Year 2, with the percentage climbing to 4.1% in Year 4. All of this clearly indicates that gang members are more likely than nonmembers to be carriers or owners throughout the course of the study.

It is also informative to examine the differences between owning and carrying across the two groups. There are very few differences between these rates for the nonmembers; about 4% are carriers and about 3% are owners. For the gang members, however, the rate of carrying without owning is considerably greater than the rate of owning: 35.7% versus 20.0% at Year 2, for example. This difference suggests that street gangs may well be suppliers of rented or borrowed guns for their members.

We now turn to a consideration of the impact of gang membership on gun carrying. In Table 7.2 we show logistic regression equations predicting both types of gun carrying. The top panel shows odds ratios and levels of statistical significance for variables predicting carrying guns at each of the three years under consideration. The bottom panel gives the same information for owning and carrying guns. The odds ratios tell us the amount of increase or decrease in the likelihood or odds of gun carrying given a one-unit increase in the predictor variable of interest. For example, because the gang member variables are dichotomies, an odds ratio of 2 for the current gang member variable would tell us that current gang members have twice the likelihood of carrying a gun than those who are not in a gang (the omitted category). Odds ratios of less than 1 indicate a decrease in the likelihood of carrying a gun given a one-unit increase in the predictor variable of interest. For example, an odds ratio of .5 would indicate that current gang members are only half as likely to carry a gun as nonmembers. The model improvement chi-square tests are statistically significant for all the equations reported here, indicating that these equations are significantly better predictors of gun carrying than equations with only the intercept term included. Predictor variables include current, future, and past gang membership, the risk factors included in the prediction equations in Chapter 6,[6] current and prior levels of violent offending, and peer gun ownership for protection.

---

[5] While the number of boys who carry guns and are gang members is relatively small, it does not impact the analysis. In the analyses to follow there are strong statistically significant effects for variables predicting this outcome and for it predicting other variables. Similarly, in logistic regression equations small numbers of cases for highly skewed dichotomies can send odds ratios to infinity because the log of zero is undefined. However, this is not a problem in the analyses reported here. The relationships between gang membership and gun carrying with other variables are so strong that a small number of cases in this group is sufficient to demonstrate significant effects.

[6] These include family poverty level, parental supervision, commitment to school, association with delinquent peers, and negative life events. These are all variables that may predict gun carrying independent of gang membership. Therefore, we hold them constant. Although these variables are included in the equations as predictors, their coefficients are not reported here to conserve space.

Table 7.2. *Odds Ratios Predicting Whether Subjects Are Gun Carriers and Gun Owners, Males Only*

Gang Status and Risk Factors	Year 2	Year 3	Year 4
Gun Carriers			
Current Gang Member	7.09**	7.72**	12.29**
Future Gang Member	2.29	1.21	–
Past Gang Member	2.08	.78	1.59
Prior Violent Delinquency	1.05	1.00	.96
Current Violent Delinquency	1.09**	1.12**	1.00
Peer Protection Gun Ownership	5.46**	1.18	6.89**
Gun Owners			
Current Gang Member	8.66**	4.00*	1.47
Future Gang Member	.00	.00	–
Past Gang Member	13.34**	1.64	.74
Prior Violent Delinquency	1.04	1.04	1.01
Current Violent Delinquency	1.13**	.98	1.47**
Peer Protection Gun Ownership	11.48*	–[a]	14.59*

Note: Control variables are family poverty level, parental supervision, commitment to school, association with delinquent peers, and negative life events.

[a]There are too few cases to estimate the odds ratio for this variable.

*p < .05 (one-tailed). **p < .01 (one-tailed).

A statistically significant odds ratio greater than 1 for the current gang member predictor variable would indicate that gang membership facilitates gun carrying. A statistically significant odds ratio greater than 1 for the future gang member variable would indicate that gangs select those who already carry guns. The same logic holds for the past gang member variable, but a significant relationship in this case would indicate that gang membership has lasting effects on gun carrying beyond the time period of actual membership. The category omitted from the analysis is never a gang member, making the current, future, and past gang member odds ratios relative to those who were never in a gang.

We control for current and prior level of violent offending because this can be a motivation for carrying a gun, independent of gang membership, and we do not want to confound the two variables. Similarly, we control for protection gun ownership by the subject's peers because peers can provide socialization into illegal gun carrying and could provide guns to the subject.

In each of the three years there is a strong and statistically significant effect of current gang membership on carrying. In Years 2 through 4, being a current gang member increases the likelihood of carrying 7- to 12-fold. This is strong evidence of the facilitation effect of gangs on gun carrying. In contrast, there is no evidence that gangs recruit those who carry guns before joining the gang; the future gang membership variable is not a statistically significant predictor of gun carrying in Years 2 and 3. In other words, there is no selection effect. Furthermore, past gang members are not significantly more likely to carry than nonmembers. So there is no lingering effect of gang membership on gun carrying.

Table 7.2 also shows that in all but the last year those who currently commit violent offenses are significantly more likely to carry a gun, independent of their gang membership. Similarly, at Years 2 and 4, having peers who own protection guns significantly and substantially increases the likelihood of carrying (five- or sevenfold). This effect is above and beyond the effect of gang membership.

As was the case for carrying guns, the bottom panel of the table shows a facilitation effect of gangs on gun ownership and carrying. In Years 2 and 3, there are statistically significant effects of current gang membership on owning. Unlike for carrying where the facilitation effect increased over time, this facilitation effect fades as the boys get older. In Year 2, current gang members are more than eight times more likely to carry a gun they own than those never in gangs. In Year 3, they are four times more likely to own and carry, and in Year 4 the effect is not significantly different than zero. There is no evidence of a selection effect. That is, gangs do not recruit those who own guns prior to gang membership. There is no statistically significant difference between future gang members and those never in gangs, in terms of the likelihood of owning. There is a statistically significant impact of past gang membership on owning, but only at the youngest age observed (Year 2). In other words, at younger ages past gang members show considerable momentum and continue to own guns when they leave the gang at a rate 13 times higher than those never in gangs.

Apart from all this, at Years 2 and 4 current violent offending and peer protection gun ownership elevate the likelihood of owning and carrying a gun. As was the case with gun carrying, the impact of peer ownership is particularly large.

In sum, gang membership consistently, strongly, and significantly increases the likelihood of carrying a gun. This is especially the case for carrying when one does not own the gun; the impact of gangs on carrying a gun that is not owned is stronger than it is for carrying guns that one also owns. Although there is no evidence of a selection effect for either outcome, it appears that this facilitation effect lingers somewhat after gang membership, but only for younger subjects who own guns. Furthermore, current violent activities and having peers who own guns for protection become motivations to carry guns.

*Predicting Offending from the Interaction of Gang Membership and
Gun Ownership*

Earlier we hypothesized that the interaction of gang membership and gun
carrying would be a particularly salient predictor of delinquent behavior. In
Tables 7.3 and 7.4 we present ordinary least squares equations predicting
general delinquency, violent delinquency, drug use, and drug sales. These tables extend the analyses presented in Tables 6.7 through 6.10 in the previous
chapter. Those analyses showed that current gang membership significantly
enhanced all four types of delinquency, indicating a facilitation effect. There
was also evidence of a weaker selection effect for general delinquency and
violent delinquency, but not drug use and drug sales. In other words, gangs
may recruit those who are already active in general and violent delinquency.
All of this was done controlling for the same risk factors as in Table 7.2.

Here we fine-tune these analyses in a number of ways. First, because we
believe that gang members who carry guns are at particularly high risk for
offending, we include interaction terms for gang membership and gun carrying. Second, we estimate these interaction terms using the carrying and
then the owning and carrying gun variables separately. To do this each equation includes three dummy variables measuring gun carrying, gang membership, and the gang-gun interaction. For half of the equations the gun
variable will be gun carriers (Table 7.3) and for the other half it will be gun
owners who carry (Table 7.4). This will show the differential impact of the
gang–gun carrying interactions for both types of carrying. We hypothesize
that the effect of the gang-gun interaction will be more profound for those
who own the gun that they carry.

Third, the equations divide the "not current gang member" variable used
in Chapter 6 into two dummy variables: future gang member and past gang
member, as was done in Appendix C. This allows us to evaluate the differential impact of gang membership selection (future gang member) versus
the momentum of gang membership (past gang member) on delinquency.
In all equations the omitted category is composed of those who were never
gang members *and* who do not own or carry guns. These equations also
control for the risk factors included in the equations in Chapter 6 as well
as peer protection gun ownership, but because their effects are largely un-
changed from prior analyses, we do not report them here.[7] Unstandardized
regression coefficients are reported in these tables.[8]

---

[7] These risk factors include family poverty level, parental supervision, commitment to school,
association with delinquent peers, negative life events, prior delinquency of the type being
explained in any particular equation, and peer protection gun ownership.

[8] Due to their skewness, the dependent variables in these equations are logged. This means
that one must take the antilog of the predicted value of the dependent variable in order to
know the impact of independent variables on the number of crimes committed.

Table 7.3. Predicting the Incidence of Self-Reported Delinquency and Drug Use, Gun Carriers, Males Only (unstandardized OLS regression coefficients)

	General Delinquency			Violent Delinquency			Drug Use			Drug Sales		
	Year 2	Year 3	Year 4	Year 2	Year 3	Year 4	Year 2	Year 3	Year 4	Year 2	Year 3	Year 4
Gun Carrier	1.65**	1.21**	1.80**	.19	–.17	.29*	.55**	–.48	.56*	.21	.07	.72**
Gang Member	1.25**	1.17**	.89**	.59**	.53**	.70**	.65**	.30*	.52*	.72**	.29**	.22
Gun Carrier × Gang Member	1.36**	1.71**	2.79**	1.11**	1.19**	.87**	.78**	1.05**	2.90**	.63**	1.06**	1.49**
Future Gang Member	.38	.09	–	.32**	.38**	–	.10	–.01	–	.04	–.25	–
Past Gang Member	.01	.48**	.07	–.07	.10	.21**	–.07	–.03	.20	–.11	.11	–.13
Adjusted R^2	.38	.41	.29	.31	.32	.24	.25	.36	.29	.21	.23	.25

*$p < .05$ (one-tailed). **$p < .01$ (one-tailed).

Table 7.4. *Predicting the Incidence of Self-Reported Delinquency and Drug Use, Gun Owners, Males Only (unstandardized OLS regression coefficients)*

	General Delinquency			Violent Delinquency			Drug Use			Drug Sales		
	Year 2	Year 3	Year 4	Year 2	Year 3	Year 4	Year 2	Year 3	Year 4	Year 2	Year 3	Year 4
Gun Owner	2.39**	1.81**	2.53**	–.01	.48**	.97**	.49	.51*	.64*	.80**	1.55**	2.13**
Gang Member	.98**	1.09**	1.11**	.60*	.75**	.46**	.35**	.56**	.95**	.39**	.52**	.57**
Gun Owner × Gang Member	2.79**	2.51**	4.40**	1.29**	.75**	2.44**	2.31**	.51	3.29**	2.31**	.97**	2.01**
Future Gang Member	.58*	.26	–	.33**	.39**	–	.17	–.01	–	.09	–.17	–
Past Gang Member	–.11	.44**	.04	–.06	.08	.20**	–.06	–.05	.15	–.15	.06	–.16
Adjusted R^2	.41	.43	.34	.31	.30	.40	.33	.35	.28	.36	.28	.35

*p < .05 (one-tailed). **p < .01 (one-tailed).

To begin, it is worth noting that all of the equations in the tables that follow explain more of the variance in the dependent variables than those reported in Chapter 6. In many instances the increase is rather dramatic. In addition, generally more variance is explained in the equations with the gun-owning measure (Table 7.4) as opposed to the gun-carrying measure (Table 7.3). The former does a remarkably good job of explaining the variation in delinquency with coefficients of determination varying between about 28% and 43%.

The equations in Table 7.3 show that for all three years those who carry guns have a significantly greater propensity to commit general delinquency. In other words, carrying a gun significantly contributes to general delinquency. In addition, the impact of gun carrying on violence, drug use, and drug selling is significant at Year 4. Gun carrying also contributes significantly to drug use in Year 2. In all years gang members commit more acts of delinquency, violence, and drug use than those who are not in gangs and do not carry guns. Gang membership also significantly contributes to drug sales in the first two years when the boys are younger but fades to insignificance as they age.

Adolescent males who are both gang members and gun carriers commit significantly more acts of all forms of delinquency in all of the three years. This means that there are interactions between gang membership and gun carrying that increase the number of these forms of delinquency that these boys commit. In addition, these interaction effects increase in size over time for general delinquency, drug use, and drug sales. For violent delinquency, however, the interactions decrease in size as the boys get older. Perhaps they are less compulsive with regard to using violence as they age. Finally, when controlling for the gun carrying and gang membership main effects and the interactions, we find evidence that future gang members do commit significantly more acts of violent delinquency in Years 2 and 3 than those who were never a gang member, but this is not true for general delinquency, drug use, or drug sales. So there is some evidence that gangs select members who have a violent past. As in Chapter 6, there is strong, consistent evidence of facilitation effects of gang membership for all types of delinquency and less consistent evidence of selection effects, in this case only for violent offenses.

Table 7.4 shows the same equations using the gun ownership variable. Similar to Table 7.3, there are statistically significant main effects of gang membership for every type of delinquency at all the years. Gun ownership, however, is a much more consistent predictor of all forms of delinquency than it was for carrying. That is, owning and carrying a gun for protection has an independent effect on delinquency for most years for all crimes, as does gang membership. In general, the size of the effect of owning increases as the boys get older. For example, the unstandardized regression

Table 7.5. *Prevalence of Gang Membership and Gun Ownership or Carrying and Percentage of Cumulative Delinquent Acts Attributable to Gang Members, Males Only*

	Gang Member Who Owns Gun (n = 590)		Gang Member Who Carries Gun (n = 597)	
	%	Ratio	%	Ratio
Gun Ownership or Carrying and Gang Membership	4.6		2.8	
Delinquent Acts				
General	18.6	4.0	17.8	6.4
Serious	39.4	8.6	24.2	8.6
Moderate	28.5	6.2	9.9	3.5
Minor	21.9	4.8	6.8	2.4
Violent	34.0	7.4	21.0	7.5
Serious Violent	46.7	10.2	28.8	10.3
Property	23.4	5.1	5.1	1.8
Public Disorder	29.0	6.3	7.4	2.6
Drug Sales	18.7	4.1	28.7	10.3
Alcohol Use	20.4	4.4	14.4	5.1
Drug Use	17.6	3.8	16.2	5.8
Arrests	12.4	2.7	8.6	3.1

coefficients for drug sales increase from .80 in Year 2 to 1.55 in Year 3 to 2.13 in Year 4.

In addition, with the exception of drug use at Year 3, for all types of delinquency the interaction between owning guns and gang membership is statistically significant. Generally these interaction coefficients are substantially larger in magnitude than were the interaction coefficients in the equations for simply carrying (Table 7.3).

Overall the pattern of these results is consistent with our core hypotheses. Gang membership consistently facilitates deviant behavior, as does gun carrying, whether the respondent owns the gun or not. Moreover, an interaction between gang membership and gun carrying is evident, and the interaction is stronger for owning and carrying than for just carrying.

Table 7.5 also assesses the impact of the interaction of gun carrying and gang membership on the number of crimes committed by these boys. The data show that 4.6% of boys own and carry guns *and* are gang members, while 2.8% of boys carry guns *and* are gang members. The lower portion of the table shows the percentage of various types of crime in the entire sample of boys committed by each of these groups. It also includes the ratio of the percentage of gun-carrying gang members to the percentage of crimes they commit.

The contribution that gang members who also carry guns make to the volume of crime is very substantial, especially for serious and violent crimes. For example, gang members who carry guns or who own and carry guns commit about 10 times more serious violent crime than one would expect from their numbers in the population. Generally speaking, gang members who carry guns commit many times the number of all types of crimes considered than would be expected from their numbers in the population. In addition, gang members who own and carry guns make particularly large contributions to moderate, minor, property, and public disorder crimes compared with gang members who carry guns but do not own them. On the other hand, gang members who carry guns they do not own are more likely to commit general delinquency and drug crimes, especially drug sales, than are gang members who own the guns that they carry. For other crimes, gang members who own and carry are about equal in the proportion of crimes they commit.

The Impact of Earlier Behavior on Later Patterns of Gun Ownership

Gun ownership (whether of legal or illegal guns) increases with age as males move through the adolescent years. Our final analysis in this chapter concerns the extent to which involvement in gangs during early adolescence and early patterns of gun carrying lead to owning and carrying a gun at Year 4. We are also interested in whether earlier gang membership and gun carrying interact in producing this outcome.

To examine this issue, we present odds ratios for logistic regressions with interactions between gun carrying and gang membership at Year 2 and at Year 3, predicting this outcome in Year 4 (Table 7.6). The omitted comparison group is neither carrying a gun nor being a gang member.

Having a history of carrying guns at Years 2 and 3 significantly and substantially increases the odds of owning and carrying a gun at Year 4. For example, being a gun carrier at Year 2 produces a 5-fold increase, and at Year 3 a 16-fold increase, in the odds of owning and carrying a gun at Year 4. Similarly, being a gun carrier and a gang member in Years 2 and 3 significantly and substantially increases the odds of owning and carrying a gun at Year 4. These enhancement effects yield between 7- and 14-fold increases depending on the year. Finally, gang membership without gun carrying also significantly increases the odds of gun ownership and carrying later, but these effects are substantially smaller than the gun-carrying combinations.

Gun carrying and the interaction of gun carrying and gang membership at an early age significantly and substantially increase the likelihood of owning and carrying guns later in life. Thus, there appears to be continuity

Table 7.6. *Odds Ratios Predicting Gun Ownership, Males Only*

	Gun Owners and Carriers at Year 4	
	Year 2	Year 3
Hidden Gun Carrier and		
Not Gang Member	5.15*	16.27**
Gang Member and		
Not Hidden Gun Carrier	4.75**	3.75**
Hidden Gun Carrier and		
Gang Member	13.85**	6.87**

*p < .05 (one-tailed). **p < .01 (one-tailed).

in this pattern of behavior over adolescence. So discouraging gun carrying early will inhibit gun ownership and carrying later.

Conclusion

This chapter examined the interplay between gang membership, the carrying of illegal guns, and the commission of crime by gang members. In particular, we were interested in determining the degree to which gangs attract those who are already heavily involved in illegal gun carrying and with the ability of gangs to facilitate gun carrying and criminal activity both during membership in the gang and after gang involvement ends. Because one need not necessarily own an illegal gun to carry one, we conduct analyses of these issues separately for those who own and carry guns and for those who carry guns but do not own them.

Substantial numbers of boys in Rochester carry guns on the street and the percentage of gang members who carry is even higher. Indeed, the rate of gun carrying, whether the gun is owned or not, is about 10 times higher for gang members as compared with nonmembers. Furthermore, there are much higher percentages of gang members carrying guns than there are of boys who carry guns they report owning. So gang membership has a profound impact on owning *and* carrying guns, but it has an even greater impact on carrying guns that are not owned.

There is no evidence that gangs select members who are either gun owners or who are gun carriers. Gang membership, however, does facilitate the carrying of guns that are owned once the boys in the Rochester sample join a gang. With regard to simply carrying guns, there is strong, consistent, and significant evidence that gangs facilitate gun carrying for the boys at all ages. In other words, boys in gangs can obtain guns for illegal use, and they do not need to own the gun to use it. The impact of gang membership on gun carrying is not small. Depending on the year the impact can be a 7- or 12-fold increase in the likelihood of carrying a gun. Moreover, the impact of gang membership is much larger and increasing over time for gun carrying compared with smaller declining effects for owning and carrying. At the youngest ages there is a strong facilitation effect of gang membership on owning and carrying.

In addition, at younger ages past gang members continue to have enhanced levels of gun owning and carrying. This suggests that contacts made in the gang may continue to provide access to the acquisition of guns to own and carry upon leaving the gang.

Gangs appear to provide an important service to their members: they open up access to guns that the members can use even if they do not own them. If true, this means that there are fewer illegal guns in the gang world than there are gang members who are willing to carry them. Therefore, interdicting a "gang gun" debilitates gun carrying for many players. Similarly, stopping a boy who already owns a gun from joining a gang does the same. When researchers study gun use among gang members, it is a mistake to ask only about guns that are owned; doing so misses a large number of boys who carry guns that they do not own.

We also analyzed the selection, facilitation, and momentum effects of gang membership and gun carrying on various forms of delinquency. Those who are gang members or who carry guns have elevated levels of delinquency. But there is also a double impact of gang membership and owning and carrying illegal guns. This interaction produces levels of all types of delinquency that are beyond what would be expected from gang membership and owning and carrying guns individually. The effects of the interaction of gang membership and owning and carrying a gun on delinquency are generally larger than the interaction effects of carrying and gang membership – perhaps because guns that are owned can be carried more frequently than those that are borrowed or rented.

As we saw in Chapter 6, gang members are high-rate offenders. Similarly, past research has shown that boys who own and use illegal guns are high-rate offenders (Wright and Rossi, 1986). However, boys in gangs who also carry guns are significantly higher-rate criminal offenders than one would expect from their gun carrying and gang membership alone. They commit many times the number of crimes than one would expect for their population size. The enhanced impact is particularly salient for serious and violent delinquency and for drug sales.

Finally, early involvement in carrying illegal guns, and in carrying illegal guns when a gang member, dramatically increases the odds of owning and carrying illegal guns later in life. Thus, deterring gun carrying in and out of gangs for young people could dramatically reduce the long-term ownership and use of illegal guns for adults.

Gangs and Other Law-Violating Youth Groups

ADOLESCENCE is a very group-oriented stage of the life course. The dominant form of social organization is the peer group, especially age-graded, same-sex peer groups. Thus, it is neither surprising that much criminological research has focused on the impact of peer group influences on delinquency nor surprising that this research has shown that group influences, in particular associating with delinquent peers, are among the strongest and most consistent predictors of delinquent behavior (Thornberry and Krohn, 1997). This observation is consistent with a fundamental proposition of social network theory – namely, that all social networks constrain the behavior of their members to be consistent with the dominant behavioral themes of the group (Krohn, 1986).

From this perspective the observation that gang members have higher rates of delinquency and violence than nonmembers may be somewhat spurious, simply reflecting the fact that gangs are one form of a delinquent peer group (Miller, 1982). If so, the "gang effect," which has been frequently noted in the literature and in previous chapters, would really be a simple "peer effect" and gangs would merely be one type of delinquent peer group, albeit at the more extreme end of the continuum. If this view is correct, we should not expect differences in the level of involvement in delinquent behavior between adolescents who are members of street gangs and nonmembers who are involved in highly delinquent social networks.

Another school of thought, however, argues that street gangs are fundamentally different from nongang delinquent peer groups. Based on her observational research, for example, Moore has concluded that "gangs are no longer just at the rowdy end of the continuum of local adolescent groups – they are now really outside that continuum" (1991: 132). Klein makes a similar point: "[S]treet gangs are something special, something qualitatively

different from other groups and from other categories of law breakers"
(1995: 197). From this perspective, gangs are predicted to exert a stronger
criminogenic influence on the behavior of their members than the influence exerted by even highly delinquent, but nongang, peer groups.

Gangs may be "qualitatively different" from delinquent peer groups in
their criminogenic effects for several reasons. They center around gang
structure and the group processes that appear to be unique to gangs. Gangs
have a more formal, hierarchical structure as compared with other adolescent peer groups. Klein (1971, 1995), for example, points to the powerful
impact that group cohesion, brought about in part by the structure of the
gang, plays in generating crime, especially violent crime. In addition, unlike
most delinquent peer groups, gangs are strongly territorial (Klein, 1996).
The staking out and protection of "turf" is another source of conflict and
violence that appears to be absent from nongang peer groups.

Another cause of the added criminogenic impact of gangs, as compared
with delinquent peer groups, is the powerful group processes associated with
them. Short and Strodtbeck (1965), Miller et al. (1961), and Jansyn (1966)
all point to the role of violence and aggression in promoting group cohesion, leadership, and solidarity in the gang. More recently, Decker (1996)
has identified a seven-step process, apparently unique to gangs, that yields
higher rates of crime, especially violent crime. According to Decker, the
process moves through the following seven steps:

1. Loose bonds to the gang;
2. Collective identification of threat from a rival gang (through rumors, sym-
   bolic shows of force, cruising, and mythic violence), reinforcing the cen-
   trality of violence that expands the number of participants and increases
   cohesion;
3. A mobilizing event possibly, but not necessarily, violence;
4. Escalation of activity;
5. Violent event;
6. Rapid de-escalation;
7. Retaliation. (1996: 262)

Gang studies that focus on the impact of structure, territory, and group processes imply that these factors are either absent or much less pronounced
in nongang peer groups. If this view is correct, then gang members should
have higher rates of delinquent behavior than do nonmembers who associate with even highly delinquent peers.

Although Moore, Klein, and other gang researchers view gangs as "qualitatively different" from other law-violating peer groups, there is actually very
little empirical evidence on this point. This chapter examines this issue by
identifying nonmembers who are involved in highly delinquent social networks and comparing their delinquent behavior with that of gang members.

We examine several types of deviant behavior to see if the impact of the gang is actually distinguishable from the impact of the delinquent peer group.

Prior Research

Preliminary examinations of this issue have been reported using data from the Rochester Youth Development Study and the Seattle Social Development Project (Battin-Pearson et al., 1998) and from the Denver Youth Survey (Huizinga, 1996).[1] Battin-Pearson et al. (1998) divided members of the Seattle sample into three groups: youths who were gang members during the past year, youths who were members of nongang but law-violating youth groups, and those who were neither. They then examined the individual offense rates, both concurrently and with one-year lags, that each group reported committing. Comparisons were made on a number of self-report indices – general delinquency, violent and nonviolent delinquency, drug selling, and use of several different substances – as well as court-recorded, official delinquency. Battin-Pearson et al. (1998) found that gang members report substantially higher levels of involvement in delinquency and substance use than do the members of the other groups. For example, the mean number of delinquent acts reported by gang members is 25.6, as compared with 13.0 for members of the nongang law-violating youth groups and 3.1 for those with nondelinquent peers.

Huizinga (1996) examined this topic using data from the Denver Youth Survey. "Youth aged 14–19 in 1991 were classified into four groups – those who had low, medium, and high involvement with delinquent friends, and those who were gang members" (Huizinga, 1996: 1). For both male and female subjects there is a substantially higher prevalence of serious assaults and total assaults for the gang members as compared with the nonmembers who had highly delinquent peers. For example, among the males 72% of the gang members reported involvement in serious assault, whereas only 20% of the nonmembers with highly delinquent peers did so. For the females, 72% of the gang members reported involvement in serious assault, whereas only 13% of the nonmembers with highly delinquent peers did so.

These earlier studies used rather generous inclusion criteria for establishing the comparison group of respondents who were not gang members but who associated with other law-violating groups. Battin-Pearson et al. (1998) included youths who were involved in highly delinquent peer networks *and* youths who were involved in more marginally delinquent peer networks in the comparison group. Huizinga (1996) included a third of the nonmembers in the high involvement group. Combining youths who fall all along this

---

[1] Because the Rochester Youth Development Study results reported by Battin-Pearson et al. (1998) are presented in more detail later in this chapter, they are not reviewed here.

continuum into one group may mute the relationship of delinquent peers and delinquency and, therefore, make the distinction between gangs and delinquent peer groups starker than it in fact is. Because of this possibility we provide a more conservative test of the hypothesis that gangs are different from delinquent peer groups, by making the definition of the delinquent peer group more extreme. First, we divide the nonmembers into quartiles based on their scores on our delinquent peer associations scale and compare the rates of delinquency of these four groups with those for gang members. Second, we compare gang members with only those nonmembers who have the most delinquent social networks. Third, we estimate regression models in which we regress delinquency and drug use on gang membership, after the variable "associations with delinquent peers" is held constant. Given the temporal distribution of gang membership by gender, all of these analyses are conducted separately for male and female respondents.

Results for Male Respondents

We begin by comparing the gang members with the nonmembers, especially those who have the highest density of delinquent friends. To do so, the respondents are divided into five groups at each wave. One group comprises respondents who indicated that they were active gang members at that wave. Respondents who were not gang members are divided into quartiles based on their association with delinquent peers at that wave. The peer association scale is based on items that ask each respondent to indicate how many of his friends, defined as the group of kids the respondent usually "hung around" with, were involved in eight delinquent activities, ranging from truancy to aggravated assault. The lowest quartile represents respondents who have the least deviant, most prosocial peers; the highest quartile represents respondents who have the most deviant, least prosocial peers.

It is instructive to compare the mean scores on the association with delinquent peers scale across these groups. Although gang membership clearly implies associations with delinquent others, being a member of a gang does not necessarily mean that one has *more* friends who are delinquent than do respondents who do not belong to a gang. This is evident in the data presented in Table 8.1.

Because scores on the peer associations scale were used to divide nongang respondents into quartiles, an increase in delinquent associations has to be found as one moves from Group I to Group IV. The most important finding, however, is that there is little difference in the level of associations with delinquent peers between gang members and the highest quartile of nonmembers. At most waves the mean scores are just about the same; only at Wave 5 do gang members have significantly more delinquent

Table 8.1. *Mean Scores on Peer Delinquency for Gang Members and Nonmembers, Males Only*

	Nonmember Quartile Groupings on Associations with Delinquent Peers				Gang Members
Wave	I (Low)	II	III	IV (High)	
2	1.00	1.12	1.30	1.89	1.79
	(158)	(176)	(110)	(124)	(85)
3	1.00	1.12	1.31	1.92	1.92
	(153)	(134)	(144)	(123)	(79)
4	1.00	1.13	1.31	1.90	1.89
	(176)	(128)	(130)	(146)	(67)
5	1.00	1.13	1.32	1.87	2.16*
	(152)	(129)	(140)	(150)	(51)
6	1.00	1.13	1.35	1.99	1.97
	(153)	(132)	(136)	(152)	(54)
7	1.00	1.14	1.36	2.00	2.05
	(140)	(130)	(153)	(141)	(35)
8	1.00	1.15	1.35	2.00	2.03
	(138)	(124)	(130)	(139)	(35)
9	1.00	1.14	1.36	1.99	2.08
	(142)	(137)	(120)	(161)	(28)

Note: The n's for each group are in parentheses. Significance tests are for the comparison between Group IV and gang members.
*$p < .05$ (two-tailed t-test).

friends than the highest quartile of nonmembers. Substantively, therefore, the delinquent quality of the peer networks of the gang members and of the nonmembers in the top quartile is essentially the same. In addition, the fact that these two types of groups have approximately the same proportion of delinquent friends provides an empirical justification for comparing the gang members with the highest quartile group in order to determine if gangs appear to be "qualitatively different" from even highly delinquent peer groups as Klein, Moore, and others have argued.

With one exception the results are presented in a series of bar graphs that compare the nonmembers in the highest quartile on association with delinquent peers to the gang members. The data for the lower three quartiles do not bear directly on the hypothesis and, as expected, the delinquency rates for these groups are lower than those in the highest quartile. With the exception of the results for general delinquency, therefore, the results for these groups are not reported. In that case the full set of results is presented to illustrate the pattern of findings. With this in mind, the central question is: are gang members more involved in delinquency and drug use than even those nonmembers whose peer social network has an equally high proportion of delinquent friends? In responding to this question, we use only the frequency of offending, not the prevalence of offending, as the outcome variable.[2] The pattern of results and the substantive conclusions are basically the same for the prevalence and frequency measures.

Quartile Comparisons

The first set of comparisons focuses on involvement in general delinquency and violence. Gang membership is often associated with violent offending, and therefore, if gangs have an impact on behavior over and above having delinquent friends, we would be most likely to observe a difference in the rates of violent offenses. It is also likely that being part of a gang places youth in positions to commit a wide variety of delinquent behaviors. Therefore, we anticipate that gang members will also have higher prevalence and incidence rates on the general delinquency index.

The pattern of results is consistent with the hypothesis that gangs are "qualitatively different" (Table 8.2). Among the nonmembers, respondents who score in the higher quartiles on the associations with delinquent peers scale also report higher rates of general delinquency at all eight waves. The differences are particularly pronounced between those in Group III and those in the highest quartile, Group IV. Even so, respondents who are gang members have the highest rates of general delinquency in all comparisons. The frequency of general delinquency among gang members is significantly higher than the rates reported by respondents in the highest quartile of associations with delinquent peers. The magnitude of the differences between gang members and these nonmembers is often quite large, especially at later waves. For example, at Wave 8 the mean frequency of delinquency is 35.07 for those with highly delinquent peers but it is almost double, 66.39, for the gang members.

If the gang members are compared with adolescents in more "run-of-the-mill" delinquent social networks, the impact of gang membership is even more pronounced. For example, comparing them with those in the next highest quartile (Group III), we see that the frequency of delinquency is about five times as great.

---

[2] The frequency measures for delinquency and drug involvement are highly skewed; most respondents commit very few acts, whereas a small number of respondents commit many acts. To reduce the impact of skewness, the natural logarithm of the frequency scores is used in the significance testing and regression analysis to follow. In tables presenting mean frequency scores, however, the actual means (not the log-transformed means) are presented to provide the reader a better sense of the magnitude of the effects.

Table 8.2. *Frequency of Self-Reported General Delinquency for Gang Members and Nonmembers, Males Only*

Wave	Nonmember Quartile Groupings on Associations with Delinquent Peers				Gang Members
	I (Low)	II	III	IV (High)	
2	1.25	2.54	5.03	20.46	34.71*
3	0.34	2.19	5.88	21.28	56.06*
4	0.72	3.14	8.50	20.69	41.45*
5	1.23	3.71	6.47	20.06	44.17*
6	1.67	1.42	5.04	29.05	38.01*
7	1.06	6.35	6.62	26.30	38.79*
8	3.12	8.07	12.64	35.07	66.39*
9	1.69	4.54	12.24	33.11	79.33*

Note: The n's for these groups are the same as those in Table 8.1. Significance tests are for the comparison between Group IV and gang members.
*p < .05 (one-tailed t-test).

The pattern for general delinquency is also evident for violent crimes (Figure 8.1). The rates of violent offenses for male gang members are significantly, and often substantially, higher than those for the nonmembers in the highest quartile at all eight waves. The differences for violent offending are particularly large at the earlier waves (Waves 2 through 4). The nonmembers report an average of about two violent offenses per six months at these ages, whereas the gang members report four times as many – about eight violent offenses.

Matched Sample Comparisons

Although the division of respondents who are not gang members into quartiles based on the degree to which they associate with delinquent peers is similar to the strategy used by Battin-Pearson et al. (1998) and Huizinga (1996), the use of quartiles is somewhat arbitrary. For example, there are substantially more subjects in the highest quartile nonmember group than there are in the gang member group at each of the waves, which increases the risk of including subjects who are not involved in highly delinquent networks (see Table 8.1). Another strategy to test the hypothesis is to compare gang members with an equal number of nonmembers based on the highest density of delinquent peers in their social network. To accomplish this we did the following. At each wave, if the number of gang members is *n*, we selected

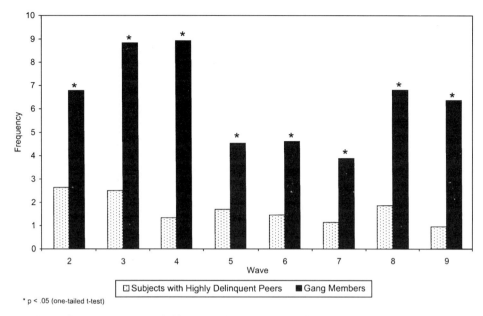

* p < .05 (one-tailed t-test)

Figure 8.1. Frequency of Self-Reported Violence for Gang Members and Subjects with Highly Delinquent Peers (Quartile Measure), Males Only

the top n nonmembers on the associations with delinquent peers measure as the comparison group. Because of tied scores, the numbers are not exact matches. At Wave 2, for example, there were 86 male gang members and we compare them with the 88 nonmembers with the highest delinquent peers scores. We refer to these nonmembers as the "matched" group.

Again, we begin the analysis by comparing the two groups on our measure of associations with delinquent peers. The data in Table 8.3 show that the matched group of nonmembers actually reports having a significantly greater number of delinquent peers than do the gang members. This finding is unexpected, given the common stereotype of the street gang as the most extreme form of delinquent peer network. It underscores the observation that gang members are versatile in many aspects of life (Short and Strodtbeck, 1965) and that they do not only associate with delinquent others. More important, it provides a very conservative test of the hypothesis that the gang is "qualitatively different," for now the issue is whether gang members are more involved in delinquency than are nonmembers, even though the nonmembers report, on average, a greater proportion of delinquent friends.

Figure 8.2 presents the data for general delinquency. Gang members have higher frequency rates at six of the waves and the differences are statistically significant at Waves 3, 4, 5, and 8. When we turn to violent offenses

Table 8.3. *Mean Scores on Peer Delinquency for Gang
Members and a Matched Number of Nonmembers, Males Only*

Wave	Matched Number of Nonmembers	Gang Members
2	2.04	1.79*
	(88)	(86)
3	2.12	1.92*
	(82)	(80)
4	2.20	1.89*
	(76)	(68)
5	2.34	2.16*
	(51)	(51)
6	2.36	1.97*
	(58)	(55)
7	2.61	2.05*
	(39)	(36)
8	2.68	2.03*
	(35)	(35)
9	2.83	2.08*
	(29)	(28)

*p < .05 (two-tailed t-test).

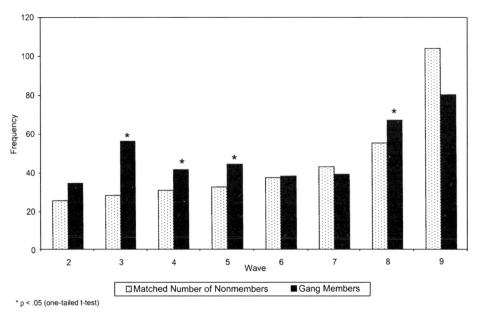

* p < .05 (one-tailed t-test)

Figure 8.2. Frequency of Self-Reported General Delinquency for Gang Members and
a Matched Number of Nonmembers, Males Only

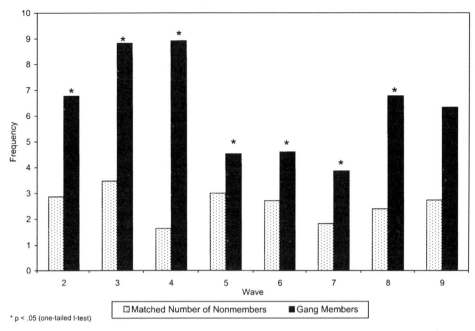

* p < .05 (one-tailed t-test)

Figure 8.3. Frequency of Self-Reported Violence for Gang Members and a Matched Number of Nonmembers, Males Only

(Figure 8.3), we see even stronger support for the hypothesis. At all waves gang members have a higher frequency of violence. All of the differences are statistically significant except those at Wave 9, when the number of gang members is the lowest, making statistical significance difficult to obtain.

Summary

Comparing the frequency of both general delinquency and violence for male gang members and nonmembers suggests that the impact of membership in a street gang is greater than the impact of associations with even highly delinquent peers. When we compare gang members with the group of nonmembers who ranked in the highest quartile in terms of delinquent peer associations, gang members have significantly higher rates of general delinquency and violent delinquency than do the nonmembers. When we restrict the comparison to an equal number of nonmembers, the same trend is evident. Even though the matched sample has a higher density of delinquent peers than do the gang members, the gang members exhibit a greater involvement in violence and, to a lesser extent, general delinquency. It appears that being a member of a gang has an impact on delinquency that cannot be attributed simply to the fact that the gang provides a setting in which it is relatively easy to associate with delinquent friends.

Table 8.4. *Mean Scores on Peer Delinquency for Gang*
Members and Nonmembers, Females Only

	Nonmember Quartile Groupings on Associations with Delinquent Peers				Gang Members
Wave	I (Low)	II	III	IV (High)	
2	1.00	1.11	1.36	1.94	1.64*
	(48)	(54)	(57)	(47)	(42)
3	1.00	1.12	1.36	2.11	1.65*
	(62)	(44)	(55)	(46)	(36)
4	1.00	1.13	1.34	1.85	1.76
	(64)	(63)	(43)	(55)	(19)

Note: Significance tests are for the comparison between Group
IV and gang members.
*p < .05 (two-tailed t-test).

Results for Female Respondents

As noted earlier, there are fewer female gang members than male gang
members. In fact, after Wave 4 there are too few gang members to make
reliable comparisons; therefore, comparisons are examined only for Waves 2
through 4.

Comparing female gang members and nonmembers in terms of their
associations with delinquent peers yields similar results to those found for
males (Table 8.4). Indeed, the highest quartile of female nonmembers has
significantly *more* delinquent friends than the female gang members in two
of the three waves.

Female gang members report a higher frequency of general delinquency than do those in the highest quartile of nonmembers (Figure 8.4).
The comparisons at Waves 2 and 4 attain statistical significance. For violence
(Figure 8.5), female gang members have higher frequency rates at all three
waves. All of these differences are significant and rather substantial. For
example, at Wave 4 the nonmembers report less than one violent offense
on average, whereas the female gang members report about six.

When the female gang members are compared with an equal number
of nonmembers who have high associations with delinquent peers, the
matched group of nonmembers reports having *more* delinquent friends than
do the gang members at all three waves (see Table 8.5). Despite this, female
gang members generally have a higher frequency of both general delinquency and violent offenses (Figures 8.6 and 8.7, respectively). For general
delinquency the frequency comparisons are significant at Waves 2 and 4; for
violence all comparisons are significant.

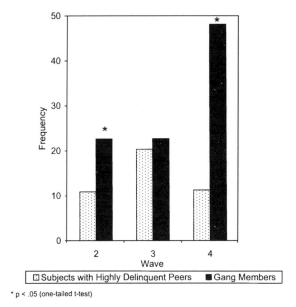

* p < .05 (one-tailed t-test)

Figure 8.4. Frequency of Self-Reported General Delinquency for Gang Members and Subjects with Highly Delinquent Peers (Quartile Measure), Females Only

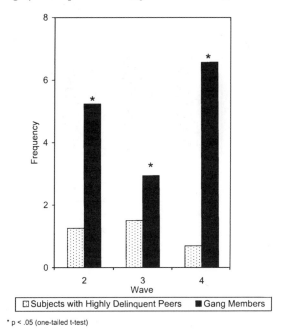

* p < .05 (one-tailed t-test)

Figure 8.5. Frequency of Self-Reported Violence for Gang Members and Subjects with Highly Delinquent Peers (Quartile Measure), Females Only

Table 8.5. *Mean Scores on Peer Delinquency for Gang Members*
and a Matched Number of Nonmembers, Females Only

Wave	Matched Number of Nonmembers	Gang Members
2	1.94	1.64*
	(47)	(42)
3	2.22	1.65*
	(39)	(37)
4	2.19	1.76*
	(22)	(19)

*$p < .05$ (two-tailed t-test).

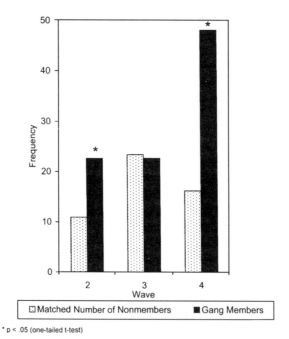

Figure 8.6. Frequency of Self-Reported General Delinquency for Gang Members and a Matched Number of Nonmembers, Females Only

Summary

Gang membership among females is, by and large, limited to the early teenage years and therefore comparisons of female gang members with nonmembers are limited to Waves 2 through 4. Results are similar to those found for the male respondents. Female gang members have a higher

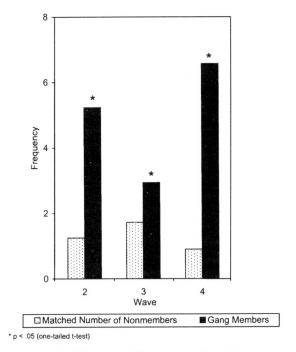

Figure 8.7. Frequency of Self-Reported Violence for Gang Members and a Matched Number of Nonmembers, Females Only

prevalence and frequency of general delinquency and violence than do even those nonmembers who score high on the delinquent associations scale.

The pattern of results for both the male and female subjects suggests that gangs may well be "qualitatively different" from simple delinquent peer groups in terms of the delinquency of their members. Gang members report higher rates of delinquency and violence than nonmembers in highly delinquent peer groups. When the comparisons are to somewhat less delinquent peer groups, for example, those near the median (results not shown except for Table 8.2), the differences are even starker.

Drug Use and Drug Sales

Hypotheses about the impact of gang membership on both the use and sale of drugs are less clear-cut than they are for delinquency. Drug use may be higher among gang members simply because they are more likely to find themselves in situations and with people who have access to and who use drugs. On the other hand, adolescents who associate with delinquent friends may be in similar situations. Given the relative ease of access to drugs and the widespread use of drugs among adolescents, gang membership may not be particularly important, relative to simple delinquent peer groups, in generating drug use.

In contrast, there has been some suggestion that gangs have become heavily involved in the sale of drugs (see Jankowski, 1991; Skolnick et al., 1988) as a means of generating income. The organization of the gang, however loose, may facilitate this type of activity. Klein (1995), Decker, Bynum, and Weisel (1998), and Decker (2000) argue, however, that although gang *members* may be involved in the sale of drugs, *gangs* are typically not organized around such activity. In the analysis to follow, we examine whether gang membership is associated with both the use and sale of drugs, over and above the effects of associating with delinquent peers. Again the analyses are separated by gender.

Comparisons for Male Respondents

Figure 8.8 presents comparisons in the rates of drug use between male gang members and nonmembers in the highest quartile of association with delinquent peers. Gang members generally have higher frequency rates of drug use than the nonmembers with the most delinquent social networks. The differences between the gang members and nonmembers are significant at Waves 3, 4, 5, and 9. When male gang members are compared with the matched group of nonmembers, however (Figure 8.9), none of the differences is significant.

We anticipate stronger gang effects for the sale of drugs than were found for drug use. Figure 8.10 contains the results comparing the frequency of selling drugs for the male gang members and the nonmembers in the highest quartile. Gang members have a higher rate of drug selling at six of the eight waves, and the differences are significant at five of eight waves. When the comparison between male gang members and nonmembers is limited to the matched group of nonmembers, these differences are not evident, however (Figure 8.11). Indeed, none of the differences is statistically significant. Overall, there is no clear pattern for drug sales.

Comparisons for Female Respondents

We now turn to the data for the female subjects, beginning with the quartile comparisons. Female gang members have significantly higher rates of drug use than do nongang females for two of the three waves for which comparisons can be made (Figures 8.12 and 8.13). This is true when

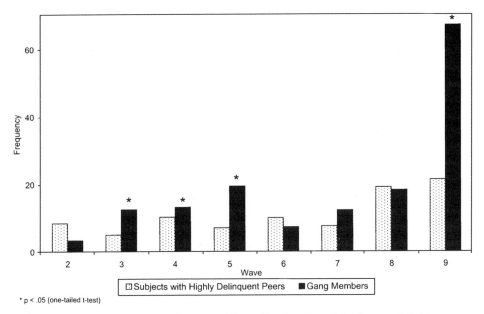

* p < .05 (one-tailed t-test)

Figure 8.8. Frequency of Self-Reported Drug Use for Gang Members and Subjects with Highly Delinquent Peers (Quartile Measure), Males Only

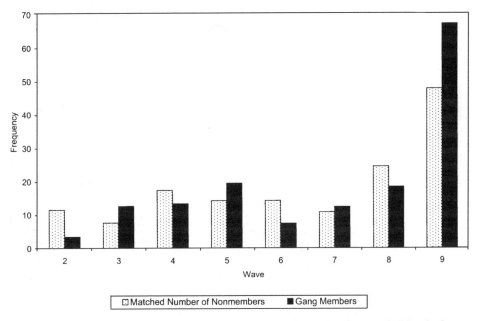

Figure 8.9. Frequency of Self-Reported Drug Use for Gang Members and a Matched Number of Nonmembers, Males Only

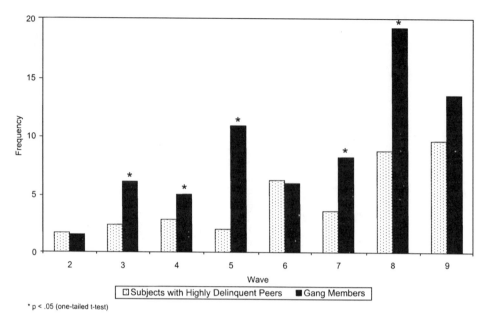

Figure 8.10. Frequency of Self-Reported Drug Sales for Gang Members and Subjects with Highly Delinquent Peers (Quartile Measure), Males Only

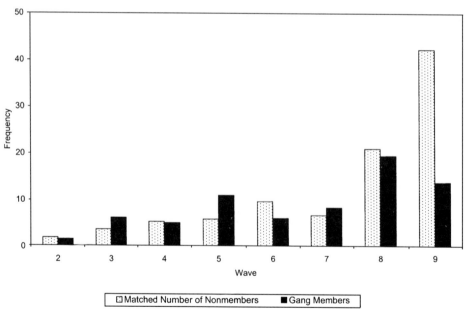

Figure 8.11. Frequency of Self-Reported Drug Sales for Gang Members and a Matched Number of Nonmembers, Males Only

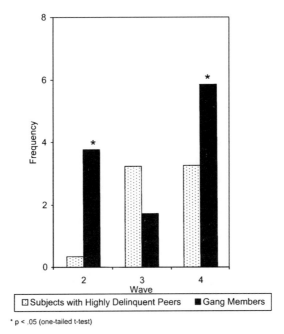

* p < .05 (one-tailed t-test)

Figure 8.12. Frequency of Self-Reported Drug Use for Gang Members and Subjects with Highly Delinquent Peers (Quartile Measure), Females Only

gang members are compared with the highest quartile of nonmembers (Figure 8.12) and in the more conservative comparison (Figure 8.13), which uses an equal number of nonmembers who associate with highly delinquent friends.

Female gang members also have higher rates of drug selling than nonmembers whether the comparisons are made to the highest quartile or to the matched group (Figures 8.14 and 8.15, respectively). In general, the frequency rates of selling drugs are at least three times as high for female gang members as they are for nonmembers who have many delinquent friends. Only one of the six comparisons (Figure 8.14; Wave 4) is statistically significant, however. For females, the failure to find significant differences between gang members and nonmembers may be due to the limited involvement that females have in drug selling.

Summary

Starting with drug use, the results suggest that, for the male members of the Rochester sample, gang members have somewhat higher rates of use than adolescents who associate with highly delinquent peer groups.

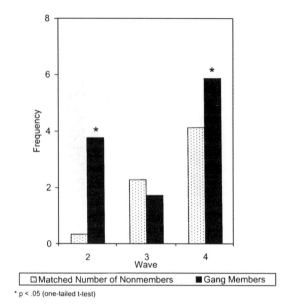

* p < .05 (one-tailed t-test)

Figure 8.13. Frequency of Self-Reported Drug Use for Gang Members and a Matched Number of Nonmembers, Females Only

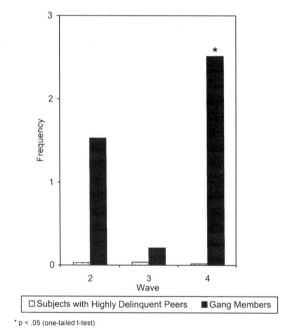

* p < .05 (one-tailed t-test)

Figure 8.14. Frequency of Self-Reported Drug Sales for Gang Members and Subjects with Highly Delinquent Peers (Quartile Measure), Females Only

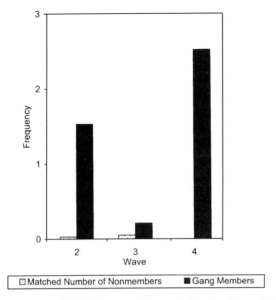

Figure 8.15. Frequency of Self-Reported Drug Sales for Gang Members and a Matched Number of Nonmembers, Females Only

The differences observed here, however, are not as great or as consistent as those observed for the delinquency measures. For females, the gang context does seem to lead to somewhat more drug use, perhaps because it leads to associations with older males who use drugs. These relatively weak gang effects on drug use are not unexpected. Drug use is more widely dispersed in the juvenile population than some other forms of delinquent behavior, for example, violence. Therefore, although associating with others is a key factor in increasing the probability of use, doing so within a gang context does not appear to be particularly important for males.

The results for drug sales demonstrate a slightly greater impact of gang membership. Both male and female gang members are more likely to engage in drug selling than the highest quartile of nonmembers. For males, however, when the comparison is made to the matched group of nonmembers, there is no evidence of a significant gang effect on the frequency of drug selling. Female gang members are at least three times more likely to sell drugs than nonmembers regardless of how nonmembers are categorized. Because of the low prevalence and frequency rates, however, these differences are generally not statistically significant.

Regression Analysis

An alternate way to investigate the relative impact of gang membership and associations with delinquent peers is to include measures of each of

Table 8.6. *The Relative Impact of Gang Membership and Association with Delinquent Peers on Delinquency, Males Only (standardized regression coefficients)*

	Year 1	Year 2	Year 3	Year 4
General Delinquency				
Gang Membership	.21**	.33**	.18**	.06
Delinquent Peers	.54**	.25**	.38**	.35**
Adjusted R^2	.42	.23	.23	.14
Violence				
Gang Membership	.31**	.34**	.20**	.15**
Delinquent Peers	.47**	.17**	.26**	.31**
Adjusted R^2	.42	.18	.15	.15
Drug Use				
Gang Membership	.05	.18**	−.04	.07*
Delinquent Peers	.44**	.28**	.45**	.38**
Adjusted R^2	.21	.15	.18	.17
Drug Sales				
Gang Membership	.13**	.24**	.12**	−.06
Delinquent Peers	.30**	.25**	.24**	.30**
Adjusted R^2	.13	.17	.09	.08

Note: The dependent variable in each equation is logged.
*$p < .05$ (one-tailed test). **$p < .01$ (one-tailed test).

these concepts in the same regression equation predicting delinquency. If the coefficient for gang membership is not significant when the impact of associations with delinquent peers is held constant, it would suggest that what appears to be a gang effect is simply a peer effect, produced by high associations with delinquent peers. On the basis of the previous group comparisons, however, we hypothesize that being a gang member will contribute to the explanation of delinquency over and above the variance explained by associations with delinquent peers. To conduct this analysis, we combined adjacent waves of data on delinquency and drug involvement into yearly rates. The peer delinquency scale and a dummy variable indicating whether the respondent was a gang member are used to predict the frequency of each of the four indicators of delinquency and drug involvement.

Table 8.6 presents the results for the male respondents. Association with delinquent peers is significantly related to each of the four measures of delinquency in each of the four years. Given the extensive literature indicating the importance of delinquent peers in predicting delinquency (see Thornberry and Krohn, 1997), these findings are certainly anticipated. In addition, however, after the effect of associations with delinquent peers is held constant,

Table 8.7. *The Relative Impact of Gang Membership and Association with Delinquent Peers on Delinquency, Females Only (standardized regression coefficients)*

	Year 1
General Delinquency	
Gang Membership	.26**
Delinquent Peers	.51**
Adjusted R^2	.39
Violence	
Gang Membership	.42**
Delinquent Peers	.27**
Adjusted R^2	.30
Drug Use	
Gang Membership	.25**
Delinquent Peers	.35**
Adjusted R^2	.23
Drug Sales	
Gang Membership	.13*
Delinquent Peers	.32**
Adjusted R^2	.13

Note: The dependent variable in each equation is logged.
*$p < .05$ (one-tailed test).
**$p < .01$ (one-tailed test).

current gang membership is generally related to general delinquency, violent delinquency, drug use, and drug sales. These effects are significant at all four years for violence, at the first three years for general delinquency and drug sales, and at Years 2 and 4 for drug use.

Parallel data for the female respondents are presented in Table 8.7. Because of the limited number of females in gangs after Wave 4, only Year 1 data are used to estimate these regression equations. The results indicate that for females, gang membership is significantly related to all four types of delinquent behavior, after the effect of associations with delinquent peers is held constant.

Summary

Prior research has clearly demonstrated that associations with delinquent peers and membership in street gangs are each a powerful predictor of delinquent behavior. Because these concepts are conceptually interrelated, though, these two findings may be redundant. That is, street gangs may be nothing more than one variant of a delinquent peer group, and really all that is involved in the impact of gangs on behavior is a specific version of the well-established impact of peers. Gang researchers often disagree with this view, however. Many of them (e.g., Klein, 1995; Moore, 1991) have suggested that gangs are qualitatively different from peer groups, generating an enhanced involvement in delinquency, over and above that generated by simple association with delinquent peers.

The Rochester Youth Development Study data indicate that gang membership is indeed different from associations with delinquent peer groups. Even though gang members have the same density of delinquent peers in their social networks as the nonmembers in the highest quartile group and fewer delinquent friends than the nonmember matched group, they generally exhibit higher rates of delinquency and drug involvement.

It is important to bear in mind that these findings are based on a conservative test of the hypothesis: gang members are only compared with nonmembers in highly delinquent networks. When comparisons are made to those in more average or typical delinquent peer networks, the differences are far more dramatic.

The findings presented here are particularly strong for those behaviors that are typically associated with gangs. The most convincing evidence of the effect of gang membership is for violent delinquent behavior. Gang membership also has the expected effect on the sale of drugs. In contrast, for drug use, a behavior that is widely dispersed in the juvenile population, being a member of a gang has no greater impact than associations with delinquent peers.

These findings have important implications for understanding the dynamics of delinquency, especially serious and violent delinquency. Future work must examine what it is about the organization and culture of a gang that produces this effect on behavior. For, in combination with the results presented in Chapters 6 and 7, these results highlight the strong, short-term criminogenic effect of the gang. Gang membership appears to facilitate delinquency, violence, drug involvement, and gun carrying. Moreover, this effect seems to be due to the specific impact of the gang, and not merely the fact that gangs provide access to delinquent peers. If gangs have this short-term impact on their members, do they also exert a long-term toll, interrupting the normal course of development? That is the last issue we address – the long-term consequences of gang membership.

Long-Term Consequences of Gang Membership

GANGS HAVE A POWERFUL, contemporaneous effect on the lives of the adolescents who become involved with them. It is also reasonable to expect that gang membership will have long-term consequences as well, interfering with the normal course of adolescent development and affecting the transition to adult roles and statuses. Although reasonable, there has been surprisingly little research conducted in this area. As early as 1971 Klein commented that "Though the need is great, there has been no careful study of gang members as they move on into adult status" (1971: 136), a view more recently advanced by Hagedorn (1998) and by Decker and Lauritsen (1996). In this chapter we examine whether adolescent involvement in street gangs has long-term consequences in such important developmental areas as family formation, parenthood, and employment. We begin by introducing basic concepts from the life-course perspective to guide the analysis.

Life-Course Perspective

The life-course perspective recognizes that as people age they enter and move along various trajectories. Trajectories are age-graded patterns of development with respect to major social institutions such as family, school, and work. They capture the long view of development, "linking social and psychological states over a substantial portion of the life span" (Elder, 1997: 955). Short-term changes in the life course, including movement into and out of trajectories, are referred to as transitions.

One of the most volatile stages of human development occurs as individuals move from adolescence to adulthood. These years are "demographically dense" (Rindfuss, 1991) because they involve transitions in multiple institutional arenas. The important transitions that adolescents are expected to make include completing their education, leaving the parental home,

163

beginning a stable pattern of employment, getting married, and having children (Kamerman, 1981). Transitions are normative in that they are expected to take place in roughly the order just presented and at particular ages in the life cycle. In fact, however, the sequence of transitions tends to be more complicated and is often quite disorderly (Rindfuss, Swicegood, and Rosenfeld, 1987).

Disorder in the life course can be thought of in at least three different ways. One is the failure to complete some developmental tasks before moving on to later, age-graded roles. For example, school dropouts fail to complete one of the most fundamental requisites of adolescent development – their basic education – before they move on to other trajectories like work and family. A second source of disorder in the life course is transitions that are out of sequence. In our culture, for example, it is expected that marriage will precede parenthood. A third sense in which there is disorder in the life course is when transitions are made off time – either too early or too late. Teen parenthood is a good example of an early or "precocious" transition.

Disorder in the life course is not simply a descriptive concept; disorder often has problematic consequences. Failure to complete developmental tasks and off-time, out-of-sequence transitions often reduce long-term economic prospects and increase economic burdens, stress, and depression when one tries to assume a role for which one is not prepared. In addition, disorder in life-course transitions often has cumulative, cascading effects, creating hardship in multiple domains. For example, teenage parenthood can necessitate dropping out of school, which in turn may limit job opportunities, increase economic disadvantage, reduce prospects of marriage, and disrupt parenting behaviors. Because of these and other consequences, it is essential that we understand the causes of disorder in the life course.

Gangs, Crime, and Disorder in the Life Course

Among the probable contributing factors, recent interest has focused on deviant behavior, including adolescent delinquency and drug use (Jessor et al., 1991; Krohn, Lizotte, and Perez, 1997; Newcomb and Bentler, 1988; Sampson and Laub, 1993). Although the long-term deleterious effects of involvement in adolescent deviance have been recognized since criminologists began to study delinquency systematically, not until researchers obtained longitudinal data could the effect of deviance on the life course be empirically investigated. A growing number of studies have found that involvement in delinquent behavior increases the likelihood that a person will experience disorderly transitions in the domains just identified. Children who either use drugs or are involved in other forms of delinquent behavior are more likely to drop out of school (Fagan and Pabon, 1990;

Kaplan and Liu, 1994; Krohn et al., 1995; Mensch and Kandel, 1988), to become pregnant (or impregnate someone else) or become a teenage parent (Newcomb and Bentler, 1988; Smith, 1997; Thornberry et al., 1997), and to be unemployed in their early adult years (Caspi et al., 1998; Kandel, Chen, and Gill, 1995; Kandel et al., 1986; Newcomb and Bentler, 1988). They are also likely to experience disorderly transitions in multiple areas of development. Clearly these consequences can have a dramatic effect on their ultimate social, emotional, and economic well-being as well as their subsequent antisocial behavior, as these youths enter and traverse their adult years. Having found that childhood antisocial behavior predicts adult employment status, occupational status, job stability, income, and mobility, Lee Robins concluded that "antisocial behavior [in childhood] predicts class status more efficiently than class status predicts antisocial behavior" (1966: 305).

For various reasons early involvement in misbehavior predicts later disorder in the life course. Participating in illegal behaviors may distract one from conventional pursuits; for example, drug use can lower performance in school. Involvement in deviance may also lead the individual to be labeled and excluded from conventional pursuits.

Another, much less studied pathway from deviance to disorderly transitions concerns the impact of deviant behavior on social networks. First, participation in deviance discourages friendships with conventional others and reduces the individual's social capital. Prosocial friends, teachers, and family members can assist individuals in getting through school, obtaining a job, and selecting a mate. Involvement in adolescent deviance can cut the person off from these conventional social networks and sources of social capital (Coleman, 1988, 1990).

Second, exclusion from conventional social networks is also likely to encourage involvement in social networks that arise in opposition to conforming norms. Recent studies have established that involvement in deviant behavior leads to increasing association with deviant peers (Krohn et al., 1996; Thornberry et al., 1994). Hagan (1997) has suggested that when normative opposition forms in groups, the effect has added salience. Often there is a closure of networks within these groups, generating a form of social embeddedness that leads to "criminal capital" (Hagan, 1997). This process leads to the integration of youths into the criminal underworld and further distances them from the job market and other conventional institutions. Indeed, Hagan argues that embeddedness in crime networks seals the economic fate of these youths.

This perspective suggests that not only does involvement in deviant *behavior* lead to an increased probability of disorder in the life course, but that involvement in deviant *social networks* should have an added, independent impact on creating disorderly transitions. Social network theory argues that all social networks constrain the actor's behavior to be consistent with that of the network (Krohn, 1986). It further suggests that the tighter the social network, the stronger the constraint on the actor's behavior. Involvement in a social network whose members regularly participate in deviant behavior will, therefore, facilitate deviance on the part of each network member and impair the actor's ability to make successful transitions to adult statuses.

Juvenile street gangs can be viewed as prototypical deviant social networks whose actors are embedded in a culture and behavior system that both facilitates deviant behavior and isolates the individual from prosocial networks. Because of that, we hypothesize that adolescent gang membership will have a disruptive influence on life-course trajectories, leading to off-time and disorderly transitions. This influence should be observed even after involvement in delinquent behavior and associations with deviant peers are taken into account. Moreover, members of a gang who are more committed to that social network should be particularly likely to experience problematic transitions. Hence, we hypothesize that gang members who remain in the gang for an extended period of time will be more likely to experience problematic transitions than short-term members.

Experiencing precocious transitions, especially multiple precocious transitions, can lead to either continuing antisocial behavior or initiating antisocial behavior in early adulthood. Therefore, we examine the hypothesis that precocious transitions will mediate the relationship between being a member of a gang during adolescence and being arrested as a young adult.

Examining these hypotheses provides an interesting test of the power of gang membership to influence life-course development as there is a substantial temporal lag between the period of gang membership and the occurrence of these transitions. Recall from Chapter 3 that gang membership was most prevalent at ages 14 and 15, especially for females. Most of the transitions examined here occur well after that point; for example, teen parenthood extends through age 19 and our measure of employment covers ages 19 to 21.

Prior Research

As noted earlier there has been relatively little research on the impact of gang membership on precocious transitions. One exception is Hagedorn's work with gangs in Milwaukee. He reinterviewed the sample of gang members, originally studied as adolescents, when they were in their early 20s and again in their late 20s (Hagedorn, 1998: 124ff., 171ff.). Of the male gang members, only a third had a high school diploma and about a third were working. About two-thirds were still gang-involved, more than 60% had been to jail, and many of them had resorted to the drug trade as a source of financial support. The female gang members fared no better. About two-thirds did not graduate from high school and, while few were still gang involved (5%), half had been to jail and half had used cocaine "to some degree." Almost all were mothers (88%), only 6% were married, and more than half (58%) were supported by welfare (Aid to Families with Dependent Children, or AFDC). All of these results are descriptive, bivariate findings, and it is not clear if gang membership causally contributed to these outcomes. There are no comparison subjects, and the impact of other variables (e.g., prior criminal behavior) is not controlled. Nevertheless, Hagedorn's results do suggest that former gang members are at risk for later disorder in the life course.

Moore's (1991) results in Los Angeles are similar. Only about 40% of the former gang members were employed (1991: 115–116), and the female gang members had high rates of early parenthood and were more responsible for raising their children than were the male gang members (1991: 114).

These earlier findings suggest that adolescent gang membership may well contribute to disorder in the life course. To address this issue more fully, we examine the impact of gang membership on several precocious or off-time transitions: dropping out of school, early pregnancy, teenage parenthood, living independently from one's parents (early nest leaving), unstable employment patterns, and cohabiting.[1]

Measures

School dropout was measured by the respondent's self-report of dropping out of high school before graduation. If respondents indicated that they were not in school and had not graduated from high school as of Wave 10 (when they were 19–21 years of age), they are considered to have dropped out of high school. Thirty-seven percent of the females and 42% of the males left school prematurely.

Female respondents were asked whether they had ever been pregnant and male respondents were asked whether they had ever gotten a girl pregnant. *Early pregnancy* is determined by an affirmative response at or prior to Wave 9, when the mean age of the respondents was 17.4 and they should have been in the spring term of their 11th or 12th grade. Using this definition, 37% of the females and 23% of the males were considered to have experienced this precocious transition during their high school years.

Teenage parenthood is indicated by whether the respondent had a child prior to his or her twentieth birthday. This measure is based on items on

---

[1] Another precocious transition that is frequently studied is marriage before graduating from high school. Early marriage was eliminated from the analysis because so few (7%) of our total sample had experienced this transition.

which respondents self-reported becoming a parent and provided the birth-dates of their children. Forty-six percent of the females and 22% of the males reported having biological children by age 20.[2] We also asked the respondent's parent or guardian if their son or daughter had a biological child. There is over 95% agreement between parent reports and respondent self-reports of the respondent having become a parent (see Thornberry et al., 1997).

Adolescents who no longer resided with a parent or guardian *and* who had not graduated from high school by Wave 9 are considered to have experienced the precocious transition of *early nest leaving*. Twenty-five percent of the females and 7.6% of the males indicated that they were living away from the home of their parents or guardians by Wave 9.

To measure *unstable employment* patterns we calculated the percentage of months from age 19 to age 21 that the subject did *not* have a job. For our purposes, respondents were considered to be "employed" if they were working, in the military, or still attending school. The number of months unemployed ranges from 0 (complete employment) to 36 (complete unemployment) over this three-year period. Unstable employment refers to those respondents above the median in terms of the percentage of months they were unemployed. Forty-one percent of the males and 59% of the females are categorized as having unstable employment.

Cohabitation is indicated if unmarried subjects reported living with a partner in either Wave 10, 11, or 12. Thirty-two percent of the male respondents and 30% of the female respondents are considered to have cohabited.

In addition to the variables measuring separate transitions, we constructed a variable that summed the total number of transitions each respondent experienced. Early pregnancy is not included in this sum because it is highly correlated with teenage parenthood. The total number of transitions ranges from 0 to 5.

In addition to these precocious transitions, we also examine the extent to which adolescent gang membership increases the chances of being arrested during the early adult years, ages 19 to 22. This measure is based on official arrest histories collected in Rochester and in New York State (see Chapter 2).

Results

As in previous chapters, we present results separately for male and female respondents. For the males we compare respondents who were never gang

---

[2] The prevalence of parenthood is higher than the prevalence of pregnancy because the former refers to becoming a parent prior to age 20, while "early pregnancy" refers to prior to the end of high school.

Table 9.1. *Bivariate Relationships between Gang Membership and Precocious Transitions, Males Only (%)*

	Nonmembers	Gang Members	
		Short-Term	Stable
School Dropout (n = 555)	33.6	45.2	71.5[a,b]
Early Nest Leaving (n = 547)	7.7	6.1	7.6
Early Pregnancy (n = 572)	14.9	31.7[a]	46.9[a]
Teenage Parenthood (n = 576)	19.3	22.0	55.0[a,b]
Unstable Employment (n = 536)	37.0	45.8	59.2[a]
Cohabitation (n = 537)	25.3	44.8[a]	58.5[a]

[a]Significantly different from nonmembers, $p < .05$ (one-tailed).
[b]Significantly different from short-term members, $p < .05$ (one-tailed).

members with the short-term gang members, that is, those who report being members for less than a year, and with the more stable, long-term members, those who were members for a year or more. We hypothesize that nonmembers are the least likely to experience precocious transitions and that stable gang members are the most likely to do so. Because of the smaller number of cases for the females, we use the simple ever-prevalence gang measure, comparing nonmembers with those who were ever a member of a street gang.

We begin by examining bivariate relationships between gang membership and the various transitions. We then examine multivariate models in which other predictors of these transitions are held constant.

Bivariate Relationships: Male Respondents

The six dichotomous transitions variables are presented in Table 9.1. The effect of gang membership is strong on five of the six transitions for the male respondents. Whereas 33.6% of those who were never members of a gang dropped out of high school, 45.2% of the short-term and 71.5% of the stable gang members did. Thus, there is not only a general effect of gang membership but also an increased impact with long-term exposure to the gang environment.

Similar effects are seen for the two indicators of precocious sexuality – early pregnancy and teenage parenthood. The effect of gang membership on early pregnancy is fairly linear. Of the nonmembers, 14.9% report impregnating a girl, whereas 31.7% of the short-term members and 46.9% of the stable members do. In terms of teenage fatherhood, one-fifth (19.3%) of the males who never joined a gang report becoming a teenage father,

Table 9.2. *Bivariate Relationships between Gang Membership and Precocious Transitions, Females Only (%)*

	Nonmembers	Gang Members
School Dropout (n = 210)	30.0	46.5[a]
Early Nest Leaving (n = 209)	18.1	29.9[a]
Early Pregnancy (n = 216)	30.6	56.1[a]
Teenage Parenthood (n = 216)	40.1	60.7[a]
Unstable Employment (n = 210)	55.6	70.1[a]
Cohabitation (n = 212)	28.2	33.6

[a]Significantly different from nonmembers, $p < .05$ (one-tailed).

and this rate increases very slightly to 22.0% for the short-term members. For the stable gang members the rate of teen fatherhood increases sharply to 55.0%, however.

Earlier gang membership also increases the chances of unstable employment histories during the early adult years. Thirty-seven percent of the nonmembers are above the median in terms of the percent of time spent unemployed, as compared with 45.8% of the short-term and 59.2% of the long-term gang members.

Stable gang membership also has an impact on cohabitation. Among stable gang members, 58.5% have cohabited in early adulthood, whereas only 25.3% of nonmembers cohabited. Among short-term gang members, 44.8% cohabited.

The only transition for which we do not see an impact of gang membership is early nest leaving – that is, living without direct parental or adult supervision prior to finishing high school. There is a low base-rate of this outcome for the male members of this sample (7.6%) and no variation by gang membership.

Being a member of a street gang during early adolescence may have a long-term impact on a number of life-course transitions for male subjects. Gang members, especially the more stable gang members, are more likely than nonmembers to be high school dropouts, to impregnate a girl, to become a teen father, to have less stable employment careers, and to have cohabited.

Bivariate Relationships: Female Respondents

Table 9.2 presents the bivariate relationships for the dichotomous outcome variables for female respondents. Again, we see a substantial impact of gang membership on the probability of making these early, off-time transitions.

Table 9.3. *Relationship between Gang Membership and Number of Precocious Transitions (%)*

| | | Gang Members | | |
	Nonmembers	Short-Term	Stable	Total
Males (n = 577)				
Mean Number of Precocious Transitions	1.15	1.51	2.42[a,b]	
Females (n = 216)				
Mean Number of Precocious Transitions	1.67			2.30[a]

[a]Significantly different from nonmembers, p < .05 (one-tailed).
[b]Significantly different from short-term members, p < .05 (one-tailed).

Whereas 30.0% of the female respondents who never joined a gang dropped out of high school, nearly half (46.5%) of the gang members did. For the female sample members there is also a statistically significant impact on early nest leaving. Of the female nonmembers, 18.1% report living independently, whereas 29.9% of the female gang members do.

There are substantial effects on precocious sexuality. Of the nonmembers, 30.6% experienced an early pregnancy as compared with 56.1% of the gang members; 40.1% of nonmembers became teenage mothers as compared with 60.7% of the gang members.

The link between gang membership and employment patterns for the female respondents is also significant. The female gang members spend a higher percentage of time unemployed as compared with the nonmembers – 70.1% versus 55.6%.

The only precocious transition not related to gang membership for females is cohabitation. Female gang members are only slightly (33.6% vs. 28.2%) more likely to cohabit than nonmembers.

Multiple Precocious Transitions

Although precocious transitions can occur separately, they are often bundled together, in part because of common causes and in part because of the cascading impact of cumulative disadvantage triggered by each of these precocious transitions. In Table 9.3 we examine whether earlier gang membership is related to experiencing multiple transitions. Recall that five transitions – dropping out of school, teen parenthood, early nest leaving, unemployment, and cohabitation – are used in this analysis; early pregnancy is not included because of its overlap with teen parenthood.

The top panel of Table 9.3 presents the mean number of precocious transitions for male respondents. Stable gang members experience on average 2.42 precocious transitions, whereas short-term gang members experience 1.51 and nonmembers only 1.15. The differences in the means for stable gang members when compared with both short-term members and nonmembers are statistically significant.

The lower panel of Table 9.3 presents the results for the female respondents. The pattern is quite similar. Gang members experience a significantly higher number of precocious transitions than do nonmembers.

Multivariate Models

Although there appears to be a fairly strong relationship between adolescent gang membership and precocious transitions, that relationship could be spurious, produced by common antecedent variables. To examine this possibility we regress each of these transitions on gang membership, holding the effect of other variables constant. We use logistic regression to estimate the models for the dichotomous transitions variables and ordinary least squares regression to estimate the model for multiple transitions.

The control variables cover several major domains – neighborhoods, social class, family, school, peers, psychological stress, and prior deviance – that have been shown to be linked to either gang membership (see Chapter 4) or to these precocious transitions. The specific indicators are percent poverty in the census tract of residence, family poverty-level income, parental supervision, commitment to school, early dating, peer delinquency, negative life events, and general delinquency. General delinquency is measured cumulatively from Wave 2 to Wave 4; all other indicators are measured at or prior to Wave 4 to preserve temporal order. (A description of these measures appears in Chapter 2.)

Table 9.4 presents the results for the male subjects, comparing the short-term gang members and the stable gang members with the nonmembers (the omitted category). Although stable gang membership does not have a significant impact on early nest leaving, it does on school dropout, early pregnancy, teenage parenthood, unstable employment, and cohabitation net of the control variables. In contrast to nonmembers, being a stable gang member increases the likelihood of dropping out of school 3.42 times, the likelihood of early pregnancy by 2.38 times, of teen parenthood by 2.78 times, of unstable unemployment by 2.76 times, and of cohabitation by 1.94 times. The short-term gang members, however, are only significantly more likely to experience cohabitation as compared with the nonmembers.

The control variables operate much as expected. Living in impoverished neighborhoods increases the odds of early pregnancy, fatherhood, early

Table 9.4. Odds Ratios for Logistic Regression Predicting Precocious Transitions, Males Only

	School Dropout	Early Nest Leaving	Early Pregnancy	Teenage Parenthood	Unstable Employment	Cohabitation
Short-Term Gang Membership	.98	.38	1.40	.69	1.18	1.71*
Stable Gang Membership	3.42**	.84	2.38**	2.78**	2.76**	1.94*
Area Percentage in Poverty	1.01	1.04**	1.05**	1.02*	1.04**	1.02*
Family Poverty-Level Income	1.57*	1.84	1.29	1.70*	2.17**	1.85**
Parental Supervision	1.28	.94	1.03	.93	.81	.74
Commitment to School	.27**	.88	.73	1.08	.60	.48*
Early Dating	1.00	.68	1.36	1.30	.90	1.05
Peer Delinquency	.79	.74	1.05	1.11	.86	1.14
Negative Life Events	4.86**	3.33	3.58*	8.88**	1.15	5.34**
General Delinquency	2.39**	3.29**	2.72**	1.32	1.25	1.08
Model Improvement X^2	93.31†	21.65†	70.60†	66.61†	66.40†	60.56†
	(n = 490)	(n = 484)	(n = 489)	(n = 507)	(n = 471)	(n = 470)

*p < .05 (one-tailed test). **p < .01 (one-tailed test). †p < .05.

nest leaving, unstable employment, and cohabitation. Family poverty level increases the odds of dropping out of school, teenage parenthood, unstable employment, and cohabitation. Also, psychological stress, indicated here by the number of negative life events that were experienced, has a sizable effect on the likelihood of high school dropout, early pregnancy, teenage parenthood, and cohabitation. General delinquency increases the likelihood of dropping out of school, early nest leaving, and early pregnancy. Commitment to school only affects dropping out and cohabiting.

Table 9.5 presents the results for the female respondents. Gang membership has a significant impact on three of the six transitions, after the control variables are considered. Female gang members are more likely to experience an early pregnancy (OR = 2.32), to become a teen mother (OR = 2.53), and to have unstable employment patterns (OR = 2.03). Although the effects are in the expected direction for dropping out of high school and prematurely moving out of the parental home, they are not statistically significant. Surprisingly, neither gang membership nor any of the control variables significantly predicts cohabitation for females.[3] In terms of the control variables, commitment to school reduces the odds of school dropout, early nest leaving, early pregnancy, and teenage motherhood. Early dating increases the odds of early nest leaving and early pregnancy. Negative life events increase the odds of unstable employment, family poverty level increases the odds of dropping out of school, and peer delinquency increases the odds of early nest leaving. The central finding, though, is that, net of the impact of these variables, gang membership still exerts an impact on several of these precocious transitions.

Finally, we examine the impact of earlier gang membership on the likelihood of experiencing multiple precocious transitions. The results of the OLS regressions are presented in Table 9.6 for both males and females. For males there is a strong effect of stable gang membership, net of the other variables, on experiencing multiple disorderly transitions. As compared with nonmembers, being a short-term member does not significantly increase the number of transitions experienced, but being a more stable, longer-term member does. Indeed, stable gang membership has the highest standardized regression coefficient ($\beta = .23$) of all the variables in the equation. In addition, area percentage in poverty, family poverty, commitment to school, negative life events, and general delinquency all affect the number of negative transitions in the expected direction.

---

[3] The model improvement chi-square statistic is not statistically significant for this equation. This is not surprising given that there are no significant predictors in the equation. Similarly, the model improvement chi-square is insignificant for the equation in predicting unstable employment. When this equation is trimmed to include only the two significant predictors, it is statistically significant, however.

Table 9.5. *Odds Ratios for Logistic Regression Predicting Precocious Transitions, Females Only*

	School Dropout	Early Nest Leaving	Early Pregnancy	Teenage Parenthood	Unstable Employment	Cohabitation
Gang Membership	1.55	1.86	2.32*	2.53**	2.03*	.85
Area Percentage in Poverty	1.01	1.01	1.01	1.00	1.00	.99
Family Poverty-Level Income	2.24*	.58	1.06	1.28	1.33	.97
Parental Supervision	1.38	1.07	1.40	1.16	1.03	.89
Commitment to School	.34*	.14**	.18**	.33*	.60	.56
Early Dating	1.27	3.67**	2.97**	1.30	1.24	1.43
Peer Delinquency	1.15	5.36**	1.89	2.11	.90	1.88
Negative Life Events	3.70	.92	2.97	1.57	6.65**	.33
General Delinquency	.85	.28*	.36*	.44*	.54	1.94
Model Improvement X^2	18.57†	30.09†	31.39†	18.36†	14.06	12.17
	(n = 195)	(n = 193)	(n = 195)	(n = 200)	(n = 194)	(n = 196)

*$p < .05$ (one-tailed test). **$p < .01$ (one-tailed test). †$p < .05$.

Table 9.6. *OLS Regression Predicting Total Number of Transitions*

	Males		Females	
Gang Membership			.45*	(.14)
Short-Term Gang Membership	.02	(.01)		
Stable Gang Membership	.87**	(.23)		
Area Percentage in Poverty	.02**	(.16)	.00	(.01)
Family Poverty-Level Income	.43**	(.16)	.23	(.08)
Parental Supervision	−.09	(−.03)	.01	(.00)
Commitment to School	−.40**	(−.12)	−.83**	(−.20)
Early Dating	.00	(.00)	.36*	(.12)
Peer Delinquency	−.06	(−.02)	.49	(.13)
Negative Life Events	1.03**	(.19)	.39	(.07)
General Delinquency	.29**	(.11)	−.34	(−.12)
R^2	.25		.12	
	(n = 510)		(n = 193)	

Note: Unstandardized coefficients are reported, with standardized coefficients in parentheses.
*p < .05 (one-tailed test). **p < .01 (one-tailed test).

Gang membership also significantly increases the number of transitions experienced by the female respondents. Even when other significant predictors of multiple transitions – commitment to school and early dating – are controlled, the effect of gang membership remains significant.

Gang Membership, Precocious Transitions, and Adult Arrests

Another long-term consequence of being a member of a juvenile gang and experiencing precocious transitions is that gang members will be less likely to desist from criminal behavior as they enter early adulthood and will be more likely to acquire official labels. As stated earlier, the gang can embed members in a criminal network and inhibit their participation in conventional arenas. Thus earlier gang membership is expected to be directly related to being arrested as an adult.

Gang membership is also expected to be indirectly related to adult criminality through its impact on precocious transitions. Experiencing precocious transitions directly affects the ability to fulfill adult roles and statuses successfully. Difficulty in making a living or experiencing family problems may make it more difficult for people to desist from criminal behavior. Thus, we expect that experiencing multiple precocious transitions will mediate, at least partially, the relationship between adolescent gang membership and adult arrests.

Table 9.7. *Odds Ratios for Logistic Regression Predicting Adult Arrests, Males Only*

	Equation 1	Equation 2	Equation 3
Short-Term Gang Membership	1.74*	1.24	1.21
Stable Gang Membership	4.03**	2.83**	2.01*
Number of Transitions			1.51**
Area Percentage in Poverty		1.01	1.00
Family Poverty-Level Income		1.10	.92
Parental Supervision		.77	.79
Commitment to School		.40**	.46**
Early Dating		1.02	1.01
Peer Delinquency		.79	.82
Negative Life Events		3.64**	2.41*
General Delinquency		1.46	1.29
Model Improvement X^2	25.61[†]	31.00[†]	17.02[†]
	(n = 505)	(n = 505)	(n = 505)

*p < .05 (one-tailed test). **p < .01 (one-tailed test). [†]p < .05.

We examine these hypotheses separately for males and females. Equation 1 provides the bivariate relationship between gang membership and adult arrests for males (Table 9.7). Both short-term and stable gang membership significantly increase the odds that males will be arrested as adults. Short-term gang membership increases the chances of adult arrests by 1.74 times and stable gang membership increases the chances by 4.03 times. Thus stable gang members are four times as likely as nonmembers to be arrested during their early 20s.

To see if the impact of gang membership is spurious, Equation 2 adds the same control variables that have been held constant in the previous tables in this chapter. When their effects are controlled, the impact of short-term gang membership becomes nonsignificant. The impact of stable gang membership diminishes in size, but its effect remains significant and sizable. Stable gang members are almost three times as likely as the nonmembers to have an adult arrest. In addition, commitment to school significantly reduces the odds of adult arrests (OR = .40), and negative life events significantly increase the odds of adult arrests (OR = 3.64). Finally, in the third equation we add the total number of precocious transitions experienced to examine its mediating effect on the relationship between

Table 9.8. *Odds Ratios for Logistic Regression Predicting Adult Arrests, Females Only*

	Equation 1	Equation 2	Equation 3
Gang Membership	3.98**	2.70*	2.33*
Number of Transitions			1.54**
Area Percentage in Poverty		1.04*	1.04*
Family Poverty-Level Income		1.01	.84
Parental Supervision		.79	.91
Commitment to School		1.74	2.58
Early Dating		.68	.57
Peer Delinquency		1.52	1.34
Negative Life Events		1.58	1.97
General Delinquency		1.44	1.71
Model Improvement X^2	8.88†	6.06	7.01
	(n = 198)	(n = 198)	(n = 198)

*p < .05 (one-tailed test). **p < .01 (one-tailed test). †p < .05.

gang membership and adult arrests. The total number of transitions has a significant impact on the likelihood of having an adult arrest, increasing the chances by 50%. The number of precocious transitions also mediates part of the impact of gang membership; the odds ratio drops from 2.83 to 2.01. Thus, a substantial part of the total effect of gang membership is indirect, operating through the experience of multiple precocious transitions.

Table 9.8 presents the results for the females in our sample. Gang membership significantly increases the odds of adult arrests (OR = 3.98) when examined bivariately. Female gang members are about four times as likely to be arrested as young adults as nonmembers. The impact of gang membership drops somewhat when the control variables are included (Equation 2) but remains statistically significant.

Finally, we consider the number of precocious transitions experienced. Women who experience a greater number are more likely to be arrested (OR = 1.54). Moreover, experiencing precocious transitions further mediates the impact of earlier gang membership on later arrests for the females, dropping the odds ratio for gang membership to 2.33. Thus, the impact of gang membership on arrests is largely indirect, mediated in part by disorderly transitions.

Discussion

Late adolescence is a critical time in the life course when youths are expected to prepare for and make successful transitions into adult roles and statuses. Events, behaviors, and associations all play important roles in determining whether those transitions are made at the appropriate time and in the normative order and, ultimately, whether they lead to successful adult outcomes.

Being a member of a street gang facilitates delinquent behavior (see Chapter 6), and prior research has established that delinquent behavior adversely affects transitions to adult statuses. On the premises of social network theory (Krohn, 1986), gang membership is expected to have an independent effect on the likelihood of disorderly transitions, over and above the impact of delinquent behavior. As an important and powerful social network, the gang constrains the behavior of its members, limits access to prosocial networks that may act as social capital in facilitating adult transitions, and increases the criminal embeddedness of its members. All of these characteristics cut the individual off from conventional pursuits and increase the chances of disorder in the life course.

We examined the impact of gang membership on important transitions that youths are expected to make – specifically, dropping out of school, prematurely leaving the parental home, early pregnancy, teenage parenthood, unstable employment, cohabitation, and experiencing multiple transitions. The results strongly support the general conclusion that being a member of a gang increases the likelihood that youths will experience off-time and unsuccessful transitions.

Support for the relationship between gang membership and precocious transitions is somewhat stronger for male than for female gang members. Both bivariately and in multivariate models, stable gang membership significantly increases the odds of dropping out of school, impregnating a girl, being a teenage father, unstable employment, cohabitation, and experiencing multiple transitions even when several other potential predictors of these transitions, including prior delinquency and associations with delinquent peers, are in the equation. The fact that these effects are most evident for stable gang members, but not for short-term members, provides further support for the debilitating effect of being in a gang.

For female gang members, the bivariate results indicate that gang members are significantly more likely to drop out of school, leave home early, become pregnant, become a teenage mother, have unstable employment patterns, and experience multiple transitions. When other predictors of these transitions are controlled, however, gang membership is significantly related only to early pregnancy, teen motherhood, unstable employment, and multiple transitions. The link between gang membership and precocious sexual activity is consistent with descriptions of the roles that female gang members are often portrayed as playing in the gang.

Moore (1991), for example, reports that half of male gang members view female gang members as "possessions" and objects of sexual exploitation. Although this view was challenged by many female gang members (Moore and Hagedorn, 2001), there is ample evidence that female gang members are sexually exploited (Fishman, 1995; Hagedorn, 1998; Miller, 1998; Moore, 1991; Venkatesh, 1998). As a result, these young women have high rates of teenage pregnancy and motherhood. Gang membership and the precocious transitions that it generates also appear to foreclose future opportunities for these young women. For example, in Moore's study, gang membership "virtually ruled out marrying nongang mates. Most female gang members married male gang members whose careers often involved repeated imprisonments" (Moore and Hagedorn, 2001: 8).

The consequences of experiencing disorderly transitions, for both males and females, can have devastating effects on the lives of former gang members. We followed our sample to about age 22 and examined one problematic outcome of precocious transitions – being arrested in the young adult years. Even with this short time horizon, we found that for both boys and girls, gang membership significantly increased the odds of later arrest. We also found that the number of precocious transitions experienced during adolescence increased the odds of later arrest. Consistent with our theoretical expectations, the number of transitions also mediated a substantial part of the effect of gang membership on this outcome. For the males the number of transitions mediated much of the effect of stable gang membership and rendered the impact of short-term membership insignificant. For the females the number of transitions also mediated much of the relationship between gang membership and adult arrests.

The dire effect of being a member of a youth gang on behavior in young adulthood is evident. Affiliating with a delinquent gang during the adolescent years has been shown to be related to early and inappropriate transitions to adult statuses and roles. Such problematic transitions are likely to reduce the gang member's eventual success in the conventional adult world. The effects of disorderly transitions can lead to a cascading series of difficulties that result in dysfunctional family life, unstable employment, and, in some cases, continued involvement in criminal activity. In assessing the negative impact that gangs have on society, we must take into account not only their immediate impact on crime but also their continuing impact on the life chances of gang members.

Gangs in Developmental Perspective: Substantive and Policy Implications

PREVIOUS STUDIES OF gangs and gang members have not, by and large, placed the study of gang members in a life-course perspective. As a consequence there are a variety of important topics in the study of gangs about which we have inadequate information. They include, first, studies of risk factors in which antecedent variables are linked to the odds of later gang membership and studies of causal processes that attempt to identify why certain youngsters join gangs while others do not. Second, although we know from many studies that gang members are more delinquent than nonmembers, few studies of within-individual change examine the extent to which gang membership itself may facilitate this outcome. Finally, although we have some indication of the short-term impact of gang membership on the individual, we have little information on long-term developmental consequences of being a member of a street gang during adolescence.

In this book, we have tried to flesh out the picture of gang life by focusing on developmental questions within the context of the Rochester Youth Development Study. This study has a number of design features that aid in the examination of these issues. The Rochester study has a representative, community-based sample of an initial panel of 1,000 adolescents followed from early adolescence to early adulthood. Subjects were not selected on the basis of whether they were gang members, and gang membership was observed as it naturally occurred over the life course, if it occurred at all. Prospective longitudinal data on a host of variables are measured – both before, during, and after periods of active gang membership. And, regardless of the age at which gang membership takes place, there is a group of adolescents of the same age who never joined a gang available for comparative purposes. Because of these design features we are able to study how adolescent development influences gang membership, how being a gang member influences behavior patterns, and how gang membership alters life-course trajectories. Admittedly, we do not have the rich detail offered by observational studies or their understanding of group processes. Because of that there are a number of important issues that we cannot examine. But we can, and did, examine several important links that are missing from a complete understanding of gangs. That said, what have we learned?

Overview of Findings

The lifetime prevalence of gang membership in the Rochester sample appears to be somewhat higher than expected based on previous studies. Thirty percent of the total sample, 32% of the boys and 29% of the girls, self-report being a gang member at some point during their adolescent years. Membership is more common during early adolescence, especially for the females, and by late adolescence gang membership has become rather uncommon for the members of the Rochester sample. While the lifetime prevalence rate is quite high, gang membership, on average, is not a very long-lived phenomenon. Most gang members report being in a gang for less than a year and very few report being a gang member for three or more years. Moreover, gang membership appears to be neither a highly intermittent status with a lot of movement in and out of the gang, nor a permanent status. Generally speaking, gang members join a gang, stay a member for a while, and then leave the gang permanently, or at least through their early 20s. If they do leave and rejoin, they tend to do so within relatively short time spans.

The extent to which any of these findings is a function of the newly emergent nature of gang activity in Rochester is unknown. It must be emphasized that gangs in Rochester blossomed at about the same time the Rochester Youth Development Study began. Thus the prevalence and age patterns observed here may be produced by the faddishness of newly emergent gangs and would differ from those observed in traditional gang cities. Unfortunately, data from the other longitudinal studies of gang members (e.g., Battin et al., 1998; Esbensen and Huizinga, 1993) cannot help because they too are conducted in emergent gang cities, Seattle and Denver respectively. We return to the issue of the impact of how the newly emergent nature of gangs in Rochester may have influenced our findings after we summarize the rest of the results.

Gangs and Delinquency

As compared with nonmembers, gang members self-report higher rates of delinquency, violence, drug use, and drug sales; they are also more likely to have an official arrest history. These findings are certainly expected given both previous results and the highly deviant nature of street gangs. Nevertheless, these basic, descriptive findings go beyond those reported in previous studies because of our long-term prospective measures of delinquency, the representative nature of a community-based sample, and the purity of the comparison group of youths who reported never being a gang member during adolescence.

The strong association between gang membership and delinquency is observed for both male and female respondents. Gangs appear to have every bit as strong an impact on the delinquent behavior of young girls as they do on young boys. Indeed, the female gang members generally have higher rates of delinquency than do the male nonmembers.

The basic association between gang membership and delinquency is well known. Surprisingly, though, there are very few estimates in the literature of the percentage of all delinquent acts for which gang members are responsible, a result of the absence of community-based samples in the area of gang research. It is clear from our data that gang members are responsible for the lion's share of the delinquent acts that are committed by the Rochester sample. While representing only a third of the sample, gang members are responsible for about two-thirds of the delinquencies, a disparity that becomes even larger for more serious and violent offenses. They are also much more likely to be arrested. To borrow Wright and Rossi's (1986) depiction of illegal gun carriers, we might conclude by saying that gang members do not simply contribute to the crime problem; in large measure, they are the crime problem. If so, it is imperative that we understand why some youths join gangs and whether gang membership itself contributes to their delinquent behavior.

Pathways to Gang Membership

Gang membership is clearly not produced by just a few risk factors. In an analysis that linked antecedent conditions and characteristics to the chances of later joining a gang, we demonstrated that gang members suffer from deficits in multiple developmental domains. They include social disadvantage at both the neighborhood and family levels, poor family management practices, poor performance in school, deviant peers, high stress, and prior involvement in delinquency.

The cumulation of deficits appears to be far more important than individual risk factors in accounting for gang membership, however. Adolescents who experience deficits in none or only a few of the seven domains we studied are not very likely to become gang members; adolescents who experience deficits in five or more domains are far more likely to be gang members. Indeed, 61% of the young boys and 40% of the young girls who have deficits in all seven domains were gang members.

The risk factor analyses identify antecedent variables that are related to gang membership but not the causal processes that lead to this outcome.

We examined this issue from two vantage points. First, we asked the members why they joined their gang. The gang members emphasized the importance of peer influences from friends and family, the search for excitement and fun, and the need for protection. Second, we developed a causal model based on interactional theory (Thornberry and Krohn, 2001) and tested it using the long-term prospective data available to us. The results from this analysis emphasized the role of structural disadvantage, poor social bonds (especially in the educational arena), strong antisocial influences and behaviors, and high levels of stress in leading to gang membership.

The two approaches to understanding why adolescents join gangs yield complementary findings. The causal model (and the risk factor analysis) highlights the developmental deficits in the backgrounds of these young men and women and attendant high levels of stress. The gang members' attributions suggest that street gangs – populated by friends and families, offering a ready source of fun and action, as well as protection from a hostile world – may be a viable response to the bleakness often confronting these urban, generally poor adolescents. If so, then gang membership is produced both by the push of their deficit-laden backgrounds *and* the pull of the glamour they expect to be associated with the gang.

Gangs and Delinquency: Facilitation versus Selection

Regardless of why youths join a street gang, we were interested in how gang membership influences the course of their unfolding lives, especially involvement in delinquency and drugs. Our data indicate that gang members are more delinquent than nonmembers. Is that because gangs elicit or facilitate involvement in delinquency? Or, is it because gangs select youths with a high propensity for delinquency? After all, we have just seen that gang members have multiple risk factors in their backgrounds, risk factors that are also generally associated with delinquent behavior.

We examined this issue in several ways. We first allowed each individual to act as his own control,[1] examining changes in delinquency before, during, and after periods of active gang membership. Second, at each of four years, we regressed various measures of delinquency on dichotomous variables representing current and noncurrent gang membership, while controlling for major risk factors. Finally, we estimated random effects models, which more formally control for the influence of selection effects.

The results are the same across these various techniques. First, there is no evidence to support the basic claim of a selection model – that is,

[1] This analysis was limited to the male subjects because of the smaller number of female subjects, especially at the later waves.

there is no evidence that gang members have significantly higher rates of delinquency than nonmembers before or after their period of gang membership. Second, consistent evidence is concordant with a strong facilitation effect – that is, delinquent behavior increases substantially during periods of active gang membership, and usually only during those time periods. Third, there is some evidence for what Thornberry, Krohn, et al. (1993) called an enhancement or mixed model – that is, gang members have somewhat higher rates of delinquency prior to joining the gang, but these rates then increase dramatically once they become members. Importantly, these results are observed when both major risk factors for delinquency and estimates of population heterogeneity are held constant.

A strong link also exists between carrying guns (whether or not the person owns the gun), gang membership, and delinquency. First, gang membership facilitates both carrying a gun that is owned for protection and gaining access to and carrying other guns. Second, not only does gang membership facilitate delinquent behavior and involvement with drugs, so too does gun carrying. Adolescents who carry guns are more apt to be involved in delinquency, violence, drug use, and drug sales. In addition, though, the interaction of gang membership and gun carrying is also related to these outcomes: gang members who also carry guns have very high rates of these deviant behaviors.

Street gangs appear to facilitate delinquent behavior on the part of their members, especially for general delinquency, violence, gun carrying, and drug sales, and somewhat less so for drug use. Put simply, when gang members are in a gang, their behavior worsens; when they are not in a gang, it improves.

Gangs versus Delinquent Peer Groups

Gangs are obviously a form of delinquent peer group. Perhaps the impact of gangs on behavior that we just observed is a simple peer effect, and gang members are really no different from members of highly delinquent peer groups. Veteran gang observers, such as Klein (1995) and Moore (1991), disagree with this view and think that gangs are "qualitatively different" from even highly delinquent peer groups.

The data from the Rochester sample are concordant with the views of Klein and Moore. Even though gang members have peer networks that are no more densely delinquent than those of adolescents in highly delinquent peer groups, their involvement in delinquency, violence, and drug sales is substantially higher. It would appear that gangs are not simply another form of delinquent peer group; at least when it comes to levels of delinquency, gangs do indeed appear to be qualitatively different.

Long-Term Consequences

The final empirical issue we examined concerned the long-term consequences of gang membership for transitions along major life-course trajectories. Are gang members more likely to have off-time, disorderly transitions
to adulthood as compared to nonmembers?

Based on the Rochester sample the answer is yes. For the male subjects,
stable gang members are more apt than the nonmembers to be high school
dropouts, to impregnate a girl at an early age, to be teen fathers, to cohabit, to have unstable employment patterns, and to have multiple disorderly transitions. For the female subjects, gang members are more apt than
nonmembers to become pregnant, to be teen mothers, to have unstable employment patterns, and to have multiple disorderly transitions. All of these
effects are observed net of antecedent control variables. Gang membership
in early adolescence interrupts life-course development several years later
at the beginning of the transition to adulthood.

Gang membership also increases the chances of being arrested during
the early twenties. Part of this impact is mediated by the number of precocious transitions experienced. Thus, not only does gang membership lead
to later disorder in the life course, that level of disorder has further negative
consequences like the inability to escape from criminal careers.

Street gangs have a pervasive influence on the lives of their members. The
young men and women who join gangs have multiple deficits in many developmental domains and being a member of a street gang further impedes
their prosocial development. In the short run, gang membership appears to
facilitate delinquency and drug involvement. Gang members are also more
frequently arrested than nonmembers, thereby acquiring an official label
and the accompanying stigma. In the long run gang members are more apt
to experience off-time, disorderly transitions to adulthood, even controlling
for other relevant influences, and, as a result, are more apt to continue their
criminal careers.

Substantive Implications

The findings reported here have a number of implications for the study of
street gangs. Some of them are theoretical, and some are methodological.
We begin with a discussion of the implications for the conceptual approaches
we adopted in this study and then move to a discussion of several basic
methodological issues.

Conceptual Implications

We adopted a general life-course perspective based on the work of Elder
(1994), with specific models derived from interactional theory (Thornberry,

1987; Thornberry and Krohn, 2001). Based on our results, both conceptual approaches appear to be useful for studying gangs and gang members.

The life-course conceptual framework hypothesized that the origins of gang membership are likely to be multidimensional, that the causes of membership are unlikely to be set early in the life course, and that dynamic, developmental variables proximally related to gang membership should play an important role. In particular, interactional theory predicted that structural position, prosocial bonding, and antisocial influences should all play a major role in producing elevated rates of gang membership. By and large, our empirical results, in both the risk factor analysis and the causal model, are consistent with these predictions.

To be sure, some findings are less consistent with theoretical expectations and warrant further investigation. One is the relatively weak impact of family process variables in accounting for gang membership. They play a smaller role, at least at these early adolescent ages, than anticipated, both in the Rochester data and in other investigations of risk factors for gang membership. In the Seattle data, for example, attachment is not significantly related to gang membership, and poor family management is less strongly related than are the family structure variables (Hill et al., 1999). In Montreal, LeBlanc and Lanctôt (1998) examined eight family process variables and found only two – parents' common activities and supervision – to be significant correlates of gang membership. Only supervision is related to gang membership in a multivariate discriminant function analysis, but its impact is relatively modest (LeBlanc and Lanctôt, 1998: 20). We need to continue to investigate the extent to which this holds in other data sets. It will also be important to investigate the extent to which this finding is specific to the developmental stage of early adolescence.

Another issue to investigate further is the strong role that precocious sexuality and dating play in leading to gang membership. Young adolescent boys and girls who are already dating seem to find the lure of the gang particularly attractive. Incorporating these processes, and more generally the impact of human sexuality, into conceptual models of gangs is an important issue for future conceptual development (see, e.g., Moffitt, 1997).

Both the life-course perspective and interactional theory emphasize the importance of peer and social network influences in human development. The social network of the juvenile street gang seems to be a particularly important one, serving as a turning point in the lives of these adolescents. In the short term, gang membership facilitates deviant behavior: delinquency and related behaviors increase when boys join gangs and decrease when they leave them. In the long term, gang membership increases disorderly transitions to adulthood and decreases the likelihood of desisting from crime.

Finally, our conceptual approach emphasizes the pernicious impact that continuous exposure to risk processes has on the course of human development. The longer one is exposed to these social influences, the more inertia is built into the system and the harder escape from risk is (Thornberry, 1987). The social environment of the gang is no exception. Indeed, throughout our analyses, at least for the male respondents, stable gang members had more negative and more extreme outcomes than the short-term members. The more one was exposed to the gang, the more the person's life course was bent toward deviance and away from conformity.

Measuring Gang Membership

Throughout this book we have relied on the respondent's self-report of gang membership to measure the central variable under study. Are self-report measures of gang membership adequate for the task?

There can be no definitive answer to this question. No measure has perfect validity and reliability, and certainly the measurement of a sensitive topic such as gang membership is no exception. Moreover, the measurement of gang membership is clouded somewhat by the lack of agreement in the scientific literature about the proper definition of the "gang" (see Bursik and Grasmick, 1993; Curry and Decker, 1997; and Klein, 1995, for discussions). Nevertheless, it seems to us that the self-report approach offers a reasonable measure to use in survey research.

First, the general literature assessing the psychometric adequacy of self-report measures of sensitive topics, including the measurement of delinquency and drug use, indicates that this approach has acceptable validity and reliability (Hindelang et al., 1981; Huizinga and Elliott, 1986; Thornberry and Krohn, 2000). There is no obvious reason to assume that self-reports of gang membership will behave more poorly than self-reports of delinquency and drug use. Certainly the data presented by Curry (2000) are consistent with this view. Recall that he found for a sample of Chicago adolescents that self-report measures of gang membership and gang involvement are significantly related to police-based measures of gang membership and of later official involvement.

Second, a number of recent surveys, particularly those in Denver, Seattle, and Montreal, are also based on self-reports of gang membership. When they have examined substantive topics similar to those examined here, the degree of replication across the projects is impressive and there is no case in which the results are contradictory or fundamentally different. This includes the results reported in Esbensen and Huizinga (1993), Battin et al. (1998), Hill et al. (1999), Thornberry (1998), LeBlanc and Lanctôt (1998), Lacourse et al. (forthcoming), and Huizinga (1996), all of which were reviewed in earlier chapters. If these self-reported measures of gang membership, each with a somewhat different wording, were highly unreliable, it is unlikely that they would produce such consistent results across these various samples.

Finally, because there is no "gold standard" against which to judge the self-report responses, the most appropriate way to assess the validity of this approach is to examine its construct validity, that is, the extent to which the measure is related to other constructs in theoretically expected ways. Given this criterion, the self-reports of gang membership in the Rochester data appear to be quite valid. Indeed, the whole pattern of results presented in the empirical chapters of this book is consistent with the underlying validity of the self-report measure. On the basis of this measure, we have seen that, as compared with nonmembers, gang members have greater social deficits in their backgrounds, self-report more delinquency especially when they are gang members, are arrested more often, are more delinquent than even youth with highly delinquent peer groups, and are responsible for the bulk of the serious, violent crimes. They also have particularly high rates of delinquent behaviors typically associated with gangs, for example, violence and drug selling. Perhaps the most compelling evidence concerns the long-term consequences of gang membership; adolescents who claim to be gang members in early adolescence report more disorderly life-course transitions several years later and are more apt to be arrested as adults.

Clearly, the measure we have used is consistently and powerfully related to a variety of other variables at varying stages of the life course, just as we would expect, given the theoretical expectations of how a valid measure of gang membership would behave. This explanation is certainly the most parsimonious for our findings. We conclude that a simple self-report of gang membership, while not a perfect measure, is a valid and reliable way of assessing gang membership in survey research.

Gang Membership in Emergent Gang Cities

This study has examined the impact of gang membership on adolescent development in Rochester, New York, a new or "emergent" gang city. Gangs emerged in Rochester in the mid 1980s; the Rochester Police Department reported 1985 as the year of onset to the National Youth Gang Center, an estimate that is probably as good as any. To what extent are the findings reported here influenced by this context, and to what extent would the same results be observed in other cities, especially traditional gang cities such as Chicago and Los Angeles, where the bulk of previous research on gangs has been conducted?

The pattern of findings reported here is certainly not unique to Rochester; similar results have been found in longitudinal studies in Denver (Esbensen and Huizinga, 1993), Seattle (Battin et al., 1998), and Montreal (Gatti et al., 2002; Lacourse et al., forthcoming). Unfortunately, these too are emergent gang cities and, while the replication of results is helpful, the broader question remains: are these results unique to emergent gang cities?

There are noticeable differences between emergent gang cities like Rochester and Denver and traditional gang cities like Chicago and Los Angeles.[2] Traditional gang cities are more likely to be large metropolitan areas, whereas emergent gang cities are more apt to be smaller or midsized cities. Gangs in traditional cities have existed for decades, and gangs and gang activity are well understood by the residents of the neighborhoods in which gangs flourish. Gangs in emergent cities are, by definition, newer and therefore less well understood by the residents. Klein (1996) has argued that the gang structure also differs, with gangs in the larger cities being more organized and territorial. Curry (2000) presents data indicating that, as compared with smaller cities, gangs in larger, traditional gang cities are more likely to be composed of minority group members and males, and gang members in these cities commit more serious and violent crimes. The most comprehensive comparison has been conducted by Howell et al. (2002) using data from the 1996 National Youth Gang Survey. They divided jurisdictions into six categories, ranging from before 1981 to 1995–1996, depending on when gangs emerged as a problem. The overall pattern of results is clear: gangs in the "late onset localities have younger members, slightly more females, more of a racial/ethnic mixture, are less involved in drug trafficking, and are less involved in violent crimes, including homicide" (Howell et al., 2002). These differences are not nearly as large when the localities that had gangs prior to 1981 are compared with those where gangs emerged as a problem between 1981 and 1985, Rochester's category. Thus, although gangs are different in Rochester from those found in traditional gang cities, the differences appear to be more a matter of degree than differences in kind.

Unfortunately, emergent and traditional gang cities differ on another dimension as well – the type of research design used to study gangs. The most common way of studying gangs and gang behavior has been through observational or ethnographic methods. More recently, studies have begun to examine the behavior of gang members within the context of longitudinal panel studies of general population samples, such as in the Rochester study. Having alternative methods for studying the same phenomenon is one of the bedrocks of scientific inquiry. Yet, in the study of gangs there is relatively little overlap in the cities in which these varying methods have been used. Panel studies have only been conducted in midsized, newly emergent gang cities. In contrast, observational studies, while existing in a broader array of cities, have clustered in the larger, more traditional gang cities. Thus, it is hard to determine if the findings produced by these different methods

[2] For a fuller discussion of this topic, see Thornberry and Porter (2001).

are a function of the research designs or the research setting. For example, panel studies indicate that gang membership during adolescence is quite fluid, with most gang members remaining in a gang for less than a year. That image is discordant with the image of gang membership based on observational studies. For example, many of the original gang members in Hagedorn's study of Milwaukee gangs remained involved in gangs when they were in their 20s (1998: 184–185). We do not yet know if this and other discrepancies are a function of the different methods, different research settings, or some combination of these effects.

Gangs may really be different in traditional gang cities and have a different impact on their members than those in new gang cities. After all, traditional gangs have been around for years and are larger, more organized, more territorial, and more integrated into the ongoing neighborhood scene (Klein, 1996). That being the case, perhaps such basic characteristics as the age of onset of joining and the fluidity or stability of membership are different than that suggested by the Rochester study. If so, this would suggest that the method of study is less central than the context in yielding an accurate understanding of the ways in which gangs influence the lives of gang members.

It is also plausible, though, that the findings reported here also apply to more traditional gang cities. This view is consistent with data reported by Curry (2000) based on a survey of adolescents in Chicago selected at approximately the same ages (grades 6–9) and same period (1987–1988) as the Rochester sample. He too found that gang members account for most offenses, that self-reported gang membership is strongly related to official and self-reported offending, and that it still has a strong impact on delinquent behavior when other major predictors are held constant. Although the overlap in the analyses conducted in Rochester and Chicago is not extensive, the overlap in the pattern of findings is.

The great strength of studying gang members within longitudinal panel studies is that the studies are based on representative, community samples followed over time. Observational studies are much more selective in the gangs they study and are more likely to be biased toward gangs at the extreme end of the continuum. If so, their results would not necessarily reflect the relationship between gang membership and other variables for all gangs and gang members, even in traditional gang cities.

In the end it is impossible for us to resolve this issue until individual-based longitudinal studies are conducted in traditional gang cities. The ideal design would be to conduct integrated observational and longitudinal studies. For example, one could observe gangs that the members of a longitudinal panel are likely to join if they were to join a gang. Until this type of information is available, we need to continue piecing together a more general picture of street gangs from the various studies that are available.

Finally, we should note that while the issue of how these findings from a new methodological perspective fit into the more general literature on gangs is important, the overall pattern of findings based on these different designs in these different types of gang cities is not very discordant with that in the traditional gang literature. One is struck more by the similarity of findings with respect to risk factors, the relationship between gangs and delinquency, and the short-term and long-term consequences of gang membership than the differences.

Gangs and Gender

The literature on gangs has long been dominated by the study of male gangs and male gang members. "Much of the research on gangs has ignored females or trivialized female gangs" (Moore and Hagedorn, 2001: 1). Female gangs were seen as auxiliary to male gangs and female gang members as subservient and exploited. As Spergel has noted, "The notion seems to be that female gangs and their members are 'pale imitations' of male gangs" (1995: 90). Such a view does not offer a very full understanding of the impact of gang membership on the lives of young women. The results of this study join those of a growing list of other studies (e.g., Bjerregaard and Smith, 1993; Campbell, 1990; Fishman, 1995; Miller, 2001) to suggest that this view is inadequate. Gang membership appears to be just as powerfully linked to the life course of young girls in Rochester as it is to that of young boys. Indeed, the empirical results are quite similar across gender.

Adolescent girls are almost as likely as adolescent boys to join a street gang; the ever-prevalence rates are 29.3% for girls and 32.4% for boys. One area of difference is that girls are less likely to stay a gang member and gang membership is more tightly clustered at younger ages for the girls than the boys. This may be due to the high level of teenage pregnancy and parenthood experienced by these young women (see Chapter 9; Moore, 1991). Despite this different temporal pattern, gang membership has similar antecedents and consequences for males and females.

In our examination of risk factors, we saw that males and females have many similar predictors for joining a gang. Especially important, for both males and females, is the strong association between having *multiple* deficits in *multiple* developmental domains and the likelihood of joining a gang. The shapes of the curves depicting this relationship are very similar for males and females (see Figures 4.1 and 4.2).

Gang membership is also strongly related to involvement in delinquency and drugs for both males and females. In some ways gang membership appears to have a more pronounced effect on females than males. Female gang members self-report higher rates of deviance than male nonmembers, and the disproportionate share of crime for which gang members are responsible is somewhat greater for female gang members than male gang members. These relationships hold, in particular, for serious and violent "street" crimes.

Being a gang member during early adolescence has disruptive life-course influences for both males and females. For the females, the effect is particularly strong in the areas of pregnancy, early parenthood, and work.

According to these findings, female gang members do not seem to be merely auxiliary or peripheral members of the gang who are less affected by gang life. Although we cannot study the structure of the gangs in this individual-level sample, it appears that street gangs have as many negative short-term and long-term consequences for the females as for the males.

Policy Implications

The pattern of findings presented in this book, and in the gang literature more generally, leads to one inescapable conclusion: if we are to be successful in our efforts to reduce delinquency and youth violence, we have to intervene successfully in the criminal careers of gang members. Gang members are responsible for a greater share of delinquency, especially serious and violent delinquency. More important, although they generally have higher rates of delinquency than nonmembers, their contribution to crime and to youth violence, drug selling, and gun carrying is considerably greater when they are actively involved with a gang. An important task that confronts policy makers in youth programming and in the juvenile justice system is the identification of programs to reduce gang membership, the delinquent behavior of gang members, or both. Failure to do so is likely to dampen our efforts to reduce youth crime, precisely because gang members make such a disproportionate contribution to the problem.

What then should be done? The empirical results presented in this study provide a less direct response to this question. To be sure, what we have learned about characteristics and risk factors, about the behavior patterns of gang members, and about the consequences of gang membership all provide suggestions for policies and programs, but they do not lead us directly to specific policies and programs. As is true of virtually all findings from basic research, the present ones identify some of the issues that effective programs need to address but they do not by themselves provide a detailed blueprint of what those programs should look like. Equally important, these results do not, and cannot, identify *effective* gang programs. That can only be done by rigorous experimental evaluation.

This does not mean that we should be mute about policy and programs based on our results, however. Indeed, by combining what we know from evaluation research about effective gang programs with the findings from this developmental study, we are able to say a good deal about appropriate programs. We begin with a discussion of what we know about the effectiveness of existing programs that intervene with gangs and gang members.

Gang Programming

Since the days of Frederic Thrasher (1936), researchers and policy makers have been trying to develop effective programs to prevent youths from joining gangs and to reduce the level of illegal gang behavior. Spergel (1995), Klein (1995), and Howell (1998, 2000) all provide extensive reviews of these programs. Spergel classifies gang programs into four primary categories: local community organizing and mobilization, social intervention, suppression, and social and economic opportunities provision. Klein and Howell use essentially the same tripartite classification – prevention, reform, and suppression – and Howell points out that current programs often combine aspects from two or more of these approaches in an integrated strategy (2000: 5).

Prevention refers to efforts to keep at-risk youth from succumbing to the allure of the gang and actually "signing on." Reform or intervention programs focus on those who have already joined gangs, attempting "to reform, rehabilitate and divert them to more prosocial pursuits" (Klein, 1995: 137). Prevention and reform efforts, what Klein calls the "softer" approaches, dominated the world of gang work for the better part of the twentieth century. Toward the latter part of the century, however, increasing attention was focused on "harder" approaches, or suppression programs. Spergel (1995) suggests that suppression, the strategy of apprehension and punishment of offenders in order to deter, is the dominant strategy of the federal government and the basis on which federal funds are currently disbursed. This approach emphasizes the efficient identification and tracking of gangs and targeted enforcement strategies.

There are numerous examples of each of these approaches to combating the problems posed by street gangs. Prevention programs range from the New York City Boys Club program (Thrasher, 1936) and the Chicago Area Project (Kobrin, 1959) both established in the 1930s, to the Gang Resistance Education and Training Program (G.R.E.A.T.) of the 1990s (Esbensen and Osgood, 1997). The prototypical reform or intervention program is the detached worker approach, which has been tried numerous times (e.g., Klein, 1969; Mattick and Caplan, 1962; Miller, 1962). In this approach youth workers provide social support and services to gang members in their own milieu. Examples of suppression programs include Operation Hardcore (Dahmann, 1995), Operation Cul-de-Sac (Lasley, 1998), and the Boston Gun Project (Kennedy, Piehl, and Braga, 1996). Finally, recent gang programs have combined multiple approaches in an effort to create an integrated, comprehensive strategy for dealing with gangs. One of the better-known ones is the Little Village Gang Violence Reduction Program developed by Spergel and colleagues (1997, 1998) in Chicago. This program combines elements of community mobilization, social intervention with outreach workers, and gang suppression.

Effectiveness

Although many different programs to reduce gang membership and gang delinquency have been tried over the years, the available evidence indicates that programs that have directly targeted gangs and gang members are not effective in reducing either the level of gang membership or the criminal and violent behavior of gangs. Moreover, some programs may be counter-productive and actually increase gang violence.

In his recent review of this literature, Howell (2000: 3–4) summarized the outcomes of 26 gang programs. Only one – the Ladino Hills Project (Klein, 1968) – was listed as having a "significant reduction in gang delinquency" and, as Klein points out, even that effect was not very long-lasting (1995: 146–147). Far more typical in Howell's summary are descriptions of the outcomes as "negligible," "marginal," "some positive results," and "modest reductions." Several programs were "ineffective" and one – the Group Guidance Project (Klein, 1969, 1971) – produced a "significant increase in gang delinquency." The overall conclusion is that these gang programs achieved, at best, some very modest level of success, but a level that is hardly distinguishable from chance.

This summary view is quite consistent with the more detailed assessments of the gang evaluation literature provided by Klein (1995), Spergel (1995), and Howell (1998). With respect to suppression programs, there is some suggestion that this approach generates an escalation in gang activity and in gang violence, although Spergel dismisses the observed confluence of targeted police programs and increased gang activity as being spurious. On the other hand, there is anecdotal information that more aggressive police tactics have prevented the widespread formation of gangs in some smaller and midsized cities. Spergel (1995: 207) concludes, however, that there is little reliable information that specialized suppression programs have been effective in reducing the gang problem in either large or small cities. Klein agrees with this assessment, concluding that "suppression programs have shown no evidence of success" (1995: 138).

Efforts to organize the community to prevent, redirect, or deter gang members are certainly not new. One of the earliest efforts, the Chicago Area Project, enlisted the efforts of local citizens, youth agencies, community organizations, and the criminal justice system to deal with delinquency, particularly gang delinquency. The emphasis was on using indigenous leadership to mobilize local resources to combat delinquency and to provide the community with a sense of involvement. There is no evidence that the project was effective in reducing gang delinquency, however (Howell, 1998). A similar large-scale effort – Mobilization for Youth started in New York City in the 1960s – has been characterized by Klein as "a controversial and massive failure to achieve lasting reform" (1995: 141). In brief, community organization programs, which are admittedly hard to evaluate, have not shown any evidence of success in reducing the number of gangs or the level of gang delinquency.

Reform or social intervention programs are predicated on the belief that gangs can be redirected to fit the expectations and norms of the larger society. A key component of this approach is gang outreach or detached worker programs where workers attempt to channel gang members into more prosocial activities. Workers are directed to be sensitive to the distinctive norms and behavior patterns of gangs and to establish positive relationships with members.

Some research has found that social intervention programs actually solidify the gang and maintain, rather than reduce, gang delinquency. For example, Klein's work (1971) with the Group Guidance Project in Los Angeles and Miller's work (1962) with the Roxbury Project in Boston indicated an increase in gang delinquency, especially serious delinquency, in detached worker programs (see, more generally, Klein, 1995: 141–151).

Programs that provide social opportunities include a broad spectrum of educational and job-related programs. The most promising educational programs are those that use the school as the base for a multifaceted approach that addresses school performance, antigang education, and the building of self-esteem. School-based programs have been shown to be effective in changing attitudes and increasing knowledge about gang issues, but their effect on behavioral change is unclear. Moreover, most of these programs are directed at marginal or peripheral youth rather than at committed gang members.

Recent efforts to prevent at-risk youth from joining a gang have fared little better. The G.R.E.A.T. program developed by the Bureau of Alcohol, Tobacco and Firearms is a school-based program to reduce the likelihood that teenagers will join street gangs. Although the initial evaluation (Esbensen and Osgood, 1999; Palumbo and Ferguson, 1995) showed modest positive results, they appear to have eroded over time. Esbensen et al. (2001) reported the most comprehensive evaluation of G.R.E.A.T., based on a longitudinal, quasi-experimental design conducted in six cities. The G.R.E.A.T. program had no significant impact on reducing the level of gang membership, or the delinquency rate, among the participants. It did have a modest but significant impact on five other outcome variables, including increasing negative views about gangs; however, these effects were not evident until three to four years after program participation. Given the popularity of this program, these results have to be considered disappointing.

The ultimate message from the literature evaluating the effectiveness of gang programs is disheartening. Although numerous programs that directly attempt to reduce gangs and gang delinquency have been tried over the years, there is no convincing evidence that any of these programs to prevent, reform, or suppress gang delinquency has been successful. If carefully done experimental and quasi-experimental designs are used as our benchmark of program effectiveness, there is simply no compelling evidence that they are effective. At best, some "promising" programs show signs of early or modest success (see Howell, 2000). But, if we take evidence-based programming as the criterion for recommending the general implementation of a program (Sherman et al., 1997), there are none to recommend.

The Way Forward

What then should we do? The results presented in this book point to the tremendous importance of effectively changing the behavior of gang members if we are to reduce levels of delinquency and youth violence. Yet the results derived from the evaluation of gang programs do not point us to a set of programs with demonstrated effectiveness. Resolving this conundrum is one of the most important issues confronting the field of juvenile justice today. Here are several suggestions, which in consort may lead to a general strategy for addressing the problem of street gangs.

Direct Approaches

First, we need to recognize – as researchers, program officials, policy makers, and politicians – that it is tremendously hard to intervene *directly* with adolescent peer groups, especially deviant peer groups like the gang. Although the gang may be a powerful cause of the behavior we abhor, it does not logically follow that interventions focused directly on the gang are the best way to change the situation. Indeed, the evidence suggests that such a strategy may be counterproductive.

Dishion, McCord, and Poulin (1999) have shown, using experimental designs, that peer-based interventions have iatrogenic effects – that is, they *increase* delinquency. Regardless of the level of adult involvement in intervention programs in which delinquent peers are brought together, the positive reinforcements for deviance provided by the peers outweigh the negative reinforcements by the adults. This outcome may be even more powerful in gang interventions given the impact of gang membership, as opposed to regular delinquent peer groups, that we observed in our data. This possibility is certainly consistent with the outcomes associated with detached worker programs. As Klein has long noted (1971, 1995), detached worker programs reinforce group cohesion and identity, thereby increasing gang violence.

Given these findings it may be wise to abandon, at least for the moment, programs that are directly focused on the gang or in which gang members, either from the same or different gangs, are brought together for treatment. According to the current evidence, these programs will likely be either ineffective or counterproductive. We recognize that this recommendation may appear counterintuitive, flying in the face of our desire to deal directly with what we think is a major cause of delinquency – the gang. But discretion is often the better part of valor. This may well be one of those circumstances, especially if there is an alternative.

Indirect Approaches

The alternative comes from the evidence associated with programs to prevent and treat delinquency, including serious and violent delinquency. Unlike the situation with gang programming in which it appears that little, if anything, "works," the evaluation of delinquency prevention and treatment programs has identified a number of effective programs. Because of this, our most central policy recommendation is to use gang membership as a *marker variable* to identify youths who are in need of extensive interventions in order to minimize their involvement in delinquency. The interventions they receive, however, should be divorced from the immediate context of the gang and based on the most appropriate interventions that have been shown to be effective in reducing delinquency.

A reasonable number of programs for reducing delinquency have been evaluated with acceptable scientific designs and have been shown to be effective. They range from general prevention programs aimed at relatively young children, for example, Headstart programs (Schweinhart, Barnes, and Weikart, 1993), through programs targeted at elementary-aged children who are at risk for joining gangs, for example, the Seattle Social Development Project (Hawkins et al., 1992) and the Montreal Preventive Program (Tremblay et al., 1996), to programs focused on more serious adolescent offenders, for example, the Multi-Systemic Treatment approach (Henggeler, Melton, and Smith, 1992). Several excellent reviews of programs that have demonstrated effectiveness in reducing delinquency are available. They include the work of the Office of Juvenile Justice and Delinquency Prevention's (OJJDP) Study Group on Serious and Violent Juvenile Offenders (Loeber and Farrington, 1998), especially the chapters in Part II, "Preventive Interventions and Graduated Sanctions." Additional sources include OJJDP's Guide for Implementing the Comprehensive Strategy for Serious, Violent, and Chronic Juvenile Offenders (Howell, 1995), the Blueprints Program (Elliott, 1998; Mihalic et al., 2001), the National Institute of Justice Report on Preventing Crime (Sherman et al., 1997), and the U.S. Surgeon General's Report on Youth Violence (U.S. Department of Health and Human Services, 2001).

Our proposal is straightforward: we should steer gang members and youths who are at elevated risk for gang membership into programs that have demonstrated effectiveness in reducing delinquency and promoting prosocial competencies. Across the range of these programs one can find different treatment components and modalities as well as programs that are focused on different risk factors, including family, school, and social skills.

Program Characteristics

In choosing among these programs, one need not lose sight of the fact that the focus is still on reducing gang membership and the delinquent and criminal behavior of gang members, not simply delinquent behavior. Our understanding of gang members can be matched with the characteristics of the program to identify ones that seem most relevant to this particular problem. Indeed, the empirical results of this study suggest several factors that should be taken into account in selecting and developing specific programs for dealing with gang members. Six appear to be particularly salient.

1. Relatively early prevention and reform programs, starting during the middle school years, should be given priority. Gang membership in Rochester was most common between grades 8 and 10. Waiting beyond this window to prevent youths from joining gangs may well be too late. Hence programs that target these ages, especially programs that are focused on keeping youths out of deviant social networks, may be particularly helpful in reducing the level of gang membership.

There is a second reason for emphasizing early programming. One of the most powerful findings to emerge from this analysis is the pervasive negative consequence of gang membership. It increases involvement in deviant activities and disrupts normal adolescent development and the transition to adulthood. As a result, delayed interventions will have to deal not only with gang membership but with a host of interlocking deficits generated, at least in part, by gang membership. This is a great deal to overcome and may be one reason that gang programs evidence so little success. Early programs simply have less to overcome and may therefore have somewhat higher chances of success.

2. At whatever ages they are offered, programs should be comprehensive and multifaceted, able to target multiple deficits in the individual's development. Our examination of antecedent risk factors for gang membership indicated that gang members experience risk in multiple domains of their lives. Single-focus interventions are not consistent with

this empirical observation. Programs that are able to deal with multiple deficits and the ways in which they become systematically interlocked over time are far more consistent with the characteristics of the "typical" gang member.

The risk factor analyses also identified several specific domains of adolescent development that should be given particular attention. Gang members experience substantially elevated stress, as measured by negative life events, and strong delinquent belief systems. Programs that emphasize the development of coping skills and cognitive competencies may be particularly beneficial. Similarly, we observed a strong impact of precocious sexual activity, both as a precursor and consequence of gang membership. Programs that include components focusing on teenage sexuality may also be quite helpful. Finally, strong school performance and high aspirations are strongly related to reducing the chances of gang membership. School-based programs to enhance these skills should be given priority.

3. The results of our investigation indicate that gang membership in Rochester, as in other cities, is strongly linked to minority group status, poverty, and disadvantaged neighborhoods. We should not lose sight of the central observation that gangs are, and always have been, linked to the American urban lower class. This suggests, among other things, that programs need to be culturally sensitive, tailored to the particular neighborhoods and racial and ethnic groups they serve.

It also suggests that programs designed to improve opportunities, to improve job skills and training, and to provide jobs in inner-city neighborhoods should be a fundamental part of our intervention efforts. This view is consistent with the recommendations coming from much observational research (e.g., Hagedorn, 1998; Klein, 1995; Moore, 1991).

4. It is also important that we recognize that gangs are a form of adolescent peer group and that peer influence and reinforcements appear to be central contributors to gang delinquency. Although peer-based programs may be counterproductive, that does not mean that peer influences should be ignored in treatment. To the contrary, many of the more successful programs focus explicitly on strategies – by the individual, family, and school – to combat peer effects (e.g., Hawkins et al., 1992; Henggeler et al., 1992). Programs that have strong peer components and that have demonstrated effectiveness in reducing delinquency may be particularly valuable in this context.

5. Throughout this book we have noted that gang effects are as strong for female gang members as they are for male gang members. The female members of the Rochester sample are as likely as the males to be gang members, although they stay for shorter periods of time. They are also likely to have highly elevated rates of delinquency when they are gang members, and

to experience long-term negative consequences. Because of this, programs should be made available for female gang members in their own right and not merely as auxiliary members.

6. Finally, gang membership is relatively fleeting, at least in an emergent gang city like Rochester. Programs should seize on this natural volatility by attempting to identify and intervene with new gang members before they become ensnared by the excitement and benefits of the gang. Also, programs with components that emphasize resistance to peer influence and the negative consequences of deviance may be particularly effective with newer members.

Evaluating Gang Programs

We recognize that our recommendation to focus on what we have labeled "indirect approaches" would constitute new, unevaluated programs with respect to gangs and gang members. What works for preventing and treating delinquency may or may not be effective with gang members. It is imperative that these and other programs for gang members be rigorously evaluated. We take it as axiomatic that only programs with scientifically *demonstrated* effectiveness should be implemented on a wide-scale basis (Sherman et al., 1997). Unfortunately, we have very little solid, scientific evidence on which to base policy choices in the area of gang programming.

First, very few of the hundreds and hundreds of gang programs that have been tried have ever been evaluated, a point illustrated by Klein. In 1990, California's "Office of Criminal Justice Planning ... poured almost $6 million into sixty projects" to reduce gang violence. "Yet not a dollar went to independent evaluation of the effectiveness of these projects. Sixty wasted opportunities to assess our efforts seems to be an inexcusable exercise in public irresponsibility" (Klein, 1995: 138). Second, of the programs that have been assessed, "very few rigorous scientific evaluations have been undertaken" (Howell, 2000: 1). For example, of the 26 gang evaluations listed by Howell (2000: 3–4), only 1 is based on random assignment.

The lack of fit between the quality of the evaluations of gang programs and the contribution that gang members make to the crime problem is both ironic and damaging to the formation of an overall juvenile justice policy. Precisely in the area where we need the most exacting data, we have some of the weakest. To address this imbalance we recommend that at both the federal and state levels, 10% of all resources spent on gang programming be allocated to evaluation research. This is the same level of allocation recommended by Sherman et al. (1997). We can only hope to reduce gang delinquency if we insist on building an accurate understanding of the causes and consequences of gang membership and of the programs that effectively combat it.

New Gang Programs

Earlier we argued that we should focus on indirect approaches to intervening with gangs and gang members. Given the state of gang programming at the moment, that seems like a wise choice. But that does not mean that we should entirely abandon our efforts at direct approaches. In the long run, developing effective gang prevention and treatment programs may well be desirable and we should work toward that goal. In doing so, however, we should recognize that this effort is, quite literally, experimental. We simply do not know what works in reducing gangs, gang membership, or gang behavior. One response is to take "promising" gang programs (see Howell, 1998) and variants of them, implement them on a limited basis, monitor what was actually done, and evaluate their effectiveness fully with randomized trials. Doing so gradually and carefully may ultimately lead to effective programming, but we will not get there overnight. It will take time, resources, and commitment. But it is foolhardy to think that anything less than that will be able to combat an adversary as strong as the street gang.

Future Research Directions

The findings reported in this book have complemented and extended the knowledge that we have obtained over the years from observational studies of gangs. By focusing on the individual gang member within the context of a longitudinal panel study, we have been able to address such issues as why youths join gangs, the effect of gang membership on a variety of problematic behaviors, the comparison of gang membership with delinquent peer groups, and the consequences of gang membership for the transition to adult status. Our findings on these topics, coupled with the limitations of the current study, suggest a number of directions for future research.

A major theme that has emerged from our findings is the dramatic effect joining a gang has on both short-term behavioral outcomes and longer-term transitional events. Joining a gang facilitates a variety of criminal behaviors including drug selling and illegal gun carrying. In addition, gang membership has detrimental effects on the movement to adult status because it leads to problematic transitions such as dropping out of school, becoming a teenage parent, and unemployment in the early adult years. It is particularly important to recognize that gang membership has these effects over and above the effect of simply having delinquent peers. There is something about the dynamics of being in a gang that produces these outcomes.

Because of this, one issue future research should focus on is identifying the social network characteristics of the gang, as compared with other delinquent peer groups, to see how those characteristics might generate problematic outcomes. Network structure and dynamics may distinguish the gang from delinquent peer networks in important ways. Certainly the insights from observational studies would suggest that the gang holds a special status for its members. For some it is seen as playing the role of a surrogate family; for others it constitutes an alternative life-style. However, the processes through which it plays these roles have not been documented.

Identifying the social network characteristics of gangs underscores the need for multimethod gang studies that combine both observational and survey data collection techniques. Observational studies have focused primarily on existing gang members and have provided a wealth of information on their interaction while in the gang. But observational studies do not lend themselves well to either a prospective or comparative focus. It is very difficult for observational techniques to study future gang members as the number of potential recruits make detailed observations impossible. Hence, observational studies cannot compare such things as the social networks of future gang members and those of youths who do not enter a gang. Nor do observational studies compare the social networks of gang members to those of nonmembers. A prospective survey, coupled with detailed observations of different types of youth groups, would establish the data base necessary to answer some of these intriguing and fundamental questions.

Earlier in this chapter we compared some of the different images of the gang that have been suggested by observational research with those derived from survey research and raised the question of whether these differences were methods-dependent. We also suggested that these different images may be due to the different type of research sites in which the respective methodologies have been employed. Observational studies have primarily been done in larger cities having more organized and territorial traditional gangs. The recent prospective survey studies of gangs have been done in smaller cities that have emergent gangs.

Because of the potential confounding of research site, gang type, and research methodology, it seems impossible to resolve the different images of the gang that have emerged until individual-based longitudinal studies are conducted in traditional gang cities. The ideal design would be to embed the observational study of gangs and gang processes within an ongoing longitudinal study so that the findings of one approach can inform findings from the other. For example, one could observe gangs in neighborhoods that the members of a longitudinal panel are likely to join, if they were to join a gang. Such designs would be difficult and expensive to implement, but they are necessary to resolve these issues.

Regardless of the specific methodological design or the city in which it is conducted, future research must include longer-term follow-up studies of gang members in order to assess the impact that gang membership has on the life course. Following our sample through the age of 22 has generated findings that indicate that gang membership has important detrimental effects on transitions to adult status. Life-course theories (e.g., Thornberry and Krohn, 2001) suggest that failure to make successful transitions as one enters adulthood can have a cascading effect on the life course. Are gang members less successful in their jobs than nonmembers when they reach their 30s, a time when the life course should become more stable? Do they have less successful partner relationships? Does having been a member of a gang impact their effectiveness as a parent? And what are the behavioral consequences in adulthood of having been a gang member? These questions can only be addressed if the upper age at which we assess gang members is extended well beyond that evident in most extant research.

In closing, we hope that the results of this investigation, with its somewhat different methodological approach, add to our understanding of street gangs, their origins, and consequences. For if there is one result that all research on gangs agrees upon, it is the documentation of the tremendous toll that gang membership takes on the lives of gang members: it increases serious delinquency and official labeling, it disrupts the normal course of adolescent development, and it increases the risk of later disorder in the life course. Until we more fully understand the dynamics of street gangs that lead to these pernicious outcomes, we remain ineffective in our efforts to combat them. This is a difficult challenge, both for research and for policy, but it is an essential challenge for us to meet if we are to rid contemporary society of youth crime and violence.

Delinquency Indices

The delinquency indices are based on a series of questions that begin with the phrase, "Since we interviewed you last time, have you . . ."

General Delinquency

1. Run away from home?
2. Skipped classes without an excuse?
3. Lied about your age to get into some place or to buy something (for example, lying about your age to get into a movie or buy alcohol)?
4. Hitchhiked a ride with a stranger?
5. Carried a hidden weapon?
6. Been loud or rowdy in a public place where someone complained and you got in trouble?
7. Begged for money or things from strangers?
8. Been drunk in a public place?
9. Damaged, destroyed, marked up, or tagged somebody else's property on purpose?
10. Set fire on purpose or tried to set fire to a house, building, or car?
11. Avoided paying for things, like a movie, taking bus rides, using a computer, or anything else?
12. Gone into or tried to go into a building to steal or damage something?
13. Tried to steal or actually stolen money or things worth $5 or less?
14. Tried to steal or actually stolen money or things worth $5 to $50?
15. Tried to steal or actually stolen money or things worth between $50 and $100?
16. Tried to steal or actually stolen money or things worth more than $100?
17. Tried to buy or sell things that were stolen?

18. Taken someone else's car or motorcycle for a ride without the owner's permission?
19. Stolen or tried to steal a car or other motor vehicle?
20. Forged a check or used fake money to pay for something?
21. Used or tried to use a credit card, bank card, or automatic teller card without permission?
22. Tried to cheat someone by selling them something that was not what you said it was or that was worthless?
23. Attacked someone with a weapon or with the idea of seriously hurting or killing them?
24. Hit someone with the idea of hurting them?
25. Been involved in gang or posse fights?
26. Thrown objects such as rocks or bottles at people?
27. Used a weapon or force to make someone give you money or things?
28. Made obscene phone calls?
29. Been paid for having sexual relations with someone?
30. Physically hurt or threatened to hurt someone to get them to have sex with you?
31. Sold marijuana, reefer, or pot?
32. Sold hard drugs such as crack, heroin, cocaine, LSD, or acid?

Violent Delinquency

1. Attacked someone with a weapon or with the idea of seriously hurting or killing them?
2. Hit someone with the idea of hurting them?
3. Been involved in gang or posse fights?
4. Thrown objects such as rocks or bottles at people?
5. Used a weapon or force to make someone give you money or things?
6. Physically hurt or threatened to hurt someone to get them to have sex with you?

Drug Use

1. Used marijuana, reefer, or pot?
2. Inhaled things, other than cigarettes, like glue to get high?
3. Tried LSD, acid, or cubes?
4. Tried cocaine, coke, or snow, other than crack?
5. Tried crack?
6. Tried heroin or smack?
7. Tried angel dust or PCP?
8. Tried tranquilizers, ludes, or valium?
9. Tried downers, yellow jackets, or red or blue devils?
10. Tried uppers, speed, bennies, or black beauties?

Drug Sales

1. Sold marijuana, reefer, or pot?
2. Sold hard drugs such as crack, heroin, cocaine, LSD, or acid?

Serious Delinquency

1. Gone into or tried to go into a building to steal or damage something?
2. Tried to steal or actually stolen money or things worth between $50 and $100?
3. Tried to steal or actually stolen money or things worth more than $100?
4. Stolen or tried to steal a car or other motor vehicle?
5. Attacked someone with a weapon or with the idea of seriously hurting or killing them?
6. Been involved in gang or posse fights?
7. Used a weapon or force to make someone give you money or things?
8. Physically hurt or threatened to hurt someone to get them to have sex with you?

Moderate Delinquency

1. Been drunk in a public place?
2. Damaged, destroyed, marked up, or tagged somebody else's property on purpose?
3. Tried to steal or actually stolen money or things worth $5 to $50?
4. Taken someone else's car or motorcycle for a ride without the owner's permission?
5. Forged a check or used fake money to pay for something?
6. Used or tried to use a credit card, bank card, or automatic teller card without permission?
7. Tried to cheat someone by selling them something that was not what you said it was or that was worthless?
8. Hit someone with the idea of hurting them?
9. Thrown objects such as rocks or bottles at people?
10. Made obscene phone calls?

Minor Delinquency

1. Run away from home?
2. Skipped classes without an excuse?
3. Lied about your age to get into some place or to buy something (for example, lying about your age to get into a movie or buy alcohol)?
4. Hitchhiked a ride with a stranger?

5. Been loud or rowdy in a public place where someone complained and you got in trouble?
6. Begged for money or things from strangers?
7. Avoided paying for things, like a movie, taking bus rides, using a computer, or anything else?
8. Tried to steal or actually stolen money or things worth $5 or less?

Serious Violent Delinquency

1. Attacked someone with a weapon or with the idea of seriously hurting or killing them?
2. Been involved in gang or posse fights?
3. Used a weapon or force to make someone give you money or things?
4. Physically hurt or threatened to hurt someone to get them to have sex with you?

Property Offenses

1. Damaged, destroyed, marked up, or tagged somebody else's property on purpose?
2. Set fire on purpose or tried to set fire to a house, building, or car?
3. Avoided paying for things, like a movie, taking bus rides, using a computer, or anything else?
4. Gone into or tried to go into a building to steal or damage something?
5. Tried to steal or actually stolen money or things worth $5 or less?
6. Tried to steal or actually stolen money or things worth $5 to $50?
7. Tried to steal or actually stolen money or things worth between $50 and $100?
8. Tried to steal or actually stolen money or things worth more than $100?
9. Tried to buy or sell things that were stolen?
10. Taken someone else's car or motorcycle for a ride without the owner's permission?
11. Stolen or tried to steal a car or other motor vehicle?
12. Forged a check or used fake money to pay for something?
13. Used or tried to use a credit card, bank card, or automatic teller card without permission?
14. Tried to cheat someone by selling them something that was not what you said it was or that was worthless?

Public Disorder Offenses

1. Hitchhiked a ride with a stranger?
2. Been loud or rowdy in a public place where someone complained and you got in trouble?

3. Begged for money or things from strangers?
4. Been drunk in a public place?
5. Made obscene phone calls?

Alcohol Use

1. Drunk beer or wine without your parents' permission?
2. Drunk hard liquor without your parents' permission?

Prevalence of Gang Membership

Table B.1. *Ever Prevalence of Gang Membership, Wave 2 through Wave 9 (%)*

	Nonmembers	Gang Members	n[a]
Total Sample	73.7	26.3	796
Gender			
Male	73.7[b]	26.3	579
Female	73.7	26.3	216
Race/Ethnicity			
African American	67.7	32.3*	522
Hispanic	81.5	18.5	124
White	88.3	11.7	149
Race/Ethnicity: Male			
African American	69.0	31.0*	315
Hispanic	68.3	31.7	95
White	85.6	14.4	168
Race/Ethnicity: Female			
African American	66.8	33.2*	165
Hispanic	95.8	4.2	32
White	97.3	2.7	19

Note: Results reported for the subsample of gang members who were interviewed at all eight waves (Wave 2 through Wave 9).

[a]Sample size varies across groups due to the weighting procedure used.

[b]The ever-prevalence rates are, in fact, identical for males and females.

*p < .05 (chi-square test).

Table B.2. *Annual Prevalence of Gang Membership (%)*

	Year 1	Year 2	Year 3	Year 4	n^a
Total	20.6	10.4	6.2	4.6	796
Gender					
Male	17.0	13.0	9.7	7.2	579
Female	24.2	7.8	2.7	1.9	216
Race/Ethnicity					
African American	26.6	12.4	6.2	5.1	523
Hispanic	12.1	6.7	7.8	2.7	124
White	6.7	6.4	5.0	4.2	149
Race/Ethnicity: Male					
African American	20.6	16.0	9.8	8.8	317
Hispanic	19.4	12.9	14.9	5.2	95
White	8.7	7.5	6.5	5.4	168
Race/Ethnicity: Female					
African American	30.8	9.9	3.6	2.5	165
Hispanic	4.2	0.0	0.0	0.0	32
White	0.0	2.7	0.0	0.0	19

Note: Results reported for the subsample of gang members who were interviewed at all eight waves (Wave 2 through Wave 9).
[a]Sample size varies across groups due to the weighting procedure used.

Impact of Gang Membership

Table C.1. *The Impact of Gang Membership Status on Self-Reported General Delinquency, OLS Estimates, Males Only (standardized OLS regression coefficients)*

	Self-Reported General Delinquency (logged)			
	Year 1[a]	Year 2[b]	Year 3[c]	Year 4[d]
Gang Membership Status				
Current Gang Member	.26**	.29**	.27**	.22**
Future Gang Member	.10**	.12**	.06**	–
Past Gang Member	–	.03	.09*	.02
Risk Factors				
Family Poverty Level	.02	.00	−.04	−.02
Parental Supervision	−.07*	−.01	−.01	−.10*
Commitment to School	−.12**	−.15**	−.21**	−.04
Association with Delinquent Peers	.31**	.12**	.14**	.22**
Negative Life Events	.17**	.14**	.19**	.16**
Prior General Delinquency	.23**	.15**	.15**	.13**
Adjusted R^2	.56	.34	.37	.26
	(n = 520)	(n = 526)	(n = 481)	(n = 428)

[a]Year 1 general delinquency combines data from Waves 2 and 3; risk factors are from Wave 2.
[b]Year 2 general delinquency combines data from Waves 4 and 5; risk factors are from Wave 3.
[c]Year 3 general delinquency combines data from Waves 6 and 7; risk factors are from Wave 5.
[d]Year 4 general delinquency combines data from Waves 8 and 9; risk factors are from Wave 7.
*p < .05. **p < .01.

Table C.2. *The Impact of Gang Membership Status on Self-Reported Violent Delinquency, OLS Estimates, Males Only (standardized OLS regression coefficients)*

	Self-Reported Violent Delinquency (logged)			
	Year 1[a]	Year 2[b]	Year 3[c]	Year 4[d]
Gang Membership Status				
Current Gang Member	.26**	.35**	.33**	.33**
Future Gang Member	.13**	.16**	.09	–
Past Gang Member	–	−.02	.04	.12**
Risk Factors				
Family Poverty Level	.02	−.05	.04	.03
Parental Supervision	−.05*	−.08*	−.01	−.04
Commitment to School	−.04	−.03	.01	−.03
Association with Delinquent Peers	.32**	.09**	.12**	.24**
Negative Life Events	.14**	.15**	.21**	.02
Prior Violent Delinquency	.15**	.09**	.12**	.09*
Adjusted R²	.42	.30	.27	.26
	(n = 520)	(n = 526)	(n = 481)	(n = 428)

[a]Year 1 violent delinquency combines data from Waves 2 and 3; risk factors are from Wave 2.
[b]Year 2 violent delinquency combines data from Waves 4 and 5; risk factors are from Wave 3.
[c]Year 3 violent delinquency combines data from Waves 6 and 7; risk factors are from Wave 5.
[d]Year 4 violent delinquency combines data from Waves 8 and 9; risk factors are from Wave 7.
*p < .05. **p < .01.

Table C.3. *The Impact of Gang Membership Status on Self-Reported Drug Use, OLS Estimates, Males Only (standardized OLS regression coefficients)*

	Self-Reported Drug Use (logged)			
	Year 1[a]	Year 2[b]	Year 3[c]	Year 4[d]
Gang Membership Status				
Current Gang Member	.14**	.23**	.18**	.23**
Future Gang Member	.03	.02	.00	–
Past Gang Member	–	−.00	−.04	.09*
Risk Factors				
Family Poverty Level	.01	.07*	.00	−.02
Parental Supervision	−.04	−.02	−.01	−.00
Commitment to School	−.03	−.03	−.13**	−.12**
Association with Delinquent Peers	.36**	.17**	.16**	.09*
Negative Life Events	−.02	.04	.03	.12**
Prior Drug Use	.05	.27**	.28**	.30**
Adjusted R^2	.19	.22	.22	.24
	(n = 520)	(n = 526)	(n = 481)	(n = 428)

[a]Year 1 drug use combines data from Waves 2 and 3; risk factors are from Wave 2.
[b]Year 2 drug use combines data from Waves 4 and 5; risk factors are from Wave 3.
[c]Year 3 drug use combines data from Waves 6 and 7; risk factors are from Wave 5.
[d]Year 4 drug use combines data from Waves 8 and 9; risk factors are from Wave 7.
*p < .05. **p < .01.

Table C.4. *The Impact of Gang Membership Status on Self-Reported Drug Sales, OLS Estimates, Males Only (standardized OLS regression coefficients)*

	Self-Reported Drug Sales (logged)			
	Year 1[a]	Year 2[b]	Year 3[c]	Year 4[d]
Gang Membership Status				
Current Gang Member	.23**	.33**	.22**	.15**
Future Gang Member	.00	.00	−.06	–
Past Gang Member	–	−.03	.01	−.01
Risk Factors				
Family Poverty Level	.00	.11**	.01	−.04
Parental Supervision	.04	−.04	−.01	.00
Commitment to School	−.02	.07	−.05	.03
Association with Delinquent Peers	.17**	.23**	.17**	.22**
Negative Life Events	−.03	.01	.04	.08*
Prior Drug Sales	.36**	−.01	.06	.31**
Adjusted R^2	.27	.21	.11	.21
	(n = 520)	(n = 526)	(n = 481)	(n = 428)

[a]Year 1 drug sales combines data from Waves 2 and 3; risk factors are from Wave 2.
[b]Year 2 drug sales combines data from Waves 4 and 5; risk factors are from Wave 3.
[c]Year 3 drug sales combines data from Waves 6 and 7; risk factors are from Wave 5.
[d]Year 4 drug sales combines data from Waves 8 and 9; risk factors are from Wave 7.
*p < .05. **p < .01.

References

Achenbach, Thomas M., and Craig S. Edelbrock. (1979). The child behavior profile: II. Boys aged 12–16 and girls aged 6–11 and 12–16. *Journal of Consulting and Clinical Psychology* 47:223–233.

Baltes, Paul B. (1987). Theoretical propositions of life-span developmental psychology: On the dynamics between growth and decline. *Developmental Psychology* 23:611–626.

Baltes, Paul B., and Orville G. Brim Jr. (Eds.). (1982). *Life Span Development and Behavior* (Vol. 4). New York: Academic Press.

Battin, Sara R., Karl G. Hill, Robert D. Abbott, Richard F. Catalano, and J. David Hawkins. (1998). The contribution of gang membership to delinquency beyond delinquent friends. *Criminology* 36:93–115.

Battin, Sara R., Karl G. Hill, J. David Hawkins, Richard F. Catalano, and Robert D. Abbott. (1996). Testing gang membership and association with antisocial peers as independent predictors of antisocial behavior: Gang members compared to non-gang members of law-violating youth groups. Paper presented at the annual meeting of the American Society of Criminology, Chicago, November.

Battin-Pearson, Sara R., Terence P. Thornberry, J. David Hawkins, and Marvin D. Krohn. (1998). *Gang Membership, Delinquent Peers, and Delinquent Behavior.* Juvenile Justice Bulletin. Washington, DC: U.S. Department of Justice, Office of Juvenile Justice and Delinquency Prevention.

Bjerregaard, Beth, and Alan J. Lizotte. (1995). Gun ownership and gang membership. *Journal of Criminal Law and Criminology* 86:37–58.

Bjerregaard, Beth, and Carolyn A. Smith. (1993). Gender differences in gang participation, delinquency, and substance use. *Journal of Quantitative Criminology* 9:329–355.

Blumstein, Alfred, Jacqueline Cohen, Jeffrey A. Roth, and Christy A. Visher (Eds.). (1986). *Criminal Careers and "Career Criminals"* (Vol. 1). Washington, DC: National Academy Press.

Bolger, Kerry E., Charlotte J. Patterson, William W. Thompson, and Janis B. Kupersmidt. (1995). Psychosocial adjustment among children experiencing persistent and intermittent family economic hardship. *Child Development* 66:1107–1129.

Bowker, Lee H., and Malcolm W. Klein. (1983). The etiology of female juvenile delinquency and gang membership: A test of psychological and social structural explanations. *Adolescence* 18:739–751.

Bronfenbrenner, Uri. (1979). *The Ecology of Human Development: Experiments by Nature and Design.* Cambridge, MA: Harvard University Press.

Bursik, Robert J., and Harold G. Grasmick. (1993). *Neighborhoods and Crime: The Dimensions of Effective Community Control.* New York: Lexington Books.

Bushway, Shawn D., Robert Brame, and Raymond Paternoster. (1999). Assessing stability and change in criminal offending: A comparison of random effects, semi-parametric, and fixed effects modeling strategies. *Journal of Quantitative Criminology* 15:23–61.

Campbell, Anne. (1990). Female participation in gangs. Pp. 163–182 in C. Ronald Huff (Ed.), *Gangs in America.* Newbury Park, CA: Sage.

Cartwright, Desmond S., Barbara Tomson, and Hershey Schwartz. (1975). *Gang Delinquency.* Monterey, CA: Brooks/Cole.

Caspi, Avshalom, Bradley R. E. Wright, Terrie E. Moffitt, and Phil A. Silva. (1998). Early failure in the labor market: Childhood and adolescent predictors of unemployment in the transition to adulthood. *American Sociological Review* 63:424–451.

Cicchetti, Dante, and Fred A. Rogosch. (1996). Equifinality and multifinality in developmental psychopathology. *Development and Psychopathology* 8:597–600.

Cloward, Richard A., and Lloyd E. Ohlin. (1960). *Delinquency and Opportunity: A Theory of Delinquent Gangs.* New York: Free Press.

Cohen, Albert K. (1955). *Delinquent Boys: The Culture of the Gang.* Glencoe, IL: Free Press.

Cohen, Bernard. (1969). The delinquency of gangs and spontaneous groups. Pp. 61–111 in Thorsten Sellin and Marvin E. Wolfgang (Eds.), *Delinquency: Selected Studies.* New York: Wiley.

Cohen, Marcia I., Katherine Williams, Alan M. Bekelman, and Scott Crosse. (1994). Evaluation of the National Youth Gang Drug Prevention Program. Pp. 266–275 in Malcolm W. Klein, Cheryl L. Maxson, and Jody Miller (Eds.), *The Modern Gang Reader.* Los Angeles: Roxbury.

Coleman, James S. (1988). Social capital and the creation of human capital. *American Journal of Sociology* 94:S95–S120.

——— (1990). *Foundations of Social Theory.* Cambridge, MA: Harvard University Press.

Cook, Philip J., Stephanie Molliconi, and Thomas B. Cole. (1995). Regulating gun markets. *Journal of Criminal Law and Criminology* 86:59–92.

Curry, G. David. (2000). Self-reported gang involvement and officially recorded delinquency. *Criminology* 38:1253–1274.

Curry, G. David, Richard A. Ball, and Scott H. Decker. (1996a). *Estimating the National Scope of Gang Crime from Law Enforcement Data.* Research in Brief. Washington, DC: U.S. Department of Justice, National Institute of Justice.

(1996b). Estimating the national scope of gang crime from law enforcement data. Pp. 21–36 in C. Ronald Huff (Ed.), *Gangs in America* (2nd ed.). Thousand Oaks, CA: Sage.

Curry, G. David, and Scott H. Decker. (1997). What's in a name?: A gang by any other name isn't quite the same. *Valparaiso University Law Review* 31:501–514.

(1998). *Confronting Gangs: Crime and Community.* Los Angeles: Roxbury.

Curry, G. David, and Irving A. Spergel. (1992). Gang involvement and delinquency among Hispanic and African-American adolescent males. *Journal of Research in Crime and Delinquency* 29:273–291.

Dahmann, J. (1995). *Operation Hardcore, a Prosecutorial Response to Violent Gang Criminality: Interim Evaluation Report.* Pp. 301–303 in Malcolm W. Klein, Cheryl L. Maxson, and Jody Miller (Eds.), *The Modern Gang Reader.* Los Angeles: Roxbury. (Original work published 1981)

Decker, Scott H. (1996). Collective and normative features of gang violence. *Justice Quarterly* 13:243–264.

(2000). Legitimating drug use: A note on the impact of gang membership and drug sales on the use of illicit drugs. *Justice Quarterly* 17:393–410.

Decker, Scott H., Tim Bynum, and Deborah Weisel. (1998). A tale of two cities: Gangs as organized crime groups. *Justice Quarterly* 15:393–425.

Decker, Scott H., and G. David Curry. (2000). Addressing key features of gang membership: Measuring the involvement of young members. *Journal of Criminal Justice* 28:473–482.

Decker, Scott H., and Janet L. Lauritsen. (1996). Breaking the bonds of membership: Leaving the gang. Pp. 103–122 in C. Ronald Huff (Ed.), *Gangs in America* (2nd ed.). Thousand Oaks, CA: Sage.

Decker, Scott H., and Barrik Van Winkle. (1996). *Life in the Gang: Family, Friends, and Violence.* Cambridge: Cambridge University Press.

Deschenes, Elizabeth P., and Finn-Aage Esbensen. (1999). Violence and gangs: Gender differences in perceptions and behavior. *Journal of Quantitative Criminology* 15:63–96.

Dishion, Thomas J., Joan McCord, and François Poulin. (1999). When interventions harm. *American Psychologist* 54:755–764.

Egley, Arlen, Jr. (2000). *Highlights of the 1999 National Youth Gang Survey.* Fact Sheet no. 20. Washington, DC: U.S. Department of Justice, Office of Juvenile Justice and Delinquency Prevention.

Elder, Glen H., Jr. (1985). Perspectives on the life course. Pp. 23–49 in Glen H. Elder Jr. (Ed.), *Life Course Dynamics.* Ithaca, NY: Cornell University Press.

(1994). Time, human agency, and social change: Perspectives on the life course. *Social Psychology Quarterly* 57:4–15.

(1997). The life course and human development. Pp. 939–991 in Richard M. Lerner (Ed.), *Handbook of Child Psychology:* Vol. 1. *Theoretical Models of Human Development.* New York: Wiley.

Elder, Glen H., Jr., and Avshalom Caspi. (1988). Economic stress in lives: Developmental perspectives. *Social Problems* 44:25–45.

Elliott, Delbert S. (1998). *Blueprints for Violence Prevention*. Center for the Study and Prevention of Violence. University of Colorado at Boulder.

Emery, Robert E., and K. Daniel O'Leary. (1982). Children's perceptions of marital discord and behavior problems of boys and girls. *Journal of Abnormal Child Psychology* 10:11–24.

Esbensen, Finn-Aage, and David Huizinga. (1993). Gangs, drugs, and delinquency in a survey of urban youth. *Criminology* 4:565–589.

Esbensen, Finn-Aage, David Huizinga, and Anne W. Weiher. (1993). Gang and non-gang youth: Differences in explanatory factors. *Journal of Contemporary Criminal Justice* 9:94–116.

Esbensen, Finn-Aage, and D. Wayne Osgood. (1997). *National Evaluation of G.R.E.A.T.* Research in Brief. Washington, DC: U.S. Department of Justice, National Institute of Justice.

   (1999). Gang Resistance Education and Training (GREAT): Results from the national evaluation. *Journal of Research in Crime and Delinquency* 36:194–225.

Esbensen, Finn-Aage., D. Wayne Osgood, Terrance J. Taylor, Dana Peterson, and Adrienne Freng. (2001). How great is G.R.E.A.T.?: Results from a longitudinal quasi-experimental design. *Criminology and Public Policy* 1:87–118.

Esbensen, Finn-Aage, and L. Thomas Winfree. (1998). Race and gender differences between gang and nongang youths: Results from a multisite survey. *Justice Quarterly* 15:505–526.

Fagan, Jeffrey. (1989). The social organization of drug use and drug dealing among urban gangs. *Criminology* 27:633–669.

   (1990). Social processes of delinquency and drug use among urban gangs. Pp. 183–219 in C. Ronald Huff (Ed.), *Gangs in America*. Newbury Park, CA: Sage.

   (1996). Gangs, drugs, and neighborhood change. Pp. 39–74 in C. Ronald Huff (Ed.), *Gangs in America* (2nd ed.). Thousand Oaks, CA: Sage.

Fagan, Jeffrey, and Edward Pabon. (1990). Contributions of delinquency and substance use to school dropout among inner-city youths. *Youth and Society* 21:306–354.

Fagan, Jeffrey, Elizabeth Piper, and Melinda Moore. (1986). Violent delinquents and urban youths. *Criminology* 24:439–471.

Farnworth, Margaret, Terence P. Thornberry, Marvin D. Krohn, and Alan J. Lizotte. (1994). Measurement in the study of class and delinquency: Integrating theory and research. *Journal of Research in Crime and Delinquency* 31:32–61.

Farrington, David P. (1977). The effects of public labeling. *British Journal of Criminology* 17:112–125.

   (1987). Early precursors of frequent offending. Pp. 27–50 in James Q. Wilson and Glenn C. Loury (Eds.), *From Children to Citizens*. New York: Springer-Verlag.

   (2000). Explaining and preventing crime: The globalization of knowledge – The American Society of Criminology 1999 presidential address. *Criminology* 38:1–24.

Fishman, Laura T. (1995). The vice queens: An ethnographic study of black female gang behavior. Pp. 83–92 in Malcolm W. Klein, Cheryl L. Maxson, and Jody Miller (Eds.), *The Modern Gang Reader*. Los Angeles: Roxbury.

Flanagan, Timothy J., and Kathleen Maguire (Eds.). (1992). *Sourcebook of Criminal Justice Statistics 1991*. U.S. Department of Justice, Bureau of Justice Statistics. Washington, DC: U.S. Government Printing Office.

Friedman, C. Jack, Fredrica Mann, and Alfred S. Friedman. (1975). A profile of juvenile street gang members. *Adolescence* 10:563–607.

Garmezy, Norman. (1995). Stress resistant children: The search for protective factors. Pp. 213–233 in J. E. Stevenson (Ed.), *Aspects of Current Child Psychiatry Research*. Oxford: Pergamon.

Gatti, Uberto, Frank Vitaro, Richard E. Tremblay, and Pierre McDuff. (2002). Youth gangs and violent behavior: Results from the Montreal Longitudinal Experimental Study. Paper presented at the XV World Meeting of the International Society for Research on Aggression, Montreal, July.

Gerrard, Nathan L. (1964). The core member of the gang. *British Journal of Criminology* 4:361–371.

Gottfredson, Michael R., and Travis Hirschi. (1990). *A General Theory of Crime*. Stanford, CA: Stanford University Press.

Hagan, John. (1997). Crime and capitalization: Toward a developmental theory of street crime in America. Pp. 287–308 in Terence P. Thornberry (Ed.), *Developmental Theories of Crime and Delinquency*. New Brunswick, NJ: Transaction Publishers.

Hagedorn, John H. (1998). *People and Folks: Gangs, Crime and the Underclass in a Rustbelt City* (2nd ed.). Chicago: Lake View Press.

Harris, Mary G. (1994). Cholas, Mexican-American girls, and gangs. *Sex Roles* 30:289–301.

Hawkins, J. David, Richard F. Catalano, and Janet Y. Miller. (1992). Risk and protective factors for alcohol and other drug problems in adolescence and early adulthood: Implications for substance abuse prevention. *Psychological Bulletin* 112:64–105.

Hawkins, J. David, Richard F. Catalano, Diane M. Morrison, Julie O'Donnell, Robert D. Abbott, and L. Edward Day. (1992). The Seattle Social Development Project: Effects of the first four years of protective factors and problem behaviors. Pp. 139–161 in Joan McCord and Richard E. Tremblay (Eds.), *Preventing Antisocial Behavior: Interventions from Birth through Adolescence*. New York: Guilford.

Hawkins, J. David, and Mark W. Fraser. (1985). Social networks of street drug users: A comparison of two theories. *Social Work Research Abstracts* 85:3–12.

Hawkins, J. David, Todd Herrenkohl, David P. Farrington, Devon Brewer, Richard F. Catalano, and Tracy W. Harachi. (1998). A review of predictors of youth violence. Pp. 106–146 in Rolf Loeber and David P. Farrington (Eds.), *Serious and Violent Juvenile Offenders: Risk Factors and Successful Interventions*. Thousand Oaks, CA: Sage.

Henggeler, Scott W., Gary B. Melton, and Linda A. Smith. (1992). Family preservation using multisystemic therapy: An effective alternative to incarcerating serious juvenile offenders. *Journal of Consulting and Clinical Psychology* 60:953–961.

Hetherington, E. Mavis, and Paul B. Baltes. (1988). Child psychology and life-span development. Pp. 1–19 in E. Mavis Hetherington, Richard M. Lerner, and Marion Perlmutter (Eds.), *Child Development in Life-Span Perspective*. Hillsdale, NJ: Erlbaum.

Hill, Karl G., J. David Hawkins, Richard F. Catalano, Richard Kosterman, Robert D. Abbott, and T. Edwards. (1996). The Longitudinal Dynamics of Gang Membership and Problem Behavior: A Replication and Extension of the Denver and Rochester Gang Studies in Seattle. Paper presented at the annual meeting of the American Society of Criminology, Chicago, November.

Hill, Karl G., J. David Hawkins, Richard F. Catalano, Eugene Maguin, and Richard Kosterman. (1995). The Role of Gang Membership in Delinquency, Substance Use, and Violent Offending. Paper presented at the annual meeting of the American Society of Criminology, Boston, November 17.

Hill, Karl G., James C. Howell, J. David Hawkins, and Sara R. Battin-Pearson. (1999). Childhood risk factors for adolescent gang membership: Results from the Seattle Social Development Project. *Journal of Research in Crime and Delinquency* 36:300–322.

Hindelang, Michael J., Travis Hirschi, and Joseph G. Weis. (1981). *Measuring Delinquency*. Beverly Hills, CA: Sage.

Hirschi, Travis. (1969). *Causes of Delinquency*. Berkeley: University of California Press.

Horowitz, Ruth. (1983). *Honor and the American Dream*. New Brunswick, NJ: Rutgers University Press.

Howell, James C. (1994). Recent gang research: Program and policy implications. *Crime and Delinquency* 40:495–515.

(1995). *Guide for Implementing the Comprehensive Strategy for Serious, Violent, and Chronic Juvenile Offenders*. Washington, DC: U.S. Department of Justice, Office of Juvenile Justice and Delinquency Prevention.

(1997). *Juvenile Justice and Youth Violence*. Thousand Oaks, CA: Sage.

(1998). Promising programs for youth gang violence prevention and intervention. Pp. 284–312 in Rolf Loeber and David P. Farrington (Eds.), *Serious and Violent Juvenile Offenders: Risk Factors and Successful Interventions*. Thousand Oaks, CA: Sage.

(2000). *Youth Gang Programs and Strategies*. Washington, DC: U.S. Department of Justice, Office of Juvenile Justice and Delinquency Prevention.

Howell, James C., Arlen Egley Jr., and Debra K. Gleason. (2002). *Modern-Day Youth Gangs*. Juvenile Justice Bulletin. Washington, DC: U.S. Department of Justice, Office of Juvenile Justice and Delinquency Prevention.

Hudson, Walter. (1982). *The Clinical Measurement Package: A Field Manual*. Homewood, IL: Dorsey Press.

Huff, C. Ronald. (1996). The criminal behavior of gang members and non-gang at-risk youth. Pp. 75–102 in C. Ronald Huff (Ed.), *Gangs in America* (2nd ed.). Thousand Oaks, CA: Sage.

Huizinga, David. (1996). *The Influence of Delinquent Peers, Gangs, and Co-Offending on Violence.* Fact Sheet. Washington, DC: U.S. Department of Justice, Office of Juvenile Justice and Delinquency Prevention.

——— (1997). Gangs and the Volume of Crime. Paper presented at the annual meeting of the Western Society of Criminology, Honolulu.

Huizinga, David, and Delbert S. Elliott. (1986). Reassessing the reliability and validity of self-report delinquency measures. *Journal of Quantitative Criminology* 2:293–327.

Huizinga, David, Barbara J. Morse, and Delbert S. Elliott. (1992). *The National Youth Survey: An Overview and Description of Recent Findings.* Boulder: Institute of Behavioral Science, University of Colorado.

Jang, Sung Joon. (1999). Age-varying effects of family, school, and peers on delinquency: A multilevel modeling test of interactional theory. *Criminology* 37:643–685.

Jankowski, Martin Sanchez. (1991). *Islands in the Street: Gangs and American Urban Society.* Berkeley: University of California Press.

Jansyn, Leon R., Jr. (1966). Solidarity and delinquency in a street corner group. *American Sociological Review* 31:600–614.

Jessor, Richard, John E. Donovan, and Frances M. Costa. (1991). *Beyond Adolescence: Problem Behavior and Young Adult Development.* Cambridge: Cambridge University Press.

Jessor, Richard, and Shirley L. Jessor. (1977). *Problem Behavior and Psychosocial Development: A Longitudinal Study of Youth.* New York: Academic Press.

Kamerman, Sheila B. (1981). Young people as individuals and as family members: The implications for public policy. Pp. 101–114 in Alvin C. Eurich (Ed.), *Major Transitions in the Human Life Cycle.* Lexington, MA: Lexington Books.

Kandel, Denise B. (1978). Similarity in real life adolescent friendship pairs. *Journal of Personality and Social Psychology* 36:306–312.

Kandel, Denise B., Kevin Chen, and Andrew Gill. (1995). The impact of drug use on earnings: A life-span perspective. *Social Forces* 74:243–270.

Kandel, Denise B., and Mark Davies. (1991). Friendship networks, intimacy and illicit drug use in young adulthood: A comparison of two competing theories. *Criminology* 29:441–470.

Kandel, Denise B., Mark Davies, Daniel Karus, and Kazuo Yamaguchi. (1986). The consequences in young adulthood of adolescent drug involvement. *Archives of General Psychiatry* 43:746–754.

Kaplan, Howard B., and Xiaoru Liu. (1994). A longitudinal analysis of mediating variables in the drug use–dropping out relationship. *Criminology* 32:415–439.

Kennedy, David M., Anne M. Piehl, and Anthony A. Braga. (1996). Youth violence in Boston: Gun markets, serious youth offenders, and a use-reduction strategy. *Law and Contemporary Problems* 59:147–196.

Kish, Leslie. (1965). *Survey Sampling.* New York: Wiley.

Klein, Malcolm W. (1968). *The Ladino Hills Project: Final Report.* Los Angeles: University of Southern California, Youth Studies Center.

(1969). Gang cohesiveness, delinquency, and a street-work program. *Journal of Research in Crime and Delinquency* 6:135–166.

(1971). *Street Gangs and Street Workers*. Englewood Cliffs, NJ: Prentice-Hall.

(1995). *The American Street Gang: Its Nature, Prevalence, and Control.* New York: Oxford University Press.

(1996). Gangs in the United States and Europe. *European Journal on Criminal Policy and Research* 4:63–80.

Klein, Malcolm W., and Lois Y. Crawford. (1967). Groups, gangs and cohesiveness. *Journal of Research in Crime and Delinquency* 4:63–75.

Klein, Malcolm W., Margaret A. Gordon, and Cheryl L. Maxson. (1986). The impact of police investigation on police-reported rates of gang and nongang homicides. *Criminology* 2:489–512.

Klein, Malcolm W., and Cheryl L. Maxson. (1989). Street gang violence. Pp. 198–234 in Neil A. Weiner and Marvin E. Wolfgang (Eds.), *Violent Crime, Violent Criminals*. Newbury Park, CA: Sage.

Klein, Malcolm W., Cheryl L. Maxson, and Lea C. Cunningham. (1991). Crack, street gangs, and violence. *Criminology* 29:623–650.

Kobrin, Solomon. (1959). The Chicago Area Project: A twenty-five year assessment. *Annals of the American Academy of Political and Social Science* 322: 19–29.

Krohn, Marvin D. (1986). The web of conformity: A network approach to the explanation of delinquent behavior. *Social Problems* 33:581–593.

Krohn, Marvin D., Alan J. Lizotte, and Cynthia M. Perez. (1997). The interrelationship between substance use and precocious transitions to adult statuses. *Journal of Health and Social Behavior* 38:87–103.

Krohn, Marvin D., Alan J. Lizotte, Terence P. Thornberry, Carolyn A. Smith, and David McDowall. (1996). Reciprocal causal relationships among drug use, peers, and beliefs: A five-wave panel model. *Journal of Drug Issues* 26:405–428.

Krohn, Marvin. D., James L. Massey, and Mary A. Zielinski. (1988). Role overlap, network multiplexity, and adolescent deviant behavior. *Social Psychology Quarterly* 51:346–356.

Krohn, Marvin D., Susan B. Stern, Terence P. Thornberry, and Sung Joon Jang. (1992). The measurement of family process variables: An examination of adolescent and parent perceptions of family life on delinquent behavior. *Journal of Quantitative Criminology* 8:287–315.

Krohn, Marvin D., and Terence P. Thornberry. (1993). Network theory: A model for understanding drug abuse among African-American and Hispanic youth. Pp. 102–128 in Mario De La Rosa and Juan-Luis Recio Adrados (Eds.), *Drug Abuse among Minority Youth: Advances in Research Methodology*. NIDA Research Monograph 130. Washington, DC: U.S. Department of Health and Human Services.

(1999). Retention of minority populations in panel studies of drug use. *Drugs & Society* 14:185–207.

Krohn, Marvin D., Terence P. Thornberry, Lori Collins-Hall, and Alan J. Lizotte. (1995). School dropout, delinquent behavior, and drug use: An examination of the causes and consequences of dropping out of school. Pp. 163–183 in Howard B. Kaplan (Ed.), *Drugs, Crime, and Other Deviant Adaptations: Longitudinal Studies*. New York: Plenum Press.

Krohn, Marvin D., Terence P. Thornberry, Craig Rivera, and Marc LeBlanc. (2001). Later delinquency careers. Pp. 67–93 in Rolf Loeber and David P. Farrington (Eds.), *Child Delinquents: Development, Intervention, and Service Needs*. Thousand Oaks, CA: Sage.

Lacourse, Eric, Daniel S. Nagin, Richard E. Tremblay, Frank Vitaro, and Michel Claes. (Forthcoming). Developmental trajectories of boys' delinquent group membership and facilitation of violent behaviors during adolescence. *Development and Psychopathology*.

Lahey, Benjamin B., Rachel A. Gordon, Rolf Loeber, Magda Stouthamer-Loeber, and David P. Farrington. (1999). Boys who join gangs: A prospective study of predictors of first gang entry. *Journal of Abnormal Child Psychology* 27:261–276.

Lasley, James. (1998). *"Designing Out" Gang Homicides and Street Assaults*. Research in Brief. Washington, DC: U.S. Department of Justice, National Institute of Justice.

LeBlanc, Marc, and Nadine Lanctôt. (1998). Social and psychological characteristics of gang members according to the gang structure and its subcultural and ethnic makeup. *Journal of Gang Research* 5:15–28.

Lizotte, Alan J., Trudy L. Bonsell, David McDowall, Marvin D. Krohn, and Terence P. Thornberry. (Forthcoming). Carrying guns and involvement in crime. In Robert A. Silverman, Terence P. Thornberry, Bernard Cohen, and Barry Krisberg (Eds.), *Crime and Justice at the Millennium: Essays by and in Honor of Marvin E. Wolfgang*. Boston: Kluwer Academic Publishers.

Lizotte, Alan J., Deborah J. Chard-Wierschem, Rolf Loeber, and Susan B. Stern. (1992). A shortened behavior checklist for delinquency studies. *Journal of Quantitative Criminology* 8:233–245.

Lizotte, Alan J., Gregory J. Howard, Marvin D. Krohn, and Terence P. Thornberry. (1997). Patterns of illegal gun carrying among young urban males. *Valparaiso University Law Review* 31:375–393.

Lizotte, Alan J., Marvin D. Krohn, James C. Howell, Kimberly Tobin, and Gregory J. Howard. (2000). Factors influencing gun carrying among young urban males over the adolescent-young adult life course. *Criminology* 38:811–834.

Loeber, Rolf, and David P. Farrington (Eds.). (1998). *Serious and Violent Juvenile Offenders: Risk Factors and Successful Interventions*. Thousand Oaks, CA: Sage.

Loeber, Rolf, and Magda Stouthamer-Loeber. (1986). Family factors as correlates and predictors of juvenile conduct problems and delinquency. Pp. 29–149 in Michael H. Tonry and Norval Morris (Eds.), *Crime and Justice: An Annual Review of Research* (Vol. 7). Chicago: University of Chicago Press.

Magnusson, David. (1988). *Individual Development from an Interactional Perspective: A Longitudinal Study*. Hillsdale, NJ: Erlbaum.

Mattick, Hans, and Nathan S. Caplan. (1962). *Chicago Youth Development Project: The Chicago Boys Club*. Ann Arbor, MI: Institute of Social Research.

Maxson, Cheryl L., and Malcolm W. Klein. (1990). Street gang violence: Twice as great, or half as great? Pp. 71–100 in C. Ronald Huff (Ed.), *Gangs in America*. Newbury Park, CA: Sage.

Maxson, Cheryl L., Malcolm W. Klein, and Lea C. Cunningham. (1991). *Street Gangs and Drug Sales*. Final Report. Washington, DC: U.S. Department of Justice, National Institute of Justice.

Mensch, Barbara S., and Denise B. Kandel. (1988). Dropping out of high school and drug involvement. *Sociology of Education* 61:95–113.

Mihalic, Sharon, Katherine Irwin, Delbert S. Elliott, Abigail Fagan, and Diane Hansen. (2001). *Blueprints for Violence Prevention*. Juvenile Justice Bulletin. Washington, DC: U.S. Department of Justice, Office of Juvenile Justice and Delinquency Prevention.

Miller, Jody. (1998). Gender and victimization risk among young women in youth gangs. *Journal of Research in Crime and Delinquency* 35:429–453.

(2001). *One of the Guys: Girls, Gangs and Gender*. New York: Oxford University Press.

Miller, Jody, and Rod K. Brunson. (2000). Gender dynamics in youth gangs: A comparison of male and female accounts. *Justice Quarterly* 17:419–448.

Miller, Jody, and Scott H. Decker. (2001). Young women and gang violence: Gender, street offending, and violent victimization in gangs. *Justice Quarterly* 18:115–140.

Miller, Walter B. (1958). Lower class culture as a generating milieu of gang delinquency. *Journal of Social Issues* 14:5–19.

(1962). The impact of a "total community" delinquency control project. *Social Problems* 10:168–191.

(1966). Violent crimes by city gangs. *Annals of the American Academy of Political and Social Science* 364:96–112.

(1975). *Violence by Youth Gangs and Youth Groups as a Crime Problem in Major American Cities*. Report. Washington, DC: U.S. Department of Justice, Office of Juvenile Justice and Delinquency Prevention.

(1982). *Crime by Youth Gangs and Groups in the United States*. Report. Washington, DC: U.S. Department of Justice, Office of Juvenile Justice and Delinquency Prevention.

Miller, Walter B., Hildred Geertz, and Henry S. G. Cutter. (1961). Aggression in a boys' street-corner group. *Psychiatry* 24:283–298.

Moffitt, Terrie E. (1997). Adolescence-limited and life-course-persistent offending: A complementary pair of developmental theories. Pp. 11–54 in Terence P. Thornberry (Ed.), *Developmental Theories of Crime and Delinquency*, New Brunswick, NJ: Transaction Publishers.

Moore, Joan W. (1978). *Homeboys*. Philadelphia: Temple University Press.

(1991). *Going Down to the Barrio: Homeboys and Homegirls in Change*. Philadelphia: Temple University Press.

Moore, Joan W., and John Hagedorn. (2001). *Female Gangs: A Focus on Research*. Juvenile Justice Bulletin. Washington, DC: U.S. Department of Justice, Office of Juvenile Justice and Delinquency Prevention.

Moore, John P., and Ivan L. Cook. (1999). *Highlights of the 1998 National Youth Gang Survey*. Washington, DC: U.S. Department of Justice, Office of Juvenile Justice and Delinquency Prevention.

Nagin, Daniel S., and David P. Farrington. (1992). The stability of criminal potential from childhood to adulthood. *Criminology* 30:235–260.

Nagin, Daniel S., and Raymond Paternoster. (1991). On the relationship of past and future participation in delinquency. *Criminology* 29:163–189.

National Youth Gang Center. (1997). *The 1995 National Youth Gang Survey.* Washington, DC: U.S. Department of Justice, Office of Juvenile Justice and Delinquency Prevention.

Newcomb, Michael D., and Peter M. Bentler. (1988). *Consequences of Adolescent Drug Use: Impact on the Lives of Young Adults.* Newbury Park, CA: Sage.

Newton, George D., and Franklin E. Zimring. (1969). *Firearms and Violence in American Life: A Staff Report to the National Commission on the Causes and Prevention of Violence.* Washington, DC: U.S. Government Printing Office.

Nirdorf, B. J. (1988). *Gang Alternative and Prevention Program: Program Policy and Procedure Handbook.* Los Angeles: County of Los Angeles Probation Department.

Palumbo, Dennis J., and Jennifer L. Ferguson. (1995). Evaluating Gang Resistance Education and Training (GREAT): Is the impact the same as that of Drug Abuse Resistance Education (DARE)? *Evaluation Review* 19:591–619.

Patterson, Gerald R., John B. Reid, and Thomas J. Dishion. (1992). *Antisocial Boys.* Eugene, OR: Castalia Press.

Radloff, Lenore S. (1977). The CES-D Scale: A self-report depression scale for research in the general population. *Applied Psychological Measurement* 1:385–401.

Rice, Robert. (1963, October 19). A reporter at large: Persian queens. *New Yorker* 39:139ff.

Rindfuss, Ronald R. (1991). The young adult years: Diversity, structural change, and fertility. *Demography* 28:493–512.

Rindfuss, Ronald R., C. Gray Swicegood, and Rachel A. Rosenfeld. (1987). Disorder in the life course: How common and does it matter? *American Sociological Review* 52:785–801.

Robins, Lee N. (1966). *Deviant Children Grown Up.* Baltimore: William and Mary.

Rosenberg, Morris. (1965). *Society and the Adolescent Self-Image.* Princeton, NJ: Princeton University Press.

Rosenfeld, Richard, Timothy M. Bray, and Arlen Egley. (1999). Facilitating violence: A comparison of gang-motivated, gang-affiliated, and non-gang youth homicides. *Journal of Quantitative Criminology* 15:495–516.

Rutter, Michael. (1987). Psychosocial resilience and protective mechanisms. *American Journal of Orthopsychiatry* 57:316–331.

Sampson, Robert J., and John Laub. (1993). *Crime in the Making: Pathways and Turning Points through Life.* Cambridge, MA: Harvard University Press.

Schwartz, Audrey J. (1989). Middle-class educational values among Latino gang members in East Los Angeles County high schools. *Urban Education* 24:323–342.

ıart, Lawrence J., Helen V. Barnes, and David P. Weikart. (1993). *Significant Benefits: The High/Scope Perry Preschool Study through Age 27.* Ypsilanti, High/Scope Press.

Sellin, Thorsten. (1938). *Culture, Conflict, and Crime.* Bulletin 41. New York: Social Science Research Council.

Shelden, Randall G., Ted Snodgrass, and Pam Snodgrass. (1992). Comparing gang and non-gang offenders: Some tentative findings. *Gang Journal* 1:73–85.

Sheley, Joseph F., and James D. Wright. (1993). *Gun Acquisition and Possession in Selected Juvenile Samples.* Research in Brief. Washington, DC: U.S. Department of Justice, National Institute of Justice.

(1995). *In the Line of Fire: Youth, Guns and Violence in Urban America.* Hawthorne, NY: Aldine De Gruyter.

Sherman, Lawrence W., Denise Gottfredson, Doris L. MacKenzie, John E. Eck, Peter Reuter, and Shawn Bushway. (1997). *Preventing Crime: What Works, What Doesn't, What's Promising.* Report. Washington, DC: U.S. Department of Justice, National Institute of Justice.

Short, James F., Jr. (1990). New wine in old bottles? Change and continuity in American gangs. Pp. 223–239 in C. Ronald Huff (Ed.), *Gangs in America.* Newbury Park, CA: Sage.

Short, James F., Jr., and Fred L. Strodtbeck. (1965). *Group Process and Gang Delinquency.* Chicago: University of Chicago Press.

Skolnick, Jerome H., Theodore Correl, and Roger Rabb. (1988). *The Social Structure of Street Dealing.* Sacramento: Office of the Attorney General of the State of California.

Small, Stephen A., and Tom Luster. (1994). Adolescent sexual activity: An ecological risk-factor approach. *Journal of Marriage and the Family* 56:181–192.

Smith, Carolyn A. (1997). Factors associated with early sexual activity among urban adolescents. *Social Work* 42:334–346.

Smith, Carolyn A., and Terence P. Thornberry. (1995). The relationship between childhood maltreatment and adolescent involvement in delinquency. *Criminology* 33:451–481.

Spergel, Irving A. (1964). *Slumtown, Racketville, Haulburg.* Chicago: University of Chicago Press.

(1966). *Street Gang Work: Theory and Practice.* Reading, MA: Addison-Wesley.

(1990). Youth gangs: Continuity and change. Pp. 171–275 in Michael Tonry and Norval Morris (Eds.), *Crime and Justice: A Review of Research* (Vol. 12). Chicago: University of Chicago Press.

(1995). *The Youth Gang Problem.* New York: Oxford University Press.

Spergel, Irving A., and G. David Curry. (1990). Strategies and perceived agency effectiveness in dealing with the youth gang problem. Pp. 288–309 in C. Ronald Huff (Ed.), *Gangs in America.* Newbury Park, CA: Sage.

Spergel, Irving A., and Susan F. Grossman. (1997). The Little Village Project: A community approach to the gang problem. *Social Work* 42:456–470.

Spergel, Irving A., Susan F. Grossman, and Wa Kwai Ming. (1998). The Little Village Gang Violence Reduction Program: A three year evaluation.

Unpublished report. University of Chicago, School of Social Service Administration.

Stern, Susan B., and Carolyn A. Smith. (1995). Family processes and delinquency in an ecological context. *Social Service Review* 69:703–731.

Strodtbeck, Fred L., and James F. Short Jr. (1964). An explanation of gang action. *Social Problems* 12:127–140.

Sudman, Seymour. (1976). *Applied Sampling.* New York: Academic Press.

Taylor, Carl S. (1990). Gang imperialism. Pp. 103–115 in C. Ronald Huff (Ed.), *Gangs in America.* Newbury Park, CA: Sage.

Thornberry, Terence P. (1987). Toward an interactional theory of delinquency. *Criminology* 25:863–892.

(1998). Membership in youth gangs and involvement in serious and violent offending. Pp. 147–166 in Rolf Loeber and David P. Farrington (Eds.), *Serious and Violent Juvenile Offenders: Risk Factors and Successful Interventions.* Thousand Oaks, CA: Sage.

Thornberry, Terence P., Beth Bjerregaard, and William C. Miles. (1993). The consequences of respondent attrition in panel studies: A simulation based on the Rochester Youth Development Study. *Journal of Quantitative Criminology* 9:127–158.

Thornberry, Terence P., and Marvin D. Krohn. (1997). Peers, drug use, and delinquency. Pp. 218–233 in David M. Stoff, James Breiling, and Jack D. Maser (Eds.), *Handbook of Antisocial Behavior.* New York: Wiley.

(2000). The self-report method for measuring delinquency and crime. Pp. 33–83 in David Duffee, Robert D. Crutchfield, Steven Mastrofski, Lorraine Mazerolle, David McDowall, and Brian Ostrom (Eds.), *CJ 2000: Innovations in Measurement and Analysis* (Vol. 4). Washington, DC: U.S. Department of Justice.

(2001). The development of delinquency: An interactional perspective. Pp. 289–305 Susan O. White (Ed.), *Handbook of Youth and Justice.* New York: Plenum.

Thornberry, Terence P., Marvin D. Krohn, Alan J. Lizotte, and Deborah Chard-Wierschem. (1993). The role of juvenile gangs in facilitating delinquent behavior. *Journal of Research in Crime and Delinquency* 30:55–87.

Thornberry, Terence P., Alan J. Lizotte, Marvin D. Krohn, Margaret Farnworth, and Sung Joon Jang. (1994). Delinquent peers, beliefs, and delinquent behavior: A longitudinal test of interactional theory. *Criminology* 32:47–83.

Thornberry, Terence P., and Pamela K. Porter. (2001). Advantages of longitudinal research designs in studying gang behavior. Pp. 59–77 in Malcolm W. Klein, Hans-Juergen Kerner, Cheryl Maxson, and Elmar G. M. Weitekamp (Eds.), *The Eurogang Paradox.* Dordrecht: Kluwer Academic Publishers.

Thornberry, Terence P., Carolyn A. Smith, and Gregory J. Howard. (1997). Risk factors for teenage fatherhood. *Journal of Marriage and the Family* 59:505–522.

Thrasher, Frederic M. (1927). *The Gang: A Study of 1,313 Gangs in Chicago.* Chicago: University of Chicago Press.

. The boys' club and juvenile delinquency. *American Journal of Sociology* 6–80.

ul E. (1979). Subcultural Delinquency: A Comparison of the Incidence and Seriousness of Gang and Nongang Member Offensivity. Unpublished manuscript. University of Pennsylvania, Center for Studies in Criminology and Criminal Law.

Tremblay, Richard E., Louise C. Masse, Linda Pagani, and Frank Vitaro. (1996). From childhood physical aggression to adolescent maladjustment: The Montreal Prevention Experiment. Pp. 268–298 in Ray D. Peters and Robert J. McMahon (Eds.), *Preventing Childhood Disorders, Substance Abuse, and Delinquency*. Thousand Oaks, CA: Sage.

Tremblay, Richard E., Robert O. Pihl, Frank Vitaro, and Patricia L. Dobkin. (1994). Predicting early onset of male antisocial behavior from preschool behavior. *Archives of General Psychiatry* 51:732–739.

U.S. Department of Health and Human Services. (2001). *Youth Violence: A Report of the Surgeon General.* Rockville, MD: Department of Health and Human Services.

Venkatesh, Sudhir Alladi. (1998). Gender and outlaw capitalism: A historical account of the Black Sisters United "girl gang." *Signs* 23:683–709.

Vigil, James Diego. (1988). *Barrio Gangs: Street Life and Identity in Southern California.* Austin: University of Texas Press.

Wang, Alvin Y. (1994). Pride and prejudice in high school gang members. *Adolescence* 29:279–291.

Werner, Emmy E., and Ruth S. Smith. (1982). *Vulnerable but Invincible: A Longitudinal Study of Resilient Children and Youth.* New York: McGraw-Hill.

(1992). *Overcoming the Odds: High Risk Children from Birth to Adulthood.* Ithaca, NY: Cornell University Press.

Wilson, William J. (1987). *The Truly Disadvantaged: The Inner City, the Underclass, and Public Policy.* Chicago: University of Chicago Press.

Winfree, L. Thomas, Jr., Teresa Vigil Backstrom, and G. Larry Mays. (1994). Social learning theory, self-reported delinquency, and youth gangs: A new twist on a general theory of crime and delinquency. *Youth and Society* 26:147–177.

Wister, Andrew V., and William R. Avison. (1982). Friendly persuasion: A social network analysis of sex differences in marijuana use. *International Journal of Addictions* 17:523–541.

Wright, James D., and Peter H. Rossi. (1986). *Armed and Considered Dangerous: A Survey of Felons and Their Firearms.* New York: Aldine De Gruyter.

Yablonsky, Lewis. (1962). *The Violent Gang.* New York: Macmillan.

Yamaguchi, Kazuo, and Denise B. Kandel. (1985a). Dynamic relationships between premarital cohabitation and illicit drug use: An event history analysis of role selection and role socialization. *American Sociological Review* 50:530–546.

(1985b). On the resolution of role incompatibility: A life event history analysis of family roles and marijuana use. *American Journal of Sociology* 90:1284–1325.

Index